FamilyCircle.

Quick&Easy
Cooking

Meredith® Consumer Marketing
Des Moines, Iowa

Family Circle® Quick & Easy Cooking

Meredith® Corporation Consumer Marketing
Vice President, Consumer Marketing: David Ball
Consumer Product Marketing Director: Steve Swanson
Consumer Marketing Product Manager: Wendy Merical
Business Director: Ron Clingman
Associate Director, Production: Douglas M. Johnston

Waterbury Publications, Inc.
Editorial Director: Lisa Kingsley
Associate Editor: Tricia Laning
Creative Director: Ken Carlson
Associate Design Director: Doug Samuelson
Contributing Copy Editors: Terri Fredrickson, Gretchen Kauffman, Peg Smith
Contributing Indexer: Elizabeth T. Parson

Family Circle® **Magazine**
Editor in Chief: Linda Fears
Creative Director: Karmen Lizzul
Food Director: Regina Ragone, M.S., R.D.
Senior Food Editor: Julie Miltenberger
Associate Food Editor: Michael Tyrrell
Assistant Food Editor: Cindy Heller
Editorial Assistant: Allison Baker

Meredith Publishing Group
President: Jack Griffin
Executive Vice President: Andy Sareyan
Vice President, Manufacturing: Bruce Heston

Meredith Corporation
President and Chief Executive Officer: Stephen M. Lacy

In Memoriam: E.T. Meredith III (1933–2003)

Pictured on the front cover:
Green Chile & Chicken Enchiladas
(recipe page 70)
Photography by Jason Donnelly

At the end of a long day, nothing is as welcome and satisfying as sitting down to a fresh, home-cooked meal. It's a time to slow down, fill up, and reconnect with one another. It's also a much more economical and healthier alternative to eating out or hitting the drive-through. Knowing you made something delicious and nourishing for your family just feels good.

But at the end of those long days, you can have little time or energy to cook. That's why the recipes in *Quick & Easy Cooking* were created for time-pressed cooks who want to feed their families well. With a handful of easy-to-find ingredients, simple preparation, and short start-to-finish times, most of the recipes in this book can be on the table in 30 minutes or less from the time you walk in the door.

Quick & Easy Cooking is filled with fresh, new ideas and lots of familiar dishes too. With more than 300 recipes for family-pleasing pastas, quick-to-grill meats, warming soups and stews, crisp and healthful salads, and fix-and-forget slow cooker meals, you can eat something wonderful and different every night of the week—and know that there's a dish to please every taste, season, mood, and occasion.

Knowing you have the tools at your fingertips to make a great-tasting, healthful, and doable meal for your family on even the busiest days is a great feeling. Happy cooking!

Because health and time-saving features are paramount these days, look for the following icons throughout the book:

 Healthy: The "healthy" icon means that the recipe meets certain calorie, fat, and sodium guidelines. See page 336 for more information.

 One-Pan: The "one-pan" icon means that the recipe uses a single pan in its preparation, and that translates to easy cleanup.

table of contents

28

255

315

89

When the meat of the matter is how you're going to satisfy hearty appetites, look to these beef, pork, and lamb dishes. Whether it's a casual sandwich or a special-occasion steak, it's in here.

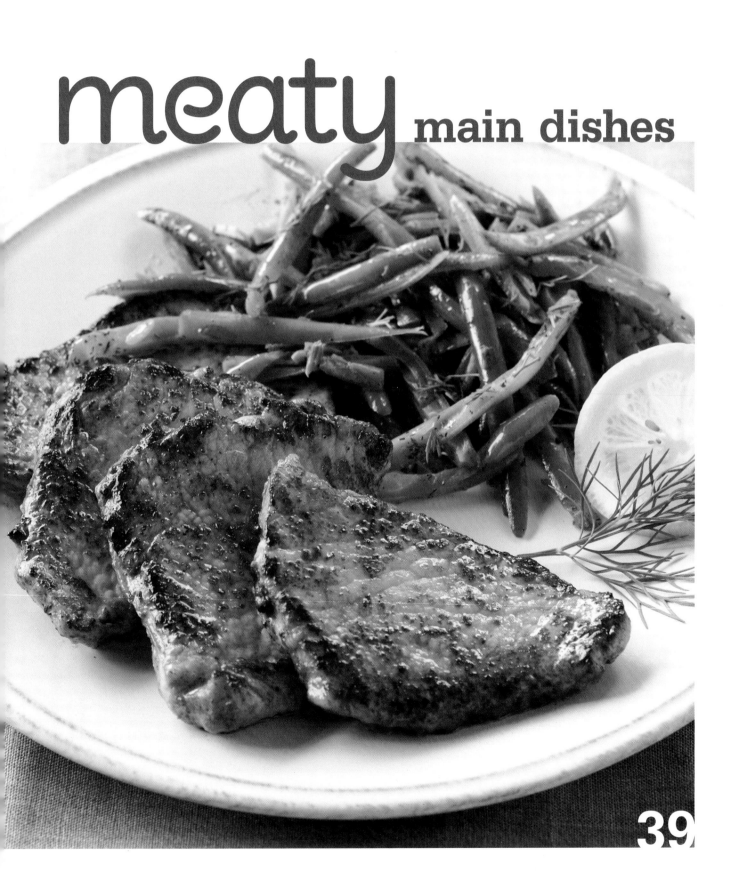

meaty main dishes

39

Blackened Beef Stir-Fry ♥

The "blackening" in this recipe comes from prepared blackened steak seasoning. Pair the meat with a mix of stir-fry vegetables that has lots of colorful peppers.

START TO FINISH 25 minutes **MAKES** 4 servings

12	ounces packaged beef stir-fry strips
2 ¼	teaspoons blackened steak seasoning
⅔	cup water
2	tablespoons tomato paste
2	teaspoons cornstarch
½	teaspoon instant beef bouillon granules
1	tablespoon cooking oil
1	16-ounce package frozen stir-fry vegetables (any combination)

❶ Sprinkle steak strips with 2 teaspoons of the blackened steak seasoning; toss to coat well. Set aside.

❷ For sauce, in a small bowl stir together the remaining ¼ teaspoon blackened steak seasoning, water, tomato paste, cornstarch, and bouillon granules. Set aside.

❸ In a large skillet or wok heat oil on medium-high heat. Add stir-fry vegetables and cook and stir for 2 to 3 minutes or until crisp-tender. Remove vegetables from skillet. Add beef strips to hot skillet. (Add more oil as necessary during cooking.) Cook and stir for 2 to 3 minutes or until meat is slightly pink in center.

❹ Push meat from center of skillet. Stir sauce; add to center of skillet. Cook and stir until thickened and bubbly. Return vegetables to skillet. Stir together to coat all ingredients with sauce. Heat through.

PER SERVING 190 cal., 6 g total fat (2 g sat. fat), 40 mg chol., 373 mg sodium, 10 g carbo., 3 g fiber, 21 g pro.

quick tip   If you can't find precut beef stir-fry strips in the meat section of your supermarket, it's easy to cut your own. Flank steak is a good cut to use for stir-fry. To make it easy to cut thin slices, place the steak in the freezer for 30 to 45 minutes or until it's partially frozen—then cut it. You'll get nice neat slices of meat.

Pan-Fried Garlic Steak & Potatoes

The trick to making this dish quickly is precooking the potatoes and garlic in the microwave—then crisping the potatoes in hot oil in the skillet right before serving.

START TO FINISH 30 minutes **MAKES** 4 servings

12	cloves garlic
1	pound tiny new potatoes, scrubbed
4	6-ounce boneless beef ribeye or beef strip steaks
2	tablespoons olive oil
1	cup grape or cherry tomatoes
	Fresh oregano (optional)

❶ Using the side of large chef's knife smash garlic; discard skins. Halve any large potatoes. Place potatoes in microwave-safe bowl. Cover with vented plastic wrap and cook on high for 5 minutes. Stir in garlic. Cover; cook 5 minutes more or until tender, stirring once. Drain.

❷ Meanwhile, heat 1 tablespoon of the olive oil in a large skillet on medium-high heat. Season steak with salt and pepper. Cook steaks, half at a time, 8 minutes for ribeye or 4 minutes for strip (145°F for medium rare or 160°F for medium), turning once halfway through cooking. Keep steaks warm while cooking remaining steaks.

❸ Add remaining 1 tablespoon oil to skillet. Add potatoes, garlic, and tomatoes. Season with salt and pepper. Cook 5 minutes or until potatoes are golden and tomatoes begin to wilt, stirring occasionally. Serve potato mixture with steak. If desired, sprinkle with fresh oregano.

PER SERVING 434 cal., 20 g total fat (6 g sat. fat), 99 mg chol., 247 mg sodium, 25 g carbo., 3 g fiber, 38 g pro.

Peppered Steaks with
Asiago Cheese

Peppered Steaks with Asiago Cheese 🎬

Look for an Asiago cheese that has been aged at least 6 months or, even better, for 1 year. The longer it ages, the more flavor it has and the easier it is to shave.

START TO FINISH 20 minutes   **MAKES** 4 servings

- 4 beef tenderloin steaks, cut ¾ inch thick (about 1 pound)
- 1 teaspoon coarsely ground black pepper
- 1 tablespoon olive oil
- ¼ cup low-sodium beef broth
- 2 4-ounce packages sliced cremini, shiitake, or portobello mushrooms or one 8-ounce package sliced button mushrooms (about 3 cups)
- 1 ounce Asiago cheese, shaved
- ¼ cup fresh spinach leaves, shredded (optional)

❶ Trim fat from steaks. Rub both sides of steaks with pepper. In a large skillet heat olive oil on medium-high heat. Add steaks; reduce heat to medium. Cook 7 to 9 minutes for medium rare (145°F) to medium (160°F), turning once halfway through cooking. Transfer steaks to serving platter; keep warm.

❷ Add beef broth to skillet. Cook and stir until bubbly to loosen any brown bits in bottom of skillet. Add mushrooms; simmer, uncovered, for 4 minutes. To serve, spoon sauce over steaks. Sprinkle with shaved cheese. If desired, garnish with fresh spinach leaves.

PER SERVING 352 cal., 26 g total fat (10 g sat. fat), 82 mg chol., 165 mg sodium, 3 g carbo., 1 g fiber, 26 g pro.

---

quick tip   Slightly reduced beef broth and mushrooms make a light sauce for this hearty steak. If you'd like the sauce to be thicker, increase the broth to ½ cup and stir in ¼ teaspoon cornstarch before adding the broth to the skillet.

Bistro Beef Steak with Wild Mushroom Ragoût ♥

Herbes de Provence is a South of France blend of dried herbs that usually contains basil, fennel seeds, lavender, marjoram, rosemary, sage, savory, and thyme.

MAKES 6 servings

- 3 8-ounce boneless beef top loin steaks, cut ¾ inch thick
- 3 cloves garlic, minced
- 1 teaspoon herbes de Provence
- ½ teaspoon black pepper
- ¼ teaspoon salt
- 1 tablespoon olive oil
- ⅓ cup finely chopped shallots
- 2 cloves garlic, minced
- 8 ounces assorted wild mushrooms (oyster, cremini, and/or shiitake), sliced
- ¼ cup dry sherry (optional)
- 1 14-ounce can low-sodium beef broth
- 1 tablespoon cornstarch
- 1 teaspoon herbes de Provence

❶ Preheat broiler. Trim fat from beef steaks. In a small bowl combine the 3 cloves minced garlic, 1 teaspoon herbes de Provence, pepper, and salt. Sprinkle herb mixture over all sides of the steaks; rub in with your fingers. Place steaks on the unheated rack of broiler pan. Broil 3 to 4 inches from the heat for 9 to 11 minutes for medium rare (145°F) to medium (160°F), turning once halfway through broiling.

❷ Meanwhile, for mushroom ragoût, in a large nonstick skillet heat oil on medium-high heat until hot. Add shallots and the 2 cloves minced garlic; cook for 1 to 3 minutes or until shallots are tender. Add mushrooms; cook for 6 to 7 minutes or until mushrooms are tender and any liquid evaporates, stirring occasionally. Remove from heat. If desired, stir in sherry. Return to heat. Bring to boiling. Cook, uncovered, for 30 to 60 seconds or until liquid evaporates.

❸ In a medium bowl stir together broth, cornstarch, and 1 teaspoon herbes de Provence. Stir broth mixture into mixture in skillet. Cook and stir on medium heat until thickened and bubbly. Cook and stir for 2 minutes more.

❹ To serve, cut each steak in half. Serve steaks with the mushroom ragoût.

PER SERVING 206 cal., 8 g total fat (2 g sat. fat), 66 mg chol., 291 mg sodium, 4 g carbo., 1 g fiber, 27 g pro.

Thai Beef Pasta

Thai seasoning infuses foods with the magic of Thai cooking in one jar. It usually contains ground chiles, ginger, coriander, red pepper, cumin, cinnamon, star anise, garlic, lemon peel, shallots, and dried jalapeño peppers.

START TO FINISH 30 minutes   **MAKES** 4 servings

    8   ounces dried angel hair pasta
    ¾   cup unsweetened coconut milk
    1   teaspoon Thai seasoning
    1   tablespoon cooking oil
   12   ounces beef top round steak, trimmed and cut into thin bite-size strips
    1   cup fresh pea pods, trimmed
    ½   cup shredded carrot
    ¼   cup chopped dry-roasted peanuts

❶ Cook pasta according to package directions; drain well. Return pasta to pan; cover and keep warm. For sauce, in a small bowl stir together coconut milk and Thai seasoning; set aside.

❷ Meanwhile, in a large skillet or wok heat oil on medium-high heat. Cook and stir beef in hot oil for 2 to 3 minutes or until desired doneness. Remove beef from skillet (drain, if necessary). Add pea pods and carrot to skillet. Cook and stir for 1 minute. Push from center of skillet. Stir sauce; add to center of skillet. Cook and stir until bubbly. Add beef and cooked pasta to wok. Stir to coat all ingredients with sauce. Sprinkle with peanuts.

PER SERVING 516 cal., 22 g total fat (10 g sat. fat), 50 mg chol., 223 mg sodium, 49 g carbo., 2 g fiber, 29 g pro.

Skillet Tostadas

Condensed nacho cheese soup and salsa create a quick and creamy sauce for these tasty tostadas.

START TO FINISH 25 minutes   **MAKES** 4 servings

    8   ounces ground beef
    ½   cup chopped onion
    1   15-ounce can light red kidney beans, rinsed and drained
    1   11-ounce can condensed nacho cheese soup
    ⅓   cup bottled salsa
    8   tostada shells
    1   cup shredded taco cheese (4 ounces)
        Shredded lettuce
        Chopped tomatoes
        Sour cream or guacamole (optional)

❶ In a large skillet cook ground beef and onion until meat is brown and onion is tender. Drain off fat. Stir kidney beans, nacho cheese soup, and salsa into beef mixture. Heat through.

❷ Divide beef-salsa mixture among tostada shells. Top with cheese. Top with lettuce and tomatoes. If desired, serve with sour cream or guacamole.

PER SERVING 576 cal., 33 g total fat (15 g sat. fat), 81 mg chol., 1,277 mg sodium, 42 g carbo., 11 g fiber, 26 g pro.

---

quick tip   When shopping for ground beef, consider the fat content of the meat. Meat that is labeled simply "ground beef" is usually about 75 percent lean—the highest fat content. Ground chuck is 80 percent lean; ground sirloin is around 85 percent lean; and the leanest choice, ground round, is generally 90 percent lean.

{ Prepared spice mixes, salsas, and bottled sauces simplify making your favorite foods. }

Skillet Beef Tenderloin

Pasta with Beef & Asparagus

Just a smidge of honey softens the tartness of the sour cream in the rich-tasting sauce for this beef and pasta dish.

START TO FINISH 30 minutes **MAKES** 4 servings

8	ounces boneless beef top sirloin steak
1	pound fresh asparagus
8	ounces dried bow tie pasta
1	8-ounce carton light sour cream
2	tablespoons all-purpose flour
⅔	cup water
1	tablespoon honey
½	teaspoon salt
¼	teaspoon black pepper
2	tablespoons finely chopped shallot
1	teaspoon cooking oil
2	teaspoons snipped fresh tarragon
	Fresh tarragon sprigs (optional)

1 If desired, partially freeze steak before slicing. Cut off and discard woody bases from fresh asparagus. If desired, scrape off scales. Bias-slice asparagus into 1-inch pieces; set aside. Cook pasta according to package directions, adding asparagus for the last 3 minutes of cooking. Drain well; keep warm.

2 Meanwhile, trim fat from steak. Thinly slice steak across the grain into bite-size strips. In a medium bowl stir together sour cream and flour. Stir in the water, honey, salt, and pepper. Set aside.

3 In a large nonstick skillet cook and stir the meat and shallot in hot oil over medium-high heat about 5 minutes or until meat is brown. Drain off fat.

4 Stir sour cream mixture into meat mixture in skillet. Cook and stir until thickened and bubbly. Cook and stir for 1 minute more. Stir in drained pasta, asparagus, and snipped tarragon. Heat through. If desired, garnish with tarragon sprigs.

PER SERVING 421 cal., 11 g total fat (4 g sat. fat), 107 mg chol., 373 mg sodium, 54 g carbo., 3 g fiber, 26 g pro.

Skillet Beef Tenderloin

Swiss chard is sometimes referred to as a "vegetable valedictorian" for its fabulous nutritional content. It's loaded with vitamins K, A, and C and—like many dark leafy greens—lots of iron.

START TO FINISH 30 minutes **MAKES** 4 servings

4	6-ounce beef tenderloin steaks (½ to ¾ inch thick)
1	tablespoon butter
1	teaspoon cooking oil or olive oil
4	shallots, quartered if large, or ½ medium red onion, cut in wedges
2	tablespoons cognac, brandy, or dry red wine
½	cup beef broth
1	tablespoon butter, softened
	Snipped fresh parsley
	Crushed pink peppercorns (optional)
1	recipe Braised Swiss Chard

1 Sprinkle steaks with salt and pepper. In an extra-large skillet heat 1 tablespoon butter and oil on high heat. Cook steaks 1 to 2 minutes until bottoms are brown. Reduce heat to medium. Turn steaks; cook 6 minutes more or until desired doneness (145°F for medium rare). Remove steaks; keep warm.

2 Add shallots to skillet. Cook 5 minutes or until crisp-tender. Remove skillet from heat. Add cognac; return to medium heat. Cook 2 minutes, stirring to scrape up brown bits from pan. Add broth. Reduce heat to medium-low. Whisk in 1 tablespoon softened butter until smooth. Return steaks to skillet. Heat, spooning sauce over steaks. Top with parsley and, if desired, peppercorns. Serve with Braised Swiss Chard.

BRAISED SWISS CHARD: Trim stems off 1 pound green, red, or rainbow Swiss chard. Wash and dry leaves. In a Dutch oven heat 2 tablespoons cooking oil or olive oil on medium heat. Add chard leaves. Cover and cook 2 to 3 minutes or just until tender, stirring occasionally. Season to taste with salt and freshly ground black pepper.

PER SERVING 434 cal., 25 g total fat (9 g sat. fat), 129 mg chol., 763 mg sodium, 7 g carbo., 2 g fiber, 40 g pro.

Pepper Steak with Horseradish Sauce

Taking a minute to score the meat on both sides makes it more tender. To serve it, cut the cooked meat diagonally across the grain into thin slices.

PREP 20 minutes **GRILL** 17 minutes **MAKES** 4 to 6 servings

½	cup mayonnaise or salad dressing
2	tablespoons vinegar
1	tablespoon snipped fresh parsley
1	to 2 tablespoons prepared horseradish
1	to 1 ½ pounds beef flank steak
2	teaspoons cracked black pepper
	Grilled small sweet peppers (optional)
	Grilled onions (optional)

① For sauce, in a small bowl stir together mayonnaise, vinegar, parsley, and horseradish. Set aside.

② Trim fat from meat. Score both sides of meat in a diamond pattern by making shallow diagonal cuts at 1-inch intervals. Sprinkle both sides of meat with cracked black pepper, gently pressing into surface.

③ For a charcoal grill, grill meat on the rack of an uncovered grill directly over medium coals for 17 to 21 minutes for medium (160°F), turning once halfway through grilling. (For a gas grill, preheat grill. Reduce heat to medium. Place steak on grill rack over heat. Cover and grill as above.)

④ To serve, thinly slice meat diagonally across the grain. Serve meat with sauce and, if desired, grilled sweet peppers and onions.

PER SERVING 301 cal., 21 g total fat (7 g sat. fat), 68 mg chol., 253 mg sodium, 6 g carbo., 0 g fiber, 23 g pro.

---

quick tip   When a recipe directs you to slice meat across the grain, what does that mean? It means to cut across rather than with the direction that the meat fibers run. In flank steak, these fibers are easily identifiable. If you cut meat with the grain, it will shred. If you cut it across the grain, you get nice, compact slices.

Tenderloins with Rosemary & Port

The quickest way to strip the leaves off the woody rosemary stem is to hold the top of the stem with the fingers of one hand, then pull down the stem with the fingers of your other hand. Put the leaves in a small bowl or cup, then snip them into smaller pieces with a pair of kitchen shears.

START TO FINISH 20 minutes **MAKES** 4 servings

4	4- to 5-ounce beef tenderloin steaks, cut ¾ inch thick
	Salt
	Coarsely ground black pepper
1	tablespoon olive oil or cooking oil
1½	teaspoons snipped fresh rosemary
⅓	cup port wine
⅓	cup water
¼	cup whipping cream

① Sprinkle both sides of steaks with salt and pepper. Add oil to a large skillet. Heat skillet on medium-high heat. Add steaks. Reduce heat to medium and cook for 10 to 13 minutes or until desired doneness, turning steaks once halfway through cooking (145°F for medium rare or 160°F for medium). Transfer steaks to a serving platter; keep warm.

② For sauce, add rosemary to drippings in skillet. Cook and stir 1 minute to loosen any brown bits in bottom of skillet. Carefully stir port and water into skillet. Bring to boiling. Boil, uncovered, about 3 minutes or until mixture is reduced by half. Stir in whipping cream. Return to boiling; boil gently for 2 to 3 minutes or until slightly thickened. Spoon sauce over steaks.

PER SERVING 295 cal., 18 g total fat (7 g sat. fat), 90 mg chol., 132 mg sodium, 3 g carbo., 0 g fiber, 24 g pro.

Mexican Beef Hash
with Eggs

Weeknight Steak with Vegetables 🍲

Here's a trick if you don't like the strings on celery: Run a vegetable peeler down the rounded side of each celery stalk to remove the strings before slicing.

START TO FINISH 30 minutes **MAKES** 4 servings

- 2 tablespoons olive oil
- 2 medium zucchini and/or yellow summer squash, cut into 1-inch pieces
- 1 large red onion, cut into thick wedges
- 2 stalks celery, cut into 1-inch-thick slices
- 3 cloves garlic, sliced
- 1 teaspoon dried rosemary, crushed
- 1 pound boneless beef sirloin steak, cut ½ to ¾ inch thick
  Salt
  Black pepper
- ½ cup dry red wine
- 1 14½-ounce can diced tomatoes with basil, oregano, and garlic, undrained

❶ In a large skillet heat 1 tablespoon of the oil on medium heat. Add zucchini or yellow summer squash, onion, celery, garlic, and rosemary; cook for 6 to 8 minutes or just until vegetables are crisp-tender, stirring occasionally. Remove from skillet.

❷ Cut beef into 4 serving-size pieces. Sprinkle with salt and pepper. Add remaining 1 tablespoon oil to skillet. Add beef to hot skillet. Cook on medium heat about 4 minutes on each side or until desired doneness (145°F for medium rare to 160°F for medium). Remove meat from skillet; cover and keep warm.

❸ Carefully add wine to skillet, stirring up brown bits from bottom of skillet. Add undrained tomatoes. Bring to boiling. Boil gently, uncovered, about 5 minutes or until slightly thickened. Return vegetables to skillet. Cook and stir just until heated through. Spoon vegetable sauce over beef.

PER SERVING 294 cal., 11 g total fat (2 g sat. fat), 69 mg chol., 691 mg sodium, 16 g carbo., 3 g fiber, 27 g pro.

Mexican Beef Hash with Eggs 🍲

This is a terrific use for leftover beef roast, steak, or brisket—and it's great for either supper or a hearty brunch.

START TO FINISH 30 minutes **MAKES** 4 servings

- ¼ cup thinly sliced green onions (2)
- 2 fresh jalapeño or serrano peppers, seeded and finely chopped (see note, below)
- 2 cloves garlic, minced
- 2 tablespoons cooking oil
- 8 ounces cooked beef, chopped
- 1 teaspoon ground cumin
- ¼ teaspoon finely shredded lime peel
- 1 tablespoon lime juice
- 8 eggs
- 1 tablespoon water
  Salt
  Black pepper
- ¼ cup sour cream
- ¼ cup shredded cheddar cheese (1 ounce)
  Snipped fresh cilantro

❶ In a large nonstick skillet cook onions, jalapeños, and garlic in 1 tablespoon of the hot oil on medium heat until tender. Stir in beef, cumin, lime peel, and lime juice. Cook and stir until heated through. Divide beef mixture among 4 plates; keep warm.

❷ In the same skillet heat the remaining 1 tablespoon oil on medium heat. Carefully break 4 eggs into skillet. When whites are set, add water. Cover skillet and cook until desired doneness (3 to 4 minutes for soft-set yolks or 4 to 5 minutes for firm-set yolks). Remove from skillet; keep warm. Repeat with remaining eggs.

❸ Top each serving of beef mixture with 2 fried eggs. Season to taste with salt and black pepper. Top with sour cream, shredded cheese, and cilantro.

PER SERVING 366 cal., 24 g total fat (8 g sat. fat), 475 mg chol., 374 mg sodium, 3 g carbo., 1 g fiber, 32 g pro.

quick tip Because hot chile peppers, such as jalapeños, contain volatile oils that can burn your skin and eyes, avoid direct contact with chiles as much as possible. When working with chile peppers, wear plastic or rubber gloves. If your bare hands do touch the chile peppers, wash your hands well with soap and water.

Corned Beef, Cabbage, Carrots & New Potatoes

The strategy for this super-quick dish involves precooking the vegetables in the microwave, then giving them a slow-roasted effect with a quick trip under the broiler to beautifully brown them.

START TO FINISH 25 minutes   **MAKES** 4 servings

- 1   pound small new potatoes, halved
- 1   pound small carrots, halved lengthwise
- ¼   cup water
- 1   small head savoy cabbage, cut into wedges
- 2   tablespoons olive oil
     Salt
     Black pepper
- 1   pound cooked deli corned beef, sliced
- 2   tablespoons spicy brown mustard
- 2   tablespoons honey

❶ In a 2½- to 3-quart microwave-safe casserole, combine potatoes, carrots, and 2 tablespoons of the water. Cover and microwave on high for 8 minutes, stirring once. Add cabbage. Cover and microwave on high about 4 minutes more or until cabbage is crisp-tender. Drain.

❷ Heat broiler. Place potatoes, carrots, and cabbage in a 15×10×1-inch baking pan. Drizzle with oil; sprinkle with salt and pepper. Broil 3 to 4 inches from heat for 5 minutes.

❸ Meanwhile, heat an extra-large skillet on medium-high heat. Add corned beef slices; cook for 2 minutes, turning once. Add the remaining 2 tablespoons water; reduce heat to low. Cover and cook until heated through.

❹ In a small bowl combine mustard and honey. Divide cabbage, corned beef, carrots, and potatoes among 4 plates; drizzle with pan juices. Serve with mustard mixture.

PER SERVING 537 cal., 29 g total fat (8 g sat. fat), 111 mg chol., 1,657 mg sodium, 44 g carbo., 8 g fiber, 25 g pro.

Cranberry Meatball Skillet 🍲

Potatoes, carrots, and prepared meatballs make this sweet-tart and saucy dish a delicious one-pot meal.

START TO FINISH 20 minutes   **MAKES** 4 servings

- 1   16-ounce can whole cranberry sauce
- ⅓   cup water
- 2   tablespoons cider vinegar
- 1   12-ounce package frozen cooked Swedish-style meatballs
- 1   cup peeled fresh baby carrots
- 8   ounces tiny new potatoes, halved
     Salt
     Black pepper

❶ In a large skillet stir together cranberry sauce, water, and vinegar. Add frozen meatballs, carrots, and potatoes. Bring to boiling; reduce heat. Cover and simmer for 12 to 15 minutes or until potatoes are tender. Season with salt and pepper.

PER SERVING 492 cal., 22 g total fat (9 g sat. fat), 30 mg chol., 857 mg sodium, 62 g carbo., 5 g fiber, 12 g pro.

Greek Beef & Pasta Skillet

The "Greek" touch here is not just the feta cheese, but also a bit of cinnamon stirred into the pasta sauce. The Greeks like to pair the warm, sweet spice of cinnamon with both beef and lamb.

START TO FINISH 30 minutes   **MAKES** 4 servings

- 8   ounces dried rotini
- 12 ounces boneless beef sirloin steak or top round steak
- 1   tablespoon cooking oil
- 1   26-ounce jar ripe olive and mushroom pasta sauce or marinara pasta sauce
- ¼   teaspoon salt
- ¼   teaspoon ground cinnamon
- ½   of a 10-ounce package frozen chopped spinach, thawed and well drained
- ⅓   cup crumbled feta cheese

❶ Cook pasta according to package directions; drain. Meanwhile, trim fat from beef. Thinly slice meat across the grain into bite-size strips.

❷ In a large skillet cook and stir meat strips in hot oil for 2 to 3 minutes or until brown. Add pasta sauce, salt, and cinnamon. Cook and stir until sauce bubbles. Add cooked pasta and spinach. Cook and stir until heated through. Sprinkle with feta cheese.

PER SERVING 483 cal., 12 g total fat (3 g sat. fat), 63 mg chol., 1,063 mg sodium, 60 g carbo., 6 g fiber, 32 g pro.

Southwestern Tortilla Wedges

Southwestern Tortilla Wedges ♥

When you tire of pizza, this fun finger-food dish is just the thing for noshing on movie night or while you watch the big game on TV.

PREP 20 minutes **BAKE** 5 minutes **OVEN** 400°F
MAKES 4 servings

Nonstick cooking spray

6 ounces lean ground beef

½ cup bottled salsa or picante sauce

¼ cup water

1 teaspoon fajita seasoning

4 8-inch spinach-flavored, tomato-basil-flavored, or plain flour tortillas

¼ cup light sour cream

½ cup canned red kidney beans, rinsed and drained

¼ cup canned whole kernel corn with sweet peppers, drained

½ cup shredded Monterey Jack cheese with peppers or shredded Colby-Jack cheese (2 ounces)

1 tablespoon snipped fresh cilantro

Chopped tomato (optional)

Shredded lettuce (optional)

Bottled salsa or picante sauce (optional)

❶ Preheat oven to 400°F. In a medium nonstick skillet cook ground beef until brown. Drain off fat. Stir in the ½ cup salsa, water, and fajita seasoning. Bring to boiling; reduce heat. Simmer, covered, for 5 minutes.

❷ Spread 1 side of each tortilla with some of the sour cream. Top evenly with beef mixture, beans, and corn. In a small bowl combine shredded cheese and cilantro. Sprinkle cheese mixture evenly on tortillas. Place on a very large baking sheet (or use 2 regular baking sheets).

❸ Bake for 5 to 7 minutes or until heated through and cheese melts. Cut into wedges to serve. If desired, top with chopped tomato and shredded lettuce and serve with additional salsa.

PER SERVING 275 cal., 12 g total fat (6 g sat. fat), 44 mg chol., 448 mg sodium, 26 g carbo., 3 g fiber, 17 g pro.

Hearty Hamburger Stroganoff 🍲

Hearty and comforting, this nostalgic take on traditional long-simmered stroganoff is a great choice for a cold winter's weeknight.

START TO FINISH 25 minutes **MAKES** 4 or 5 servings

1 pound ground beef

½ cup chopped onion (1 medium)

1 clove garlic, minced

8 ounces fresh mushrooms, sliced

1 10½-ounce can condensed beef broth

3 tablespoons lemon juice

1 tablespoon dry red wine (optional)

4 ounces dried angel hair pasta, broken

1 8-ounce carton sour cream

Salt

Black pepper

❶ In an extra-large skillet cook beef, onion, and garlic until meat is brown and onion is tender. Drain off fat.

❷ Stir in mushrooms; cook and stir about 5 minutes or until mushrooms are tender. Stir in broth, lemon juice, and, if desired, wine. Bring to boiling; reduce heat. Stir in uncooked pasta.

❸ Cover and simmer about 5 minutes more or until pasta is tender. Stir in sour cream. Cook and stir until heated through. Season with salt and pepper.

PER SERVING 543 cal., 34 g total fat (15 g sat. fat), 106 mg chol., 780 mg sodium, 30 g carbo., 1 g fiber, 31 g pro.

Spaghetti with Cincinnati-Style Marinara

"Cincinatti-style" chili refers to a regional version of "red" to which sweet spices such as cloves and/or cinnamon are added and that's most often served over spaghetti.

START TO FINISH 30 minutes   **MAKES** 6 servings

- 12 ounces dried spaghetti
- 1   pound ground beef
- 1   cup chopped onion (1 large)
- 1   to 2 tablespoons chili powder
- ¼   teaspoon ground cinnamon
- 1   15-ounce can red kidney beans, rinsed and drained
- 1   14-ounce jar marinara sauce
- ½   cup water
- 1   cup shredded cheddar cheese (4 ounces)

❶ Cook spaghetti according to package directions. Meanwhile, in a large skillet cook beef and onion until meat is brown and onion is tender. Drain off fat. Stir chili powder and cinnamon into meat mixture; cook and stir for 2 minutes.

❷ Add kidney beans, marinara sauce, and water. Cook on medium heat until boiling, stirring occasionally.

❸ Place hot cooked spaghetti in a large serving bowl. Spoon sauce over spaghetti; sprinkle with cheddar cheese.

PER SERVING 522 cal., 17 g total fat (7 g sat. fat), 67 mg chol., 527 mg sodium, 62 g carbo., 7 g fiber, 32 g pro.

Barbecue Beef Cups

Kids will love these flaky biscuit cups filled with sweet and saucy ground beef. Pair them with some fresh fruit or steamed baby carrots and dinner is done.

PREP 15 minutes   **BAKE** 12 minutes   **OVEN** 400°F
MAKES 5 servings

- 1   pound ground beef
- ¼   cup chopped onion
- ⅔   cup bottled barbecue sauce
- 2   tablespoons packed brown sugar
- 1   10- to 12-ounce package refrigerated biscuits (10 biscuits)
- ½   cup shredded cheddar cheese (2 ounces)

❶ Preheat oven to 400°F. In a large skillet cook ground beef and onion until meat is brown. Drain off fat. Stir in barbecue sauce and brown sugar.

❷ Press a biscuit into the bottom and up the side of a 2½-inch muffin cup; repeat with remaining biscuits to make 10 biscuit-lined cups. Spoon ground beef mixture into biscuit-lined cups. Sprinkle with cheese. Bake about 12 minutes or until biscuit edges are golden brown. Loosen and carefully remove from muffin cups.

PER SERVING 483 cal., 24 g total fat (10 g sat. fat), 76 mg chol., 1,011 mg sodium, 44 g carbo., 1 g fiber, 22 g pro.

{ Just a handful of ingredients and less than 30 minutes yield a wholly satisfying supper. }

Spaghetti with Cincinnati-Style Marinara

Beef & Bean
Taco Salad

Beef & Bean Taco Salad

This fresh and crunchy version of taco salad calls for lean ground beef, baked tortilla strips—without the cheese and sour cream—to keep it light.

PREP 15 minutes   **COOK** 10 minutes   **MAKES** 4 servings

- ¾   pound lean ground beef
- 1½ cups no-salt-added pinto or navy beans, drained
- ½   teaspoon chili powder
- ¼   teaspoon salt
- ⅛   teaspoon pepper
- ½   cup salsa
- 1   tablespoon lime juice
- 1½ cups shredded lettuce
- ½   avocado, chopped
- 1   small chopped tomato
- ¼   cup red onion strips
      Baked tortilla strips

1 In a large skillet cook beef on medium heat until brown. Drain off fat. Add beans, chili powder, salt, and pepper; cook for 1 minute. Stir in ¼ cup of the salsa and heat through.

2 In a small bowl combine remaining salsa and lime juice; set aside. Divide lettuce among 4 serving bowls. Add meat mixture, avocado, tomato, red onion, and salsa mixture. Serve each salad with some of the tortilla strips.

PER SERVING 347 cal., 16 g total fat (5 g sat. fat), 58 mg chol., 430 mg sodium, 24 g carbo., 8 g fiber, 22 g pro.

---

quick tip Most of the avocados sold in grocery stores are too firm to use immediately. Let them sit on your counter for 2 to 3 days until they fully ripen. A ripe avocado will yield slightly to gentle pressure. The simplest way to seed an avocado is to cut around it horizontally, then twist both halves to separate. Use a large spoon to pop out the seed.

Meat-&-Cheese-Sandwich Loaf

The clever construction method employed in this recipe allows you to make a batch of toasted, melty, yummy sandwiches all at once.

PREP 10 minutes   **BAKE** 15 minutes   **OVEN** 375°F
MAKES 6 servings

- ¼   cup creamy Dijon mustard blend
- 1   tablespoon prepared horseradish
- 1   unsliced loaf Italian bread (about 12 inches long)
- 1   6-ounce package Swiss cheese slices
- 2   2½-ounce packages very thinly sliced smoked chicken or very thinly sliced smoked turkey
- 1   2½-ounce package very thinly sliced pastrami

1 Preheat oven to 375°F. In a small bowl stir together mustard blend and horseradish. Set aside.

2 Cut bread loaf into 1-inch-thick slices by cutting from the top to, but not through, the bottom crust. (You should have 11 pockets.)

3 To assemble sandwich loaf, spread about 1 tablespoon of the mustard blend in every other pocket in the bread loaf, starting with the first pocket on one end and spreading mustard blend evenly over both sides of the pocket.

4 Divide cheese, chicken, and pastrami among the mustard-spread pockets. Place the bread loaf on a baking sheet. Bake about 15 minutes or until heated through.

5 To serve, cut bread loaf into sandwiches by cutting through the bottom crusts of the unfilled pockets.

PER SERVING 394 cal., 15 g total fat (7 g sat. fat), 55 mg chol., 1,058 mg sodium, 42 g carbo., 2 g fiber, 21 g pro.

Italian-Style Sloppy Joes 🍲

Switch up the flavor profile of everyone's favorite saucy loosemeat sandwich with oregano, basil, and Parmesan cheese. You'll need a lot of napkins.

PREP 15 minutes   **COOK** 15 minutes   **MAKES** 6 servings

12	ounces very lean ground beef
½	cup chopped onion (1 medium)
1	8-ounce can tomato sauce
¼	teaspoon dried oregano, crushed
¼	teaspoon dried basil, crushed
6	whole wheat hamburger buns, split and toasted
½	cup shredded reduced-fat mozzarella cheese (2 ounces)
¼	cup finely shredded Parmesan cheese (1 ounce)

❶ In a large skillet cook ground beef and onion until meat is brown and onion is tender. Drain off fat. Stir in tomato sauce, oregano, and basil. Bring mixture to boiling; reduce heat. Simmer, covered, for 15 minutes.

❷ Divide beef mixture among hamburger bun bottoms; sprinkle with mozzarella and Parmesan cheese. Add bun tops.

PER SERVING 281 cal., 10 g total fat (5 g sat. fat), 50 mg chol., 583 mg sodium, 25 g carbo., 3 g fiber, 20 g pro.

Italian-Style Sloppy Joes

Tarragon Pot Roast with Fruit ♥ 🍲

Spaetzle are small, chewy German-style dumplings. Dried spaetzle can be found in the pasta aisle in most grocery stores. If you can't find them, egg noodles work just as well.

START TO FINISH 25 minutes   **MAKES** 4 servings

1	tablespoon butter
2	tablespoons finely chopped shallot
1	16- to 17-ounce package refrigerated cooked beef roast au jus
2	tablespoons tarragon vinegar
2	cups fresh fruit wedges (such as apples, plums, pears, and/or nectarines or peeled peaches)
	Hot cooked spaetzle or wide noodles (optional)
1	teaspoon snipped fresh tarragon

❶ In a large skillet cook shallot in hot butter for 1 minute. Add beef roast and juices from package; reduce heat. Cover and simmer about 10 minutes or until roast is heated through.

❷ Add vinegar to skillet. Spoon fruit on top. Cover and heat about 4 minutes or until heated through. If desired, serve with hot cooked noodles. Sprinkle with tarragon.

PER SERVING 225 cal., 11 g total fat (6 g sat. fat), 68 mg chol., 422 mg sodium, 12 g carbo., 1 g fiber, 22 g pro.

quick tip   Tarragon has a licoricelike flavor, similar to basil but a bit more intense. It's often paired with chicken. If you don't have fresh tarragon, basil makes a fine substitute. Its clovelike flavor is a nice match with the fruit in this dish.

Asian Pork Skillet

Mediterranean Lamb Skillet

Lamb rib chops are those that have the delicate bone as a kind of "handle" and a small scallop of meat on the end. Lamb loin chops (used in the recipe at right) are thicker and meatier and have a "T-bone" that separates the loin end from the filet end.

START TO FINISH 25 minutes   **MAKES** 4 servings

- ½   **cup dried orzo**
- 8   **lamb rib chops, cut 1 inch thick**
-     **Salt**
-     **Black pepper**
- 2   **teaspoons olive oil**
- 3   **cloves garlic, minced**
- 1   **14.5-ounce can diced tomatoes with basil, garlic, and oregano, undrained**
- 1   **tablespoon balsamic vinegar**
- 2   **teaspoons snipped fresh rosemary**
- ⅓   **cup halved, pitted kalamata olives**
- 2   **tablespoons pine nuts, toasted (see tip, below)**
-     **Fresh rosemary sprigs (optional)**

❶ Cook orzo according to package directions; drain and keep warm. Meanwhile, trim fat from chops. Sprinkle with salt and pepper. In a large skillet heat olive oil on medium heat. Add chops; cook in hot oil for 9 to 11 minutes for medium (160°F), turning once halfway through cooking. Remove chops from skillet; keep warm.

❷ Stir garlic into drippings in skillet. Cook and stir for 1 minute. Stir in undrained tomatoes, vinegar, and snipped rosemary. Bring to boiling; reduce heat. Simmer, uncovered, for 5 minutes. Stir in orzo and olives. Spoon mixture onto 4 serving plates; arrange 2 chops on each plate. Sprinkle with pine nuts and, if desired, top with rosemary sprigs.

PER SERVING 678 cal., 51 g total fat (20 g sat. fat), 105 mg chol., 886 mg sodium, 28 g carbo., 2 g fiber, 27 g pro.

quick tip   Spread nuts, seeds, or shredded coconut in a single layer in a shallow baking pan. Bake in a 350°F oven for 5 to 10 minutes or until the pieces are golden brown, watching carefully and stirring once or twice so they aren't getting too brown.

Lamb Chops with Cinnamon Apples

Good choices for cooking apples (because they hold their shape best when subjected to heat) include Granny Smith, Fuji, Jonathan, and Rome Beauty.

START TO FINISH 25 minutes   **MAKES** 4 servings

- 8   **lamb loin chops, cut 1 inch thick (about 2 pounds)**
- 1   **tablespoon butter or margarine**
- 1   **tablespoon water**
- 3   **medium red cooking apples, cored and sliced (3 cups)**
- 1   **tablespoon packed brown sugar**
- ¼   **teaspoon salt**
- ¼   **teaspoon ground cinnamon**

❶ Trim fat from chops. In a large skillet cook chops in hot butter on medium heat for 9 to 11 minutes for medium doneness (160°F), turning once. Transfer chops to a serving platter; keep warm.

❷ Add water to skillet. Cook and stir until bubbly to loosen any brown bits in bottom of skillet. Add apple slices. Cook about 5 minutes or until apples are tender, stirring occasionally. Add brown sugar, salt, and cinnamon. Cook and stir about 2 minutes or until sugar dissolves. Spoon apple mixture over chops.

PER SERVING 394 cal., 14 g total fat (6 g sat. fat), 153 mg chol., 287 mg sodium, 19 g carbo., 4 g fiber, 47 g pro.

Asian Pork Skillet

This dish can be on the table in less time than it takes to pick up the phone and order Chinese takeout.

START TO FINISH 18 minutes   **MAKES** 4 servings

- 2   **tablespoons vegetable oil**
- 12   **ounces boneless pork, cut into bite-size strips**
- 1½   **cups water**
- 1   **3-ounce package oriental- or pork-flavor ramen noodles, broken**
- 2   **tablespoons hoisin sauce**
- 2   **cups fresh snow pea pods**
- 2   **orange, red, and/or yellow sweet peppers, cut into bite-size strips**
-      **Black pepper**

❶ In a large skillet heat oil on medium-high heat. Add pork; cook and stir about 2 minutes or until light brown.

❷ Add the water to the skillet; bring to boiling. Add noodles, seasoning packet, hoisin sauce, pea pods, and sweet pepper. Return to boiling; reduce heat. Simmer, covered, for 5 minutes. Season to taste with black pepper.

PER SERVING 312 cal., 15 g total fat (2 g sat. fat), 54 mg chol., 646 mg sodium, 21 g carbo., 2 g fiber, 23 g pro.

Pork Chops Dijon ♥

You can use either regular or coarse-ground Dijon in this dish. Coarse-ground mustard will add a bit of texture to the sauce, with toothsome little bites of mustard seed.

START TO FINISH 30 minutes   **MAKES** 4 servings

- 3 **tablespoons Dijon mustard**
- 2 **tablespoons bottled reduced-calorie Italian salad dressing**
- ¼ **teaspoon black pepper**
- 4 **pork loin chops, cut ½ inch thick (about 1½ pounds total)**
    Nonstick cooking spray
- 1 **medium onion, halved and sliced**

❶ In a small bowl combine mustard, Italian dressing, and pepper; set aside. Trim fat from the chops. Coat an unheated large skillet with cooking spray. Preheat the skillet on medium-high heat; add the chops; cook until brown on both sides, turning once. Remove chops from skillet.

❷ Add onion to skillet. Cook and stir on medium heat for 3 minutes. Push onion aside; return chops to skillet. Spread mustard mixture over chops. Cover and cook on medium-low heat about 15 minutes or until done (160°F). Spoon onion mixture over chops.

PER SERVING 163 cal., 5 g total fat (2 g sat. fat), 53 mg chol., 403 mg sodium, 2 g carbo., 0 g fiber, 22 g pro.

Pork Chops Dijon

Pork & Pumpkin Noodle Bowl

If the chewiness of whole wheat pasta prevents you from eating it, overcook it by just a minute or two. It will soften up significantly but will remain al dente, or "to the tooth."

START TO FINISH 30 minutes   **MAKES** 4 servings

- 8 **ounce whole wheat linguine**
- 1 **small red onion, thinly sliced**
- 1 **tablespoon olive oil**
- 1 **pound pork loin, cut into ½-inch-thick slices**
- 3 **tablespoons reduced-sodium soy sauce**
    Black pepper
- 12 **fresh sage leaves**
- 1 **teaspoon minced garlic (2 cloves) or ½ teaspoon garlic powder**
- 1 **cup canned or frozen pureed pumpkin or butternut squash**
- 1 **cup water**
- ¼ **cup blue cheese crumbles (optional)**

❶ Cook pasta according to package directions, adding onion during last 5 minutes of cooking time. Drain and keep warm.

❷ Meanwhile, in an extra-large skillet heat oil. Brush pork with some soy sauce and generously sprinkle with pepper. Cook sage leaves in hot oil until crisp. Drain on paper towels. Add pork to skillet and cook for 2 minutes on each side or until golden outside and slightly pink inside. Remove pork from skillet; cover to keep warm.

❸ In the same skillet combine remaining soy sauce, garlic, ¼ cup of the pumpkin, and water. Bring to boiling and reduce sauce slightly. Add pasta and onions to skillet; heat through. In a small skillet heat remaining pumpkin.

❹ Divide pasta among 4 bowls. Serve pork with pasta, pumpkin, sage leaves, and blue cheese.

PER SERVING 414 cal., 9 g total fat (2 g sat. fat), 71 mg chol., 645 mg sodium, 51 g carbo., 2 g fiber, 34 g pro.

Pork Cutlets with
Brussels Sprouts

Pork Cutlets with Brussels Sprouts

This dish will convince avoiders of Brussels sprouts to embrace the little green globes. Cooked in hot butter, they get browned and crisp and flavorful. Yum!

START TO FINISH 30 minutes **MAKES** 4 servings

4	½-inch-thick boneless pork chops
¼	cup all-purpose flour
2	teaspoons paprika or smoked paprika
½	teaspoon salt
½	teaspoon black pepper
1	pound Brussels sprouts, trimmed and halved
2	tablespoons butter
1	8-ounce carton light sour cream
2	tablespoons milk or half-and-half
1	teaspoon packed brown sugar

1 Using a meat mallet or heavy rolling pin, pound pork, layered between plastic wrap, to ¼-inch thickness. In a shallow dish combine flour, half the paprika, salt, and pepper. Coat pork in flour mixture; set aside.

2 In a large skillet cook Brussels sprouts in hot butter on medium-high heat for 5 to 8 minutes until crisp-tender and edges are brown. Remove from skillet. Cover and keep warm.

3 In the same skillet cook pork 4 to 5 minutes, turning once, until golden outside and slightly pink in center (add additional butter, if needed). Remove from skillet. Cover; keep warm.

4 For sauce, combine sour cream, milk, and brown sugar. Whisk into skillet. Heat through (do not boil). Sprinkle paprika on sauce. Serve sauce over pork and sprouts.

PER SERVING 395 cal., 22 g total fat (11 g sat. fat), 108 mg chol., 480 mg sodium, 22 g carbo., 5 g fiber, 29 g pro.

Quick Mu Shu Pork ♨

Bias-slicing the green onions (cutting them at an angle) takes no more time than cutting them straight on—and it pretties up the dish just a bit.

START TO FINISH 20 minutes **MAKES** 4 servings

12	ounces boneless pork top loin chops, cut into thin strips
1	tablespoon cooking oil
1	8-ounce package sliced button mushrooms
½	cup bias-sliced green onions (4)
4	cups packaged shredded cabbage with carrot (coleslaw mix)
2	tablespoons soy sauce
1	teaspoon toasted sesame oil
⅛	teaspoon crushed red pepper
8	7- to 8-inch flour tortillas, warmed
	Bottled hoisin or plum sauce

1 In a large skillet cook pork strips in hot oil on medium-high heat for 4 to 5 minutes or until no longer pink. Remove meat from skillet. Add mushrooms and green onions to skillet; cook for 3 minutes or until softened. Add coleslaw mix and cook about 1 minute until wilted. Return meat to skillet. Add soy sauce, sesame oil, and crushed red pepper. Heat through.

2 Serve pork mixture with warm tortillas and hoisin sauce.

PER SERVING 412 cal., 14 g total fat (3 g sat. fat), 47 mg chol., 1,066 mg sodium, 43 g carbo., 4 g fiber, 26 g pro.

---

quick tip Warming tortillas in the microwave may be the quickest way, but it's not the best way: You run the risk of toughening them. The best way to warm tortillas is to wrap a stack tightly in foil, then warm them in a 300°F oven for 10 to 12 minutes.

Sweet-&-Sour Pork Lo Mein

You don't need bottled sweet and sour sauce to make this dish. If you've got marmalade and cider vinegar, you've got the ingredients you need to whip up your own sauce.

START TO FINISH 18 minutes   **MAKES** 4 servings

1	9-ounce package refrigerated linguine
2	tablespoons vegetable oil
1½	cups packaged julienne or shredded fresh carrots
1	large onion, cut into thin wedges
12	ounces boneless pork loin, cut into thin strips
⅓	cup orange marmalade
¼	cup cider vinegar
	Salt
	Black pepper
	Chopped peanuts (optional)

❶ If desired, snip linguine into 2- to 3-inch lengths. Cook linguine according to package directions; drain.

❷ Meanwhile, in a large skillet heat 1 tablespoon of the oil on medium-high heat. Add carrots and onion; cook and stir about 4 minutes or until onion is tender. Remove vegetables from skillet.

❸ Add the remaining 1 tablespoon oil and pork to skillet; cook and stir for 3 to 4 minutes or until pork is no longer pink. Return vegetables to skillet. Add linguine, marmalade, and vinegar; toss to mix. Heat through. Season to taste with salt and pepper. If desired, sprinkle with chopped peanuts.

PER SERVING 452 cal., 12 g total fat (3 g sat. fat), 121 mg chol., 252 mg sodium, 60 g carbo., 4 g fiber, 27 g pro.

Maple-Bourbon Smoked Chops

You may not use it every day on your toaster waffles, but splurge, if you can, on a bottle of pure maple syrup for occasions like making this recipe. There is nothing quite like the intense, authentic flavor of real maple syrup.

START TO FINISH 30 minutes   **MAKES** 4 servings

2	teaspoons cooking oil
1	medium onion, halved lengthwise and sliced
¼	cup pure maple syrup or maple-flavored syrup
1	tablespoon bourbon
1	tablespoon Dijon mustard
⅛	teaspoon crushed red pepper
2	cloves garlic, minced
4	cooked smoked boneless pork chops, cut ¾ inch thick (about 1 pound total)
	Cooked broccolini (optional)

❶ In a large skillet heat oil on medium heat. Add onion; cook for 4 to 5 minutes or until tender, stirring occasionally. Increase heat to medium-high; cook and stir for 3 to 4 minutes more or until onion is golden. Remove onion from skillet with a slotted spoon, reserving drippings. In a medium bowl stir together cooked onion, syrup, bourbon, mustard, red pepper, and garlic; set aside.

❷ Trim fat from chops. In the same skillet cook chops in reserved drippings on medium heat for 5 minutes. Turn chops over. Add onion mixture to skillet. Cook, uncovered, for 4 to 5 minutes more or until chops are heated through.

❸ To serve, transfer chops to a serving platter. Spoon onion mixture over chops. If desired, serve with broccolini.

PER SERVING 229 cal., 8 g total fat (2 g sat. fat), 60 mg chol., 1,382 mg sodium, 16 g carbo., 0 g fiber, 20 g pro.

{ There is something about the flavor of pork that makes it especially suited to the sweetness of marmalade and maple syrup. }

Maple-Bourbon
Smoked Chops

Pork Medallions with
Lemon-Dill Green Beans

Pork Medallions with Lemon-Dill Green Beans ♥ 📽

A purchased premarinated pork tenderloin gives you a head start on this quick-cooking skillet dish.

START TO FINISH 20 minutes **MAKES** 4 servings

- 1 1- to 1½-pound honey-mustard-marinated pork tenderloin
- 1 tablespoon butter or margarine
- 1 9-ounce package frozen French-cut green beans, thawed
- 1 teaspoon dried dill
- 1 teaspoon lemon juice
   Fresh dill sprigs
   Lemon slices

❶ Cut pork tenderloin into ¼-inch slices. In a very large skillet cook pork in hot butter on medium heat for 4 to 6 minutes or until juices run clear, turning once. Remove meat from skillet; reserve drippings. Keep warm.

❷ Add green beans and dill to drippings in skillet. Cook and stir for 3 to 4 minutes or until beans are tender. Stir in lemon juice. Transfer beans and pork slices to a serving platter. If desired, garnish with fresh dill and lemon slices.

PER SERVING 189 cal., 8 g total fat (4 g sat. fat), 53 mg chol., 531 mg sodium, 8 g carbo., 2 g fiber, 21 g pro.

---

quick tip This recipe calls for dried dill for convenience, but if you have some fresh dill on hand, by all means use it. The general rule of substituting dried herbs for fresh is 1 tablespoon of fresh herb for every 1 teaspoon of dried (and vice versa), which is a three-to-one ratio.

Pork & Noodle Salad Bowls

This dish takes the concept of the Asian-style lettuce-wrap appetizer and turns it into a main dish.

START TO FINISH 15 minutes **MAKES** 4 servings

- 1 3-ounce package ramen noodles (any variety)
- 1 17-ounce package cooked pork roast au jus, unheated
- 1 cup fresh pea pods, strings and tips removed
- ¼ cup cider vinegar
- 3 tablespoons salad oil
- 1 tablespoon soy sauce
- 8 butterhead (Boston or Bibb) lettuce leaves
- ⅓ cup butter toffee glaze-flavored sliced almonds

❶ Cook noodles according to package directions, except discard seasoning packet; drain. Meanwhile, remove pork roast from au jus; discard au jus. Cut pork into large chunks and place in a large bowl. Add hot noodles and pea pods to pork in bowl.

❷ In a screw-top jar combine vinegar, oil, and soy sauce; cover and shake well. Pour over pork mixture; toss to combine.

❸ Place lettuce leaves on 4 dinner plates. Spoon pork mixture into lettuce leaves. Sprinkle with almonds.

PER SERVING 409 cal., 24 g total fat (5 g sat. fat), 72 mg chol., 832 mg sodium, 19 g carbo., 2 g fiber, 30 g pro.

{ Pork has the delightful quality of being crisp-cooked on the outside while juicy on the inside. }

Pork & Hominy Skillet 🍲

It used to be that any dish that had rice in it required at least 15 minutes of cooking time just for the rice. Thanks to precooked rice, the whole dish takes just 20 minutes.

START TO FINISH 20 minutes   **MAKES** 4 servings

- 1 tablespoon vegetable oil
- 1 large sweet onion, cut into wedges
- 2 medium carrots, thinly sliced
- 1 17-ounce package refrigerated cooked pork roast au jus
- 2 8.8-ounce pouches cooked whole grain brown rice
- 1 15-ounce can yellow hominy, rinsed and drained
- ⅔ cup water
  Black pepper

❶ In a very large skillet heat oil on medium heat. Add onion and carrots; cook for 5 minutes.

❷ Add pork with juices, breaking up meat with the back of a wooden spoon. Add rice, drained hominy, and water. Cook, covered, about 5 minutes, stirring occasionally, until heated through. Season to taste with pepper.

PER SERVING 503 cal., 14 g total fat (3 g sat. fat), 72 mg chol., 742 mg sodium, 63 g carbo., 5 g fiber, 32 g pro.

Easy Skillet Lasagna

This weeknight lasagna is cooked completely on top of the stove—in 25 minutes, start to finish.

START TO FINISH 25 minutes   **MAKES** 4 to 6 servings

- 1 pound bulk Italian sausage
- 1 8-ounce package sliced fresh mushrooms
- ¾ cup chopped green sweet pepper (1 medium)
- ½ cup chopped onion (1 medium)
- 8 ounces dried campanelle or mafalda pasta
- 1 26-ounce jar mushroom pasta sauce
- 1 cup shredded Italian cheese blend
  Snipped fresh parsley (optional)

❶ In an extra-large skillet cook sausage, mushrooms, sweet pepper, and onion on medium heat until sausage is no longer pink and vegetables are tender. Drain off fat.

❷ Meanwhile, cook pasta according to package directions; drain.

❸ Stir pasta and pasta sauce into mixture in skillet. Return to a simmer. Sprinkle with cheese. Cook, covered, on low heat until cheese melts. If desired, sprinkle with parsley.

PER SERVING 892 cal., 49 g total fat (19 g sat. fat), 106 mg chol., 1,881 mg sodium, 78 g carbo., 8 g fiber, 36 g pro.

Apple-Glazed Pork Loaf

Each person gets his or her own apple-infused mini meatloaf served on a slice of toasted chewy ciabatta.

START TO FINISH 30 minutes   **OVEN** 425°F   **MAKES** 4 servings

- ½ cup apple jelly
- 1 tablespoon Dijon mustard
- 2 small apples
- 2 eggs, lightly beaten
- 1 pound ground pork
- ½ teaspoon salt
- ½ teaspoon black pepper
- 1 medium sweet potato, chopped
- 1 tablespoon olive oil
  Salt
  Black pepper
- ⅛ teaspoon cayenne pepper (optional)
- 2 ciabatta sandwich rolls, split and toasted

❶ Preheat oven to 425°F. Grease a 15×10×1-inch baking pan; set aside. For apple glaze, in a small microwave-safe bowl microwave jelly on high about 30 seconds or until jelly melts. Stir in mustard. Set aside. Chop one of the apples; set aside.

❷ In a large bowl combine eggs, ground meat, half of the chopped apple, the ½ teaspoon salt, and the ½ teaspoon pepper. Form into four 6×2-inch loaves. Place in prepared baking pan. Spoon a small amount of apple glaze over each loaf. Bake for 10 minutes.

❸ Meanwhile, thinly slice the remaining apple. Top loaves with some of the apple slices; drizzle loaves with a little more apple glaze. Bake for 5 to 10 minutes more or until internal temperature is 160°F on an instant-read thermometer.

❹ Place sweet potato in a large microwave-safe bowl. Microwave, uncovered, on high about 4 minutes or until nearly tender.

❺ Meanwhile, in a large skillet heat oil on medium-high heat. Add sweet potato and the remaining chopped apple. Season with salt, black pepper, and, if desired, cayenne pepper. Cook and stir for 3 to 4 minutes or until potato and apple are tender and golden.

❻ Place a pork loaf on each roll half. Serve with the sweet potato mixture. Drizzle with any remaining apple glaze.

PER SERVING 697 cal., 32 g total fat (11 g sat. fat), 187 mg chol., 842 mg sodium, 74 g carbo., 5 g fiber, 28 g pro.

Pan-Seared Pork Burgers
with Peppers & Mushrooms

Pan-Seared Pork Burgers with Peppers & Mushrooms

The peppers in this dish go in two places—mixed into the meat and quickly sauteed, along with mushrooms, as a topping for the finished burgers.

START TO FINISH 25 minutes   **MAKES** 4 servings

2	small red and/or green sweet peppers
1	banana, jalapeño, or other chile pepper, seeded and chopped (see note, page 19) (optional)
1	pound ground pork
1	tablespoon Worcestershire or soy sauce
2	teaspoons cracked black pepper
8	ounces sliced fresh mushrooms
4	pita bread rounds or other flatbread
½	cup mayonnaise
	Black pepper

❶ Slice one of the sweet peppers and half of the chile pepper (if using) into rings; set aside. Chop the remaining sweet pepper and chile pepper. In a medium bowl combine chopped peppers, pork, 2 teaspoons of the Worcestershire sauce, and cracked black pepper. Shape into four ¾-inch-thick patties. Heat a large skillet on medium-high heat; add patties. Cook patties for 10 to 12 minutes or until done (165°F); turning once halfway through cooking. Transfer to a plate; keep warm.

❷ In the same skillet cook pepper rings and mushrooms in drippings for 3 minutes; sprinkle with salt.

❸ Wrap bread in paper towels. Microwave on high for 30 seconds.

❹ For sauce, in a small bowl stir together mayonnaise and the remaining 1 teaspoon Worcestershire sauce. Season to taste with black pepper.

❺ Serve burgers on bread topped with pepper-mushroom mixture. Pass sauce.

PER SERVING 693 cal., 47 g total fat (12 g sat. fat), 92 mg chol., 734 mg sodium, 40 g carbo., 3 g fiber, 27 g pro.

Sausage-Fruit Kabobs

If you have mustard in your refrigerator and honey in your pantry, you always have the makings for honey mustard on hand.

START TO FINISH 20 minutes   **MAKES** 4 servings

3	tablespoons spicy brown or Dijon mustard
3	tablespoons honey
12	ounces cooked smoked sausage, bias-cut into ½-inch slices
1	apple, cored and cut into ½-inch wedges
1	medium zucchini, halved and cut into ¼-inch slices
6	ounces crusty bread, cut into 1-inch pieces

❶ Preheat broiler. In a bowl stir mustard into honey.

❷ On four 12-inch skewers* alternately thread sausage, apples, and zucchini, leaving ¼ inch between pieces. Brush with some of the honey mustard; reserve remaining honey mustard. Place on rack of unheated broiler pan. Broil 4 to 5 inches from heat for 4 minutes.

❸ Meanwhile, thread bread on four 12-inch skewers; lightly brush with olive oil. Add bread skewers to broiler; turn sausage skewers. Broil 3 minutes more or until sausage is heated through and bread is toasted, turning bread once. Serve with reserved honey mustard.

PER SERVING 527 cal., 32 g total fat (9 g sat. fat), 52 mg chol., 1,138 mg sodium, 33 g carbo., 3 g fiber, 11 g pro.

*NOTE: If using wooden skewers, soak them in water for at least 30 minutes before grilling.

quick tip   If you don't use a lot of honey at your house, even small jars or bottles of it can become crystallized over time. Don't throw it away—just place the jar or bottle in a pan of very warm water until the honey softens enough to use.

Tex-Mex Skillet 📇

If you can't find bulk chorizo, you can buy it in links. Just cut the casings off before cooking it.

START TO FINISH 30 minutes   **MAKES** 4 servings

- 8 ounces ground pork
- 4 ounces bulk chorizo sausage
- 1 10-ounce can diced tomatoes and green chile peppers, undrained
- 1 cup loose-pack frozen whole kernel corn
- ¾ cup water
- ½ cup chopped red sweet pepper
- 1 cup instant rice
- ½ cup shredded cheddar cheese or Monterey Jack cheese (2 ounces)
  Flour tortillas, warmed (optional)
  Sour cream (optional)

❶ In a large skillet cook pork and sausage until brown. Drain off fat. Stir in undrained tomatoes, corn, water, and sweet pepper. Bring to boiling.

❷ Stir uncooked rice into tomato mixture in skillet. Remove from heat. Top with cheese. Cover and let stand about 5 minutes or until rice is tender. If desired, serve in flour tortillas and top with sour cream.

PER SERVING 395 cal., 20 g total fat (9 g sat. fat), 66 mg chol., 748 mg sodium, 33 g carbo., 1 g fiber, 21 g pro.

Tex-Mex Skillet

Apple Butter-Glazed Ham

This dish is a perfect choice for fall, when Brussels sprouts and sweet potatoes are at their best.

START TO FINISH 20 minutes   **MAKES** 4 servings

- 2 medium sweet potatoes, peeled and cut into 1-inch cubes
- 12 ounces Brussels sprouts, trimmed and halved
- 1 to 1¼ pounds sliced cooked ham, about ¼ inch thick
- 2 tablespoons butter
  Salt
  Black pepper
- ½ cup apple butter
- 2 tablespoons cider vinegar
  Baguette slices (optional)

❶ In a large saucepan cook potatoes and Brussels sprouts in lightly boiling salted water for 8 or 10 minutes or just until tender. Drain.

❷ Meanwhile, in an extra-large skillet cook ham in hot butter on medium-high heat for 4 to 5 minutes, turning occasionally. Remove from skillet and place on serving plates with vegetables; season to taste with salt and pepper. Keep warm. Stir apple butter and vinegar into skillet; heat through. Serve with ham, vegetables, and, if desired, baguette slices.

PER SERVING 513 cal., 16 g total fat (7 g sat. fat), 80 mg chol., 1,664 mg sodium, 71 g carbo., 8 g fiber, 23 g pro.

quick tip   When trimming Brussels sprouts, be sure to nip the very tip off the stem end with a small sharp knife. If you cut off too much, when you cut the sprouts in half, there will be nothing to hold the individual leaves together, and they will fall apart.

Ham with Leeks
& Dilled Potatoes

Ham with Leeks & Dilled Potatoes 🍲

Leeks must be cleaned before using to get out any grit from between the layers. After trimming, cut them in half horizontally, then fan the layers under cool running water before slicing them.

START TO FINISH 20 minutes **MAKES** 4 servings

- 2 tablespoons vegetable oil
- 3 cups packaged refrigerated diced potatoes
- 2 medium leeks, thinly sliced
- 1½ cups cubed cooked ham (8 ounces)
- 8 ounces fresh asparagus spears, trimmed and cut into 2-inch lengths
- ⅓ cup water
   Freshly ground black pepper
- 1 cup shredded Havarti cheese with dill (4 ounces)

❶ In a large skillet heat oil on medium heat. Add potatoes and leeks; cook for 5 minutes, turning mixture occasionally with a spatula. Fold in ham. Cook for 2 minutes more. Add asparagus and water; season with pepper. Cook, covered, for 3 minutes.

❷ Sprinkle with cheese; cover and cook for 1 minute more or until cheese melts.

PER SERVING 381 cal., 20 g total fat (1 g sat. fat), 60 mg chol., 1,158 mg sodium, 33 g carbo., 4 g fiber, 22 g pro.

Ham-Basil-Broccoli Wraps

These wraps make a terrific totable lunch. Be sure to keep them refrigerated or stored with a cold pack.

START TO FINISH 25 minutes **MAKES** 4 wraps

- 1¼ cups packaged shredded broccoli (broccoli slaw mix)
- 8 ounces smoked cooked ham or turkey, cut into bite-size strips
- 6 tablespoons bottled peppercorn ranch salad dressing or ranch salad dressing
- ¼ cup chopped walnuts, toasted (see note, page 31)
- ¼ cup oil-packed dried tomatoes, well drained and cut into thin strips
- 4 8- or 9-inch tomato or spinach flour tortillas
- 12 large fresh basil or spinach leaves

❶ In a medium bowl combine broccoli, ham, 4 tablespoons of the salad dressing, walnuts, and tomatoes.

❷ Spread tortillas with the remaining 2 tablespoons salad dressing. Top with basil leaves and ham mixture.

❸ Roll up tortillas. Halve rolls and secure with wooden picks, if necessary.

PER WRAP 481 cal., 27 g total fat (5 g sat. fat), 36 mg chol., 1,321 mg sodium, 42 g carbo., 5 g fiber, 18 g pro.

Ham with Creamed Spinach & Sweet Potatoes

This quick dish is the definition of comfort food—a creamy spinach-ham mixture studded with sweet cranberries and ladled over mashed sweet potatoes.

START TO FINISH 15 minutes **MAKES** 4 servings

- 1 22- to 24-ounce package refrigerated mashed sweet potatoes or mashed potatoes
- 1 9- to 10-ounce package frozen creamed spinach, thawed
- 2½ cups cubed cooked ham (12 ounces)
- 1 small red sweet pepper, chopped
- ¼ cup dried cranberries
   Black pepper

❶ Microwave mashed potatoes according to package directions.

❷ Meanwhile, in a large saucepan combine creamed spinach, ham, sweet pepper, and cranberries. Cook and stir on medium heat until heated through. Season to taste with black pepper.

❸ Serve spinach mixture with mashed potatoes.

PER SERVING 368 cal., 14 g total fat (4 g sat. fat), 56 mg chol., 1,357 mg sodium, 42 g carbo., 5 g fiber, 18 g pro.

quick tip The best way to core and prep a sweet pepper for cooking is to place it, bottom side down, on a cutting board. Cut each of the four sides off and you're left with a seedy core and stem you can discard—and four clean pieces of pepper you can slice or chop as needed.

Chicken and turkey are budget-friendly, fast to fix, and lend themselves to an array of flavors and cooking methods. Broiled, baked, fried, roasted, or grilled, these birds are sure to please.

50   58   93

quick poultry

69

Pan-Fried Chicken Breasts with Orange Sauce 🍲

You'll only need one orange for this recipe. Shred the peel first—most conveniently on a Microplane shredder—then cut the orange in half and juice it.

START TO FINISH 30 minutes **MAKES** 4 servings

- 4 skinless, boneless chicken breast halves
- 4 tablespoons butter
- ½ teaspoon finely shredded orange peel
- 3 tablespoons fresh orange juice
- 2 tablespoons golden raisins or raisins
- 2 teaspoons packed brown sugar
  Hot cooked rice or pasta
  Cooked sugar snap peas (optional)

❶ In a large skillet cook chicken in 1 tablespoon of the butter on medium-high heat for 12 minutes or until chicken is no longer pink (170°F), turning once. Transfer chicken to a serving platter; cover and keep warm.

❷ Add remaining butter to the skillet. Stir in orange peel, orange juice, raisins, and brown sugar. Cook and stir on medium heat about 2 minutes or until slightly thick. Add chicken to skillet to heat through. Serve with hot cooked rice and, if desired, sugar snap peas.

PER SERVING 391 cal., 14 g total fat (8 g sat. fat), 113 mg chol., 478 mg sodium, 30 g carbo., 1 g fiber, 35 g pro.

Pan-Fried Chicken Breasts with Orange Sauce

Almost a Potpie

Instead of having a pastry cap or topper, each serving of this veggie-packed chicken "potpie" is served with wedges of flaky piecrust.

START TO FINISH 20 minutes **OVEN** 425°F **MAKES** 4 servings

- ½ of a 15-ounce package rolled refrigerated unbaked piecrust (1 crust)
- 2 tablespoons vegetable oil
- 1 pound skinless, boneless chicken breast halves, cut into ½-inch pieces
- 1 cup thinly sliced carrots (2 medium) (optional)
- 3 tablespoons all-purpose flour
- 1½ cups chicken broth
- 2 cups fresh pea pods, halved crosswise
- ½ cup chopped fresh basil
  Salt
  Black pepper

❶ Preheat oven to 425°F. Follow package directions for refrigerated piecrust. Unroll piecrust on a large baking sheet; cut into 8 wedges. Separate wedges slightly. If desired, flute edges. Bake for 8 to 10 minutes or until golden.

❷ Meanwhile, in an extra-large skillet heat oil on medium heat. Add chicken and, if desired, carrots; cook until chicken is brown and carrots are crisp-tender. Stir in flour. Add broth; cook and stir until thickened and bubbly. Add pea pods; cook for 1 minute. Stir in basil. Season to taste with salt and pepper.

❸ Divide chicken mixture evenly among 4 shallow bowls. Serve with piecrust wedges.

PER SERVING 462 cal., 22 g total fat (6 g sat. fat), 72 mg chol., 782 mg sodium, 33 g carbo., 1 g fiber, 29 g pro.

---

quick tip   In most cases, using all-purpose flour to thicken sauces and gravies works just fine. However, for a little extra insurance against lumpy gravy or sauce, use an instant flour that is specifically formulated as a thickener. The most recognizable brand of instant flour is Wondra, which you will generally find in the baking aisle of your supermarket.

Herbed Chicken,
Orzo & Zucchini

Pan-Fried Italian Chicken Parmesan

Japanese panko bread crumbs are lighter and larger than traditional bread crumbs. Because they are coarser, they create a much crisper crust.

START TO FINISH 25 minutes   **MAKES** 4 servings

8	ounces dried linguine or fettuccine
1	egg
1	tablespoon cooking oil
½	teaspoon salt
¼	teaspoon coarsely ground black pepper
½	cup panko (Japanese-style bread crumbs)
¼	cup grated Parmesan cheese
1	teaspoon dried Italian seasoning, crushed
4	skinless, boneless chicken breast halves
	Salt
	Black pepper
2	tablespoons cooking oil
1	cup prepared marinara sauce
	Grated Parmesan cheese (optional)

❶ Prepare pasta according to package directions; drain.

❷ Meanwhile, in a shallow dish whisk together egg, the 1 tablespoon oil, salt, and pepper; set aside. In another shallow dish combine panko, ¼ cup Parmesan cheese, and Italian seasoning. Sprinkle chicken lightly with salt and pepper. Dip each chicken breast half in the egg mixture and then in the bread crumb mixture to coat.

❸ In a large skillet cook chicken in the 2 tablespoons hot oil on medium-high heat for 8 to 12 minutes or until no longer pink (170°F), turning once. (If chicken browns too quickly, reduce heat to medium.)

❹ Meanwhile, place marinara sauce in microwave-safe dish. Heat on high for 1 minute or until hot. Spoon about ¼ cup sauce on each chicken breast. If desired, sprinkle with additional Parmesan cheese. Serve with hot cooked pasta.

PER SERVING 456 cal., 17 g total fat (4 g sat. fat), 175 mg chol., 807 mg sodium, 31 g carbo., 1 g fiber, 42 g pro.

quick tip   If you'd like the chicken to cook even more quickly than the 8 to 12 minutes, you can make thin cutlets from the breast halves before breading. To make a chicken cutlet, place a breast half on a flat surface. Press down on it with one hand to hold it steady while you cut through it horizontally with a knife held in the other hand. Place each piece between two pieces of plastic wrap and pound lightly with a meat mallet until it is ¼ to ⅛ inch thick.

Herbed Chicken, Orzo & Zucchini

Dressed with an herbed olive oil-and-vinegar dressing, the orzo in this one-dish meal is served like a warm pasta salad accompaniment to the chicken.

START TO FINISH 20 minutes   **MAKES** 4 servings

1	cup dried orzo
4	small skinless, boneless chicken breast halves (1 to 1¼ pounds)
1	teaspoon dried basil
3	tablespoons olive oil
2	medium zucchini, sliced
2	tablespoons red wine vinegar
1	tablespoon snipped fresh dill
	Lemon wedges (optional)
	Snipped fresh dill (optional)

❶ Prepare orzo according to package directions; drain. Cover and keep warm.

❷ Meanwhile, sprinkle chicken with the basil; season with salt and pepper. In a large skillet heat 1 tablespoon of the olive oil. Add chicken and cook 12 minutes or until no longer pink (170°F), turning once. Remove from skillet. Add zucchini to skillet; cook for 3 minutes or until crisp-tender.

❸ In a bowl whisk together vinegar, remaining olive oil, and 1 tablespoon fresh dill. Add orzo; toss. Season with salt and pepper. Serve chicken with orzo and zucchini and, if desired, lemon wedges and dill.

PER SERVING 390 cal., 12 g total fat (2 g sat. fat), 66 mg chol., 233 mg sodium, 35 g carbo., 3 g fiber, 33 g pro.

Chicken-Pineapple Fajitas

To save time, look in the produce section of your supermarket for the whole fresh pineapple that is already peeled and cored.

START TO FINISH 20 minutes   **OVEN** 350°F   **MAKES** 4 servings

  8 6-inch flour tortillas
     Nonstick cooking spray
  4 1-inch slices peeled fresh pineapple
  1 pound skinless, boneless chicken breast halves
  2 small red and/or orange sweet peppers, cut into thin bite-size strips
  2 teaspoons Jamaican jerk seasoning
  ⅛ teaspoon black pepper
  1 tablespoon vegetable oil
     Fresh cilantro (optional)
     Lime wedges (optional)

❶ Preheat oven to 350°F. Wrap tortillas in foil. Place foil packet in the oven. Meanwhile, lightly coat an extra-large nonstick skillet with cooking spray; heat on medium-high heat. Add pineapple slices. Cook for 4 to 6 minutes or until light brown, turning once. Transfer pineapple to a cutting board; set aside.

❷ Meanwhile, cut chicken into thin strips. In a large bowl toss chicken and sweet peppers with jerk seasoning and pepper.

❸ In the same skillet heat oil on medium-high heat; add chicken mixture. Cook and stir for 4 to 6 minutes or until chicken is no longer pink.

❹ Meanwhile, core and coarsely chop pineapple slices. Divide pineapple and chicken mixture among the warm tortillas. If desired, serve with cilantro and lime.

PER SERVING 393 cal., 10 g total fat (2 g sat. fat), 66 mg chol., 633 mg sodium, 43 g carbo., 4 g fiber, 32 g pro.

Lemon Chicken Stir-Fry ♥

A medium size lemon will yield about ¼ cup of juice (the equivalent of 4 tablespoons).

START TO FINISH 25 minutes   **MAKES** 4 servings

  1 pound skinless, boneless chicken breast halves
  ¾ cup chicken broth
  3 tablespoons lemon juice
  1 tablespoon cornstarch
  1 tablespoon soy sauce
  2 tablespoons cooking oil
  1 16-ounce package frozen stir-fry vegetables (any blend)
  2 cups hot cooked rice
     Soy sauce (optional)

❶ Cut chicken into bite-size strips, set aside. For sauce, in a small bowl stir together chicken broth, lemon juice, cornstarch, and soy sauce; set aside.

❷ In a large skillet heat 1 tablespoon of the oil on medium-high heat. Add frozen vegetables; cook and stir for 5 to 7 minutes or until crisp-tender. Remove from skillet. Add remaining oil and half of the chicken to the skillet. Cook and stir for 2 to 3 minutes or until chicken is no longer pink. Remove from skillet. Repeat with remaining chicken (add more oil, if necessary). Return all chicken to skillet. Push chicken from center of skillet.

❸ Stir sauce; add to center of skillet. Cook and stir until thickened and bubbly. Return vegetables to skillet; stir to coat with sauce. Cook and stir for 1 to 2 minutes more or until heated through. Serve with rice. If desired, pass additional soy sauce.

PER SERVING 348 cal., 9 g total fat (2 g sat. fat), 66 mg chol., 522 mg sodium, 32 g carbo., 3 g fiber, 32 g pro.

{ Here are two different ways to define "fried chicken"—a fruited fajita dish and a lemony stir-fry. }

Blackened Chicken
with Avocado Salsa

Blackened Chicken with Avocado Salsa

There are some subtle differences between rice vinegar and rice wine vinegar, but they can be used interchangeably in most recipes—and certainly in this one.

START TO FINISH 25 minutes   **OVEN** 375°F   **MAKES** 4 servings

4	skinless, boneless chicken breast halves (1¼ to 1½ pounds total)
2	teaspoons blackened steak seasoning
1	tablespoon olive oil
2	tablespoons rice vinegar
2	tablespoons olive oil
¼	teaspoon ground cumin
⅛	teaspoon salt
	Dash black pepper
1	avocado, halved, seeded, peeled, and chopped
⅔	cup chopped fresh or refrigerated papaya
⅓	cup finely chopped red sweet pepper
¼	cup chopped fresh cilantro
	Fresh cilantro sprigs (optional)

❶ Preheat oven to 375°F. Lightly sprinkle both sides of each chicken breast half with blackened steak seasoning. In a large ovenproof skillet heat the 1 tablespoon oil on medium heat. Add chicken; cook until brown, turning once. Bake about 15 minutes or until the chicken is no longer pink (170°F).

❷ Meanwhile, for avocado salsa, in a large bowl whisk together rice vinegar, the 2 tablespoons oil, cumin, salt, and black pepper. Stir in avocado, papaya, sweet pepper, and chopped cilantro. Serve salsa with chicken. If desired, garnish with cilantro sprigs.

PER SERVING 322 cal., 17 g total fat (3 g sat. fat), 82 mg chol., 513 mg sodium, 7 g carbo., 3 g fiber, 34 g pro.

Coconut Chicken with Pineapple-Mango Salsa

This crispy, coconut-crusted chicken is baked—not fried—and served with a light and healthful tropical salsa.

START TO FINISH 30 minutes   **OVEN** 400°F   **MAKES** 4 servings

1	egg, lightly beaten
1	tablespoon cooking oil
¼	teaspoon salt
⅛	teaspoon cayenne pepper
1¼	cups flaked coconut
14	to 16 ounces chicken breast tenderloins
1	8-ounce can pineapple tidbits (juice pack), drained
1	cup chopped refrigerated mango slices (about 10 slices)
2	tablespoons snipped fresh cilantro (optional)
1	tablespoon lime juice
¼	teaspoon salt

❶ Preheat oven to 400°F. Line a large baking sheet with foil; lightly grease foil. Set aside. In a shallow dish whisk together egg, oil, salt, and cayenne pepper. Spread coconut in another shallow dish. Dip chicken, 1 piece at a time, in egg mixture, allowing excess to drip off. Coat chicken in coconut and arrange on prepared baking sheet. Bake for 10 to 12 minutes or until chicken is no longer pink (170°F).

❷ Meanwhile, for salsa, in a medium bowl combine pineapple, mango, cilantro (if using), lime juice, and salt. Serve with chicken.

PER SERVING 401 cal., 18 g total fat (12 g sat. fat), 110 mg chol., 485 mg sodium, 33 g carbo., 3 g fiber, 27 g pro.

---

quick tip   Sweet and hot flavors go particularly well together—especially in tropical salsas such as the Pineapple-Mango Salsa above. If you would like a little heat with your sweet, stir 1 seeded and finely chopped jalapeño into the salsa along with the fruit.

Chicken Piccata ♥

This classic Italian dish gets its piquancy from lemon and capers—the briny pickled buds of the Mediterranean caper bush. It's also made with scallops of veal.

START TO FINISH 20 minutes **MAKES** 4 servings

- 4   small skinless, boneless chicken breast halves (about 1½ pounds)
- 1   tablespoon Dijon mustard
     Salt
     Black pepper
- ¼   cup seasoned fine dry bread crumbs
- ¼   cup olive oil
- 2   small lemons
- 8   ounces haricots verts, trimmed if desired, or green beans, trimmed and halved lengthwise
  - 1   tablespoon capers
     Hot buttered pasta (optional)

❶ Place a chicken breast half between 2 sheets of plastic wrap. Lightly pound using the flat side of a meat mallet to an even thickness. Repeat with remaining chicken breast halves. Brush chicken lightly with Dijon mustard; sprinkle with salt and pepper. Place chicken on waxed paper-lined baking sheet. Sprinkle chicken with crumbs to coat.

❷ Heat 2 tablespoons of the oil in an extra-large skillet on medium to medium-high heat; add chicken breast halves and cook 4 minutes per side or until no pink remains.

❸ Meanwhile, slice one of the lemons. Transfer chicken to serving plates. Add remaining oil to skillet. Cook haricots verts in hot oil 4 to 5 minutes or until they are crisp tender, adding the lemon slices the last minute of cooking. Remove to plates with slotted spoon. Juice remaining lemon and add lemon juice and capers to skillet; cook 30 seconds. Drizzle on chicken and beans. Serve with pasta.

PER SERVING 362 cal., 16 g total fat (3 g sat. fat), 99 mg chol., 546 mg sodium, 13 g carbo., 4 g fiber, 42 g pro.

Crusted Chicken with Maple-Laced Squash ♥

Cornflake crumbs create the crisp crust on this autumnal chicken dish that's served with maple-dressed winter squash and topped with toasted pecans.

START TO FINISH 20 minutes **OVEN** 450°F **MAKES** 4 servings

     Nonstick cooking spray
- 14 to 16 ounces chicken breast tenderloins
     Salt
     Black pepper
- ¾   cup packaged cornflake crumbs
- 3   tablespoons pure maple syrup or maple-flavored syrup
- 1   10- to 12-ounce package frozen cooked winter squash
- ¼   cup pecan pieces

❶ Preheat oven to 450°F. Line a baking sheet with foil; lightly coat foil with cooking spray. Sprinkle chicken lightly with salt and pepper. Place crumbs in a shallow dish. Place 1 tablespoon of the syrup in a small bowl; brush syrup lightly on both sides of chicken. Coat chicken on both sides with cornflake crumbs. Place chicken on prepared baking sheet. Bake for 9 to 11 minutes or until chicken is no longer pink (170°F).

❷ Meanwhile, place squash in a microwave-safe 1½-quart casserole. Microwave, uncovered, on high for 5 to 6 minutes or until heated through, stirring twice. Stir in 1 tablespoon of the syrup. Season to taste with salt and pepper.

❸ In a small skillet heat pecans on medium-high heat for 2 to 3 minutes or until lightly toasted, stirring frequently. To serve, divide squash mixture and chicken among 4 plates. Drizzle with the remaining 1 tablespoon syrup; sprinkle with the toasted pecans.

PER SERVING 296 cal., 6 g total fat (1 g sat. fat), 58 mg chol., 333 mg sodium, 35 g carbo., 2 g fiber, 26 g pro.

{ Whether it's baked, roasted, pan-fried, or grilled, chicken is America's favorite bird. }

Lemon Chicken with
Olives & Ricotta

Lemon Chicken with Olives & Ricotta

A Meyer lemon is a cross between a lemon and an orange. Its flesh is sweeter than a regular lemon. Look for them in the specialty produce section of your supermarket. If you can't find them, a regular lemon will do just fine.

START TO FINISH 27 minutes **MAKES** 4 servings

- 8 no-boil lasagna noodles
- 1 teaspoon olive oil
- 1 Meyer lemon or lemon
- 4 small skinless, boneless chicken breast halves, halved crosswise (1 to 1¼ pounds)
  Salt
  Black pepper
- 1 tablespoon olive oil
- 1 cup garlic-stuffed or pitted green olives
- 1 cup ricotta cheese
- ½ teaspoon salt
- ½ teaspoon black pepper
  Fresh rosemary (optional)

1 In a Dutch oven bring 3 inches water to boiling. Add noodles and 1 teaspoon olive oil. Cover. Cook 6 minutes or until tender; drain. Lay noodles in single layer on waxed paper. Cover; set aside.

2 Meanwhile, shred peel from lemon; halve lemon. Juice one half; cut remaining half into wedges. Season chicken with salt, pepper, and half of lemon peel. In a skillet heat oil on medium-high heat. Add chicken. Cook 10 minutes or until no pink remains, turning once. Add olives; heat through. Remove from heat.

3 In a microwave-safe bowl combine ricotta, lemon juice, ½ teaspoon salt, and ½ teaspoon pepper. Microwave on high for 30 seconds, stirring once.

4 Spoon ricotta mixture into bowls. Top with noodles, chicken and olive mixture, remaining lemon peel, and, if desired, the fresh rosemary. Serve with lemon wedges.

PER SERVING 443 cal., 19 g total fat (7 g sat. fat), 130 mg chol., 1,053 mg sodium, 30 g carbo., 4 g fiber, 39 g pro.

Lickety-Split Lemon Chicken

Chicken with a lemony pan sauce is served over rice.

START TO FINISH 30 minutes **MAKES** 4 servings

- 12 ounces chicken breast tenderloins
- 2 tablespoons butter
- 1 8-ounce package sliced mushrooms
- 1 medium red sweet pepper, cut into strips
- 2 tablespoons all-purpose flour
- 1 14-ounce can chicken broth
- 1 teaspoon finely shredded lemon peel
- 2 tablespoons lemon juice
- 1 teaspoon dried thyme, crushed
  Salt
  Black pepper
- 1 14.8-ounce pouch cooked long grain white rice
  Lemon wedges (optional)

1 In an extra-large skillet cook chicken in hot butter on medium heat for 6 to 8 minutes or until no longer pink (170°F). Add mushrooms and sweet pepper for the last 5 minutes of cooking time. Stir in flour. Cook and stir for 1 minute more. Add chicken broth, lemon peel, lemon juice, and thyme. Cook and stir until thick and bubbly. Cook and stir for 2 minutes more. Season to taste with salt and black pepper.

2 Meanwhile, prepare rice according to package directions. Serve chicken mixture over rice. If desired, serve with lemon wedges.

PER SERVING 361 cal., 10 g total fat (4 g sat. fat), 66 mg chol., 643 mg sodium, 41 g carbo., 2 g fiber, 25 g pro.

{ The mild taste of chicken makes it a blank canvas for all kinds of herbs, seasonings, and flavors. }

Pan-Fried Chicken with Tomato Jam

This eye-catching and colorful Southern-inspired dish is gorgeous to look at and even lovelier to eat.

START TO FINISH 20 minutes   **MAKES** 4 servings

- 1 pint grape or cherry tomatoes
- 1 tablespoon packed brown sugar
- 2½ cups water
- 1 teaspoon salt
- ¾ cup quick-cooking polenta mix
- ½ cup all-purpose flour
- ½ teaspoon salt
- ½ teaspoon black pepper
- ¼ cup buttermilk
- 4 skinless, boneless chicken breast halves (about 1½ pounds)
- 3 tablespoons cooking oil
- 1 9-ounce package fresh spinach
   Salt
   Black pepper

❶ For tomato jam, pierce tomatoes with a sharp knife. Place in a microwave-safe bowl; sprinkle with brown sugar. Cover loosely with clear plastic wrap. Microwave on high about 3 minutes or until skins burst and tomatoes are soft, stirring once; set aside.

❷ In a medium saucepan bring water and the 1 teaspoon salt to boiling; stir in polenta. Reduce heat; cook 5 minutes, stirring often.

❸ In a shallow dish combine flour and the ½ teaspoon salt and ½ teaspoon pepper; add buttermilk to another dish. Dip chicken in buttermilk, then flour. Heat oil in large skillet on medium-high heat; add chicken. Cook 4 minutes per side or until no pink remains (170°F); remove from pan and keep warm.

❹ Drain and discard pan drippings. Add spinach; cook just until wilted. Season to taste with salt and pepper. Serve chicken with spinach, polenta, and tomato jam.

PER SERVING 448 cal., 9 g total fat (1 g sat. fat), 66 mg chol., 869 mg sodium, 56 g carbo., 8 g fiber, 34 g pro.

Quick Coconut Chicken

You can vary the spiciness of this dish by choosing either a mild or hot mango chutney to coat the chicken.

START TO FINISH 20 minutes   **OVEN** 450°F   **MAKES** 4 servings

- ¾ cup panko (Japanese-style bread crumbs)
- ⅓ cup shredded coconut
- ½ cup mango chutney
- 2 tablespoons butter or margarine, melted
- ¼ teaspoon salt
- ¼ teaspoon black pepper
- 14 to 16 ounces chicken breast tenderloins
- 1 fresh mango

❶ Preheat oven to 450°F. Line a baking sheet with foil; set aside. In a small bowl combine panko and coconut; set aside.

❷ Place chutney in another small bowl. Snip any large fruit pieces in chutney. Stir in melted butter, salt, and pepper. Using tongs, dip each chicken piece into the chutney mixture. Dip in panko mixture to coat. Arrange chicken on the prepared baking sheet. Sprinkle any remaining panko mixture over chicken.

❸ Bake for 10 to 12 minutes or until coating is brown and chicken is no longer pink.

❹ Meanwhile, seed, peel, and chop mango (see tip, below). Transfer chicken to a serving platter. Sprinkle with mango.

PER SERVING 339 cal., 10 g total fat (6 g sat. fat), 73 mg chol., 545 mg sodium, 35 g carbo., 2 g fiber, 25 g pro.

---

quick tip   To seed a fresh mango, first slice a thin piece off the top and then the bottom of the fruit—so it will sit flat on a cutting board. Place it upright on its large end. Using a paring knife, peel the skin from the fruit, top to bottom, in a circular motion. With a large knife cut the fruit from around the seed. Discard the seed and slice or chop the fruit as needed.

Pan-Fried Chicken
with Tomato Jam

Pecan-Crusted Chicken Thighs
with Braised Greens

Pecan-Crusted Chicken Thighs with Braised Greens

Boneless, skinless chicken breasts may be the leanest parts of the bird, but boneless, skinless thighs aren't far behind in healthfulness—and they have more flavor to boot.

START TO FINISH 30 minutes **MAKES** 4 servings

- 1 pound skinless, boneless chicken thighs
  Salt
  Black pepper
- 1 egg
- ⅓ cup finely chopped pecans
- ⅓ cup crushed saltine or wheat crackers
- ¼ teaspoon ground nutmeg
- 4 teaspoons olive oil
- 1 10-ounce package mixed salad greens
- 4 small grape clusters
- ⅓ cup frozen harvest blend or white grape juice concentrate, thawed

❶ Place each of the chicken thighs between 2 pieces of waxed paper. Using the flat side of a meat mallet, pound chicken thighs to flatten pieces slightly. Sprinkle lightly with salt and pepper. Beat egg in a shallow dish. In another shallow dish combine pecans, crackers, and nutmeg. Dip chicken into egg and then into pecan mixture, pressing to coat both sides.

❷ In an extra-large skillet heat 3 teaspoons of the olive oil on medium heat. Add chicken; cook for 10 to 12 minutes or until golden and crisp (180°F), turning once halfway through cooking. Remove chicken; cover and keep warm. Add greens to skillet; cook and stir just until greens begin to wilt. Remove from heat; season with salt and pepper.

❸ Meanwhile, in a medium skillet heat the remaining 1 teaspoon oil. Add grapes and cook for 3 to 4 minutes or just until grapes are warmed and some of the skins begin to burst. Add juice concentrate; cook for 1 minute more. Remove from heat.

❹ To serve, divide greens among 4 plates; serve with chicken and grape clusters. Drizzle with the remaining juice from skillet.

PER SERVING 367 cal., 18 g total fat (3 g sat. fat), 147 mg chol., 485 mg sodium, 27 g carbo., 3 g fiber, 27 g pro.

Mediterranean Pizza Skillet 🍲

The romaine lettuce is cooked only a minute or two—just enough for it to wilt slightly—in this unusual warm salad.

START TO FINISH 30 minutes **MAKES** 4 servings

- 3 skinless, boneless chicken breast halves, cut into ¾-inch pieces
- 2 cloves garlic, minced
- 2 tablespoons olive oil
- 4 roma tomatoes, chopped
- 1 14-ounce can artichoke hearts, drained and quartered
- 1 2.25-ounce can sliced pitted ripe olives, drained
- ½ teaspoon dried Italian seasoning, crushed
- ¼ teaspoon freshly ground black pepper
- 2 cups romaine lettuce or hearty mesclun, chopped
- 1 cup crumbled feta cheese (4 ounces)
- ⅓ cup fresh basil leaves, shredded or torn
  Crusty Italian or French bread, sliced

❶ In a large skillet cook and stir chicken and garlic in hot oil on medium-high heat until chicken is brown. Stir in tomatoes, artichokes, olives, seasoning, and pepper. Bring to boiling; reduce heat. Simmer, covered, for 10 minutes or until chicken is no longer pink (170°F).

❷ Top chicken with lettuce and cheese. Cook, covered, for 1 to 2 minutes more or until lettuce starts to wilt. Sprinkle with basil. Serve with bread.

PER SERVING 395 cal., 17 g total fat (6 g sat. fat), 82 mg chol., 1,003 mg sodium, 27 g carbo., 6 g fiber, 33 g pro.

Mediterranean Pizza Skillet

Chicken Fettuccine ♥

This recipe calls for refrigerated red pepper fettuccine, but you could just as easily use spinach or plain pasta if you'd like.

START TO FINISH 20 minutes   **MAKES** 4 servings

- 1   9-ounce package refrigerated red sweet pepper fettuccine
- ¼   7-ounce jar oil-packed dried tomato strips or pieces (¼ cup)
- 1   large zucchini or yellow summer squash, halved lengthwise and sliced (about 2 cups)
- 8   ounces packaged skinless, boneless chicken breast strips (stir-fry strips)
- 2   tablespoons olive oil
- ½   cup finely shredded Parmesan, Romano, or Asiago cheese (2 ounces)
    Freshly ground black pepper

❶ Using kitchen scissors cut fettuccine strands in half. Cook fettuccine according to package directions. Drain well. Return fettuccine to hot pan; cover to keep warm.

❷ Meanwhile, drain dried tomatoes, reserving 2 tablespoons of the oil. Set drained tomatoes aside. In a large skillet heat 1 tablespoon of the reserved oil on medium-high heat. Add zucchini; cook and stir for 2 to 3 minutes or until crisp-tender. Remove from skillet. Add the remaining 1 tablespoon reserved oil to skillet. Add chicken strips; cook and stir for 2 to 3 minutes or until no longer pink.

❸ Add chicken, zucchini, drained tomatoes, and olive oil to cooked fettuccine; toss gently to combine. Sprinkle each serving with cheese. Season to taste with pepper.

PER SERVING 384 cal., 14 g total fat (4 g sat. fat), 93 mg chol., 356 mg sodium, 37 g carbo., 4 g fiber, 28 g pro.

Chicken-Broccoli Mac & Cheese ▣

This dish features chicken, chewy rigatoni, sweet dried tomatoes, and healthful broccoli florets covered in a creamy, cheesy sauce. What kid could resist?

START TO FINISH 21 minutes   **MAKES** 4 servings

- 8   ounce dried rigatoni
- 2   cups fresh broccoli florets
- 1   2- to 2¼-pound whole roasted chicken
- 1   5.2-ounce package semisoft cheese with garlic and fine herbes
- ¾   to 1 cup milk
- ¼   cup oil-packed dried tomatoes, drained and snipped
- ¼   teaspoon freshly ground black pepper
    Fresh parsley (optional)

❶ In a large saucepan cook pasta according to package directions, adding broccoli florets during the last 3 minutes of cooking time. While pasta is cooking, remove meat from roasted chicken. Coarsely chop chicken. Drain pasta and broccoli; set aside.

❷ In same saucepan combine cheese, the ¾ cup milk, tomatoes, and pepper. Cook and stir until cheese is melted. Add pasta mixture and chicken. Heat through. If necessary, thin with additional milk. Sprinkle with fresh parsley.

PER SERVING 667 cal., 34 g total fat (15 g sat. fat), 163 mg chol., 872 mg sodium, 52 g carbo., 3 g fiber, 40 g pro.

---

quick tip   Once you've removed the meat from a whole roasted chicken, toss it in a large freezer bag and freeze. When you have two carcasses in the freezer, you can make homemade stock: Put the bones in a large stockpot along with some herbs and vegetables—such as onion, celery, and carrot—and cover with water. Cook, covered, for about 2 to 2½ hours. Remove the bones and discard. Cool the stock and skim the fat off the top. Use immediately or freeze.

{ When in doubt about what to serve for dinner, a chicken and pasta dish is sure to please. }

Chicken with Orzo

Chicken with Orzo ♥

It doesn't get much easier than this. All you have to do is cook the orzo and toss it with some lemon peel and shredded spinach leaves and season to taste. Just squeeze the lemon wedge and dig in!

START TO FINISH 20 minutes **MAKES** 4 servings

- 8 ounces dried whole wheat or plain orzo pasta (1½ cups)
- 1 lemon
- 4 cups shredded packaged prewashed fresh spinach leaves
  Salt
  Black pepper
- 1 purchased roasted chicken, skinned and cut into serving-size pieces

❶ Cook orzo according to package directions. Drain well. Return orzo to hot saucepan.

❷ Meanwhile, cut lemon in half; finely shred peel from half of the lemon. Cut remaining lemon half into wedges.

❸ Add spinach and lemon peel to orzo in saucepan; toss to mix. Season to taste with salt and pepper. Divide orzo mixture among 4 serving plates. Arrange chicken on top of orzo mixture. Serve with lemon wedges.

PER SERVING 477 cal., 12 g total fat (3 g sat. fat), 126 mg chol., 146 mg sodium, 43 g carbo., 11 g fiber, 49 g pro.

Arroz con Pollo ▥

This version of the traditional Mexican rice-and-chicken dish takes advantage of a purchased roasted chicken and prepared Spanish-style rice.

START TO FINISH 25 minutes **MAKES** 4 servings

- 1 purchased roasted chicken
- 1 14.5-ounce can diced tomatoes
- 1 4-ounce can diced green chiles
- 1 cup frozen peas
- ⅓ cup pitted green olives, sliced
- 1 8.8-ounce pouch cooked Spanish-style rice
- ⅓ cup shredded Monterey Jack cheese

❶ Remove chicken meat from bones, discarding skin and bones. Tear chicken into large pieces. Set aside 3 cups of the chicken; save remaining chicken for another use.

❷ In a large skillet combine undrained tomatoes, undrained diced green chiles, peas, and olives. Bring to boiling. Stir in rice and 3 cups chicken; heat through. Top each serving with cheese.

PER SERVING 399 cal., 14 g total fat (4 g sat. fat), 102 mg chol., 939 mg sodium, 29 g carbo., 4 g fiber, 37 g pro.

Skip-a-Step Chicken Risotto ▥

Traditional risotto usually takes about an hour and nearly constant stirring to make. This streamlined version allows you to enjoy this creamy and ultra-satisfying dish any day of the week.

START TO FINISH 20 minutes **MAKES** 4 servings

- 1 14.8-ounce pouch cooked original long grain rice
- 1 5.2-ounce container semisoft cheese with garlic and fine herbes
- 1¾ cups milk
- 12 ounces asparagus spears, trimmed and cut into 2-inch pieces
- 1 2¼- to 2½-pound purchased roasted chicken
- 2 large tomatoes, coarsely chopped
  Milk (optional)
  Salt
  Black pepper
  Finely shredded Parmesan cheese (optional)

❶ Heat rice according to package directions. Meanwhile, in a medium skillet heat semisoft cheese; stir in milk. Add rice and asparagus. Cover and cook on medium heat for 7 minutes, stirring occasionally.

❷ Meanwhile, remove skin and bones from chicken; discard. Coarsely chop chicken. Stir chicken and tomatoes into the rice mixture. Cook and stir about 1 minute more or until heated through. If necessary, stir in additional milk until desired consistency. Season to taste with salt and pepper. If desired, sprinkle with Parmesan cheese.

PER SERVING 645 cal., 35 g total fat (15 g sat. fat), 168 mg chol., 955 mg sodium, 47 g carbo., 4 g fiber, 38 g pro.

quick tip To prepare asparagus for cooking, rinse with cool water. Starting at the base of each spear, bend the spear several times, working toward the tip until you find a place where it breaks easily. Break off and discard the woody end. If desired, you can use a paring knife or vegetable peeler to remove the tiny scales on each stalk.

Soft Shell Chicken Tacos 📷

You can get this dish on the table nearly as fast as it takes to buzz through the drive-through of the nearest Mexican fast-food joint—and it's more healthful than the fare you can get there as well!

START TO FINISH 20 minutes   **MAKES** 4 soft-shell tacos

1	2¼- to 2½-pound purchased roasted chicken
4	7- to 8-inch flour tortillas
½	cup sour cream salsa- or Mexican-flavor dip
1	large red, green, or yellow sweet pepper, cut into bite-size strips
1½	cups shredded lettuce

1 Remove skin and bones from chicken and discard. Coarsely shred 2 cups of the chicken. Reserve remaining chicken for another use.

2 Spread 1 side of each tortilla with dip. Top with chicken, sweet pepper, and lettuce. Fold each tortilla in half.

PER TACO 284 cal., 13 g total fat (5 g sat. fat), 82 mg chol., 479 mg sodium, 19 g carbo., 1 g fiber, 23 g pro.

Soft Shell Chicken Tacos

Green Chile & Chicken Enchiladas

This recipe calls for chicken tenders, which break up and shred a little more easily than breast meat itself.

START TO FINISH 28 minutes   **MAKES** 4 servings

1¼	pounds chicken breast tenders
1½	cups bottled green salsa
1	4-ounce can diced green chiles
1½	cups shredded Mexican-style four-cheese blend (6 ounces)
8	6- to 7-inch flour tortillas
	Refrigerated fresh salsa (optional)
	Lime wedges (optional)

1 Preheat broiler. Cut chicken into 1-inch pieces and place in a microwave-safe bowl. Microwave, covered, on high for 7 minutes or until no pink remains, stirring twice. Drain liquid. Break up the chicken slightly in a bowl with back of wooden spoon. Add salsa and chiles. Cook 3 minutes more or until heated through, stirring once. Stir in 1 cup of the cheese.

2 Spoon chicken mixture evenly down center of tortillas. Roll tortillas around filling and place in 13×9×2-inch baking pan. Sprinkle remaining ½ cup cheese over enchiladas. Broil 3 to 4 inches from heat 1 to 2 minutes or until cheese melts.

3 To serve, if desired, top enchiladas with salsa and lime wedges.

PER SERVING 569 cal., 24 g total fat (8 g sat. fat), 120 mg chol., 1,081 mg sodium, 33 g carbo., 1 g fiber, 49 g pro.

quick tip   Refrigerated salsa has a fresher taste and chunkier texture than most of the jarred varieties—close to that of pico de gallo. You can usually find it in the produce section in both mild and hot versions.

Caesar Salad Pita Pizzas

Chicken Wraps

If you like your chicken salad with grapes, you will like these wraps that feature chicken, crunchy shredded broccoli slaw, and grapes dressed with sweet poppy seed dressing.

START TO FINISH 14 minutes   **MAKES** 4 wraps

- 1½ cups packaged shredded broccoli (broccoli slaw mix)
- 1 cup seedless red or green grapes, halved or quartered
- ⅓ cup bottled poppy seed salad dressing
- 1 2¼- to 2½-pound purchased roasted chicken
- 4 10-inch flour tortillas
  Orange wedges (optional)

1 In a medium bowl combine broccoli slaw, grapes, and salad dressing.

2 Remove skin and bones from chicken and discard. Slice or coarsely chop chicken. Divide chicken among the tortillas. Top with broccoli slaw mixture. Roll up and secure with wooden toothpicks. If desired, serve with orange wedges.

PER WRAP 510 cal., 28 g total fat (8 g sat. fat), 125 mg chol., 1,171 mg sodium, 35 g carbo., 2 g fiber, 31 g pro.

Caesar Salad Pita Pizzas

All of the great flavors and textures of the ever-popular chicken Caesar salad come together in these pita pizzas—and you can eat them with your fingers!

PREP 15 minutes   **BAKE** 12 minutes   **OVEN** 400°F
MAKES 6 pizzas

- 6 pita bread rounds
- 1 10-ounce container refrigerated Alfredo pasta sauce
- 1 9-ounce package refrigerated cooked chicken breast strips
- ¾ cup finely shredded Parmesan cheese
- 3 cups packaged chopped hearts of romaine
- ¼ cup bottled Caesar salad dressing

1 Preheat oven to 400°F. Line a very large baking sheet with foil; place pita rounds on baking sheet. Spread Alfredo sauce on pita rounds. Top with chicken breast strips; sprinkle with Parmesan cheese.

2 Bake for 12 to 15 minutes or until pitas are crisp and cheese softens.

3 In a medium bowl combine romaine and salad dressing. Top pizzas with salad mixture.

PER PIZZA 426 cal., 20 g total fat (9 g sat. fat), 62 mg chol., 1,321 mg sodium, 39 g carbo., 2 g fiber, 21 g pro.

Spring Greens & Roasted Chicken

Serve this refreshing and beautiful strawberries-and-greens main-dish salad with crusty rolls and iced tea or a crisp dry white wine.

START TO FINISH 25 minutes   **MAKES** 6 servings

- 1 purchased roasted chicken, chilled
- 1 5-ounce package mixed spring greens salad mix (about 8 cups)
- 2 cups fresh sliced strawberries or blueberries
- 1 cup Gorgonzola or blue cheese, crumbled (4 ounces)
- ½ cup honey-roasted cashews or peanuts
- 1 lemon, halved
- 3 tablespoons olive oil
- ¼ teaspoon salt
- ¼ teaspoon black pepper

1 Remove and discard skin from chicken. Pull meat from bones, discarding bones. Shred meat (you should have about 3½ cups).

2 Place greens on a platter. Top with chicken, strawberries, cheese, and nuts. Drizzle with juice from lemon and the oil; sprinkle with salt and pepper.

PER SERVING 426 cal., 31 g total fat (9 g sat. fat), 81 mg chol., 482 mg sodium, 12 g carbo., 2 g fiber, 28 g pro.

Spring Greens & Roasted Chicken

Chicken & Fruit Salad with Mango Vinaigrette

Although you may have heard that thumping a melon is the best way to tell if it's ripe, the most reliable way to tell is to press gently on the stem end. If it yields slightly and the melon has a fresh, fragrant smell, it's perfect.

PREP 20 minutes   **GRILL** 12 minutes   **MAKES** 4 servings

2	medium mangoes
½	teaspoon curry powder
¼	teaspoon coarsely ground black pepper
⅛	teaspoon salt
12	ounces skinless, boneless chicken breast halves
6	cups torn mixed greens
½	of a medium cantaloupe, seeded, peeled, and cut into 1-inch chunks
1	cup raspberries
1	small apple, cored and sliced
1	recipe Mango Vinaigrette
2	green onions, thinly bias-sliced

❶ Seed, peel, and cube the mangoes. Measure 1 cup mango cubes for use in the vinaigrette; set remaining mango cubes aside for salad.

❷ In a small bowl stir together curry powder, pepper, and salt. Sprinkle chicken evenly with curry mixture; rub in with your fingers.

❸ For charcoal grill, place chicken on the rack of an uncovered grill directly over medium coals. Grill for 12 to 15 minutes or until tender and no longer pink (170°F), turning once halfway through grilling. (For gas grill, preheat grill. Reduce heat to medium. Place chicken on grill rack over heat. Cover and grill as above.) (Or preheat broiler. Place chicken on the unheated rack of a broiler pan. Broil 4 to 5 inches from the heat for 10 to 12 minutes or until tender and no longer pink [170°F], turning once.) Cool chicken slightly; slice into ¼-inch-wide strips.

❹ Arrange greens on 4 serving plates. Top greens with chicken strips, cantaloupe, raspberries, apple slices, and reserved mango cubes. Drizzle salads with Mango Vinaigrette. Sprinkle with green onions.

MANGO VINAIGRETTE: In a blender or food processor combine the 1 cup mango cubes, 3 tablespoons orange juice, 2 tablespoons rice vinegar or white wine vinegar, 2 teaspoons honey, and 1 teaspoon Dijon mustard. Cover and blend or process until smooth. Cover and chill until serving time (up to 2 hours).

PER SERVING 253 cal., 2 g total fat (0 g sat. fat), 49 mg chol., 173 mg sodium, 39 g carbo., 7 g fiber, 22 g pro.

Thai Chicken in Lettuce Cups ♥

Boston or Bibb lettuce leaves make great serving bowls. Their crisp and sturdy leaves naturally form a bowl or cup shape. You just have to fill and eat!

START TO FINISH 25 minutes   **MAKES** 4 servings

12	ounces chicken breast tenderloins
¼	cup bottled Thai ginger salad dressing and marinade
½	cup thinly sliced red onion
4	Boston or Bibb lettuce cups
3	tablespoons coarsely chopped dry-roasted peanuts

❶ In a medium bowl combine chicken and marinade; toss to coat. Let stand at room temperature for 10 minutes.

❷ Heat a large skillet on medium-high heat for 2 minutes; add undrained chicken mixture and onion. Cook and stir for 3 to 5 minutes or until chicken is no longer pink and onion is tender.

❸ Divide chicken mixture among lettuce cups. Sprinkle with peanuts.

PER SERVING 156 cal., 5 g total fat (1 g sat. fat), 49 mg chol., 392 mg sodium, 6 g carbo., 0 g fiber, 22 g pro.

Greek Chicken Salad 🎬

Serve this speedy Greek-style salad with wedges of warm pita bread.

START TO FINISH 19 minutes   **MAKES** 4 servings

1	5-ounce package spring mix salad greens
1	purchased roasted chicken
2	small cucumbers, cut into chunks
2	medium tomatoes, cut into wedges
⅔	cup bottled Greek salad dressing with feta cheese
	Cracked black pepper

❶ Arrange greens on a serving platter. Remove skin and bones from chicken and discard. Coarsely chop chicken. Arrange chicken on the greens. Add cucumber and tomato wedges. Drizzle with salad dressing. Sprinkle with pepper.

PER SERVING 473 cal., 27 g total fat (6 g sat. fat), 136 mg chol., 433 mg sodium, 9 g carbo., 2 g fiber, 46 g pro.

Papaya & Coconut Chicken Salad

Lemony Chicken & Fruit Salad 🍲

At just 215 calories and 4 grams of fat per serving, this chicken and fruit salad is a dieter's dream.

START TO FINISH 20 minutes   **MAKES** 4 servings

- **6** cups packaged torn mixed salad greens
- **1** small cantaloupe (about 2 pounds)
- **2** 6-ounce packages refrigerated grilled chicken breast strips
- **1** cup green and/or red seedless grapes
- **1** 6-ounce carton lemon yogurt
- **2** tablespoons orange juice
- **⅛** teaspoon black pepper

1 Arrange greens on a platter. Halve cantaloupe; remove seeds and rind. Cut cantaloupe into chunks. Arrange cantaloupe, chicken, and grapes on top of greens.

2 For dressing, in a small bowl stir together yogurt, orange juice, and pepper. Spoon on top of salad.

PER SERVING 215 cal., 4 g total fat (1 g sat. fat), 58 mg chol., 824 mg sodium, 23 g carbo., 2 g fiber, 23 g pro.

Tropical Broiled Chicken ♥

A mixture of pineapple jam, orange juice, and cilantro makes a sweet glaze for this simple chicken.

START TO FINISH 30 minutes   **MAKES** 4 servings

- **4** skinless, boneless chicken breast halves
  Salt
  Black pepper
- **⅓** cup pineapple jam
- **2** tablespoons orange juice or water
- **1** tablespoon cooking oil
- **1** tablespoon snipped fresh cilantro
- **¼** teaspoon salt
- **¼** teaspoon black pepper
- **½** of a peeled, cored fresh pineapple, cut into 4 rings

1 Preheat broiler. Place chicken breast halves on the unheated rack of a broiler pan. Sprinkle lightly with salt and pepper. Broil about 5 inches from the heat for 5 minutes.

2 Meanwhile, in a small bowl combine jam, orange juice, oil, cilantro, ¼ teaspoon salt, and ¼ teaspoon pepper; brush over chicken. Turn chicken; add pineapple rings to pan. Broil 4 to 7 minutes more or until chicken is no longer pink (170°F), brushing chicken and pineapple with glaze the last 3 to 4 minutes of broiling.

3 To serve, spoon any remaining glaze over chicken breasts.

PER SERVING 262 cal., 5 g total fat (1 g sat. fat), 66 mg chol., 374 mg sodium, 27 g carbo., 1 g fiber, 27 g pro.

Papaya & Coconut Chicken Salad

This vibrant salad bears witness to the fact that the more colors you have on your plate, the more nutritious the food. Antioxidant-packed blueberries and papaya provide both powerful nutrients and visual appeal.

START TO FINISH 30 minutes   **OVEN** 450°F   **MAKES** 4 servings

- **1** pound skinless, boneless chicken breast halves
- **½** teaspoon salt
- **1½** cups flaked coconut
- **1** medium papaya
- **¼** cup cider vinegar
- **¼** cup vegetable oil
- **1** tablespoon honey
- **¼** teaspoon salt
  Dash cayenne pepper
- **1** 5-ounce package mixed salad greens
- **¾** cup blueberries

1 Heat oven to 450°F. Line a baking sheet with foil; set aside. Cut chicken in strips; season with salt. Place coconut in shallow dish. Roll chicken in coconut to coat, pressing lightly to adhere. Transfer to prepared baking sheet. Bake about 12 minutes or until coconut is golden and chicken is no longer pink.

2 Meanwhile, peel, seed, and cut papaya in cubes. For dressing, place ¼ cup papaya cubes in blender or food processor; add vinegar, oil, honey, the ¼ teaspoon salt, and cayenne. Process until smooth. Toss ¼ cup dressing with greens; divide among 4 plates.

3 Top greens with chicken, remaining papaya, and blueberries. Pass remaining dressing.

PER SERVING 526 cal., 30 g total fat (15 g sat. fat), 66 mg chol., 639 mg sodium, 35 g carbo., 6 g fiber, 30 g pro.

Raspberry-Dijon Chicken Salad

Bottled balsamic vinaigrette does double duty here—as a flavoring for the glaze for the chicken and as a dressing for the salad as well.

START TO FINISH 30 minutes   **MAKES** 4 servings

- ¼   cup seedless raspberry preserves
- 1   tablespoon Dijon mustard
- 1   tablespoon bottled balsamic vinaigrette salad dressing
- 4   skinless, boneless chicken breast halves
- ¼   teaspoon salt
- ⅛   teaspoon black pepper
- 8   cups torn mixed salad greens
- 1   cup cherry tomatoes, halved
- ¼   cup chopped pecans, toasted (see note, page 31)
- ⅓   cup bottled balsamic vinaigrette salad dressing

❶ Preheat broiler. In a small bowl stir together preserves, mustard, and 1 tablespoon dressing; set aside. Season chicken with salt and pepper; place on the unheated rack of a broiler pan. Broil 4 to 5 inches from the heat for 3 minutes per side. Brush 1 side with preserves mixture. Broil 2 minutes more. Turn and brush with remaining mixture. Broil 2 minutes more or until no longer pink (170°F). Remove from oven; cover with foil and set aside.

❷ In a very large bowl toss together greens, tomatoes, pecans, and ⅓ cup dressing. Divide among 4 serving plates. Slice chicken and place on greens.

PER SERVING 355 cal., 14 g total fat (2 g sat. fat), 82 mg chol., 606 mg sodium, 22 g carbo., 3 g fiber, 35 g pro.

Chicken-Pepper Kabobs

Strawberry-Kiwi Chicken Salad

Bagged baby spinach and a purchased rotisserie chicken make quick work of this main-dish version of classic spinach-strawberry salad.

START TO FINISH 20 minutes   **MAKES** 4 servings

- 1   2- to 2 ½-pound purchased roasted whole chicken
- 1   5-ounce bag baby spinach
- 2   cups small strawberries, halved
- 2   kiwifruits, peeled and sliced
- ⅓   to ½ cup bottled raspberry vinaigrette salad dressing
     Purchased sugared pecans (optional)

❶ Remove and discard bones and skin from chicken; cut chicken into large chunks. Arrange spinach on a large platter. Top with chicken, strawberries, and kiwifruit. Drizzle with salad dressing. If desired, sprinkle with pecans.

PER SERVING 593 cal., 38 g total fat (12 g sat. fat), 250 mg chol., 1,675 mg sodium, 16 g carbo., 3 g fiber, 55 g pro.

Chicken-Pepper Kabobs

Add some hot cooked rice to these broiled kabobs and you have a complete meal.

START TO FINISH 30 minutes   **MAKES** 4 to 6 servings

- 1   pound skinless, boneless chicken breasts, cut into 1-inch pieces
- ⅔   cup bottled balsamic vinaigrette salad dressing
- 1   red sweet pepper
- 1   green sweet pepper
- 8   green onions, trimmed and cut into 2-inch pieces
     Bottled balsamic vinaigrette salad dressing

❶ Preheat broiler. Place chicken breasts in a shallow dish. Pour the ⅔ cup dressing over chicken; stir to coat. Let marinate for 10 minutes.

❷ Meanwhile, cut sweet peppers into 1-inch pieces. Drain chicken, reserving marinade. Thread chicken, peppers, and onions on 8 metal skewers. Place on the unheated rack of a broiler pan.

❸ Broil 5 to 6 inches from heat for 8 to 10 minutes or until chicken is no longer pink, brushing with reserved marinade during the first 5 minutes and turning occasionally to brown evenly. (Discard any remaining marinade.) If desired, serve with additional salad dressing.

PER SERVING 241 cal., 10 g total fat (2 g sat. fat), 66 mg chol., 574 mg sodium, 11 g carbo., 2 g fiber, 27 g pro.

Chicken Salad with
Basil Mayonnaise

Chicken Salad with Basil Mayonnaise

You can lower the calorie and fat content of this salad significantly by using reduced-fat mayonnaise—with no detrimental effect on its taste or texture.

START TO FINISH 20 minutes **MAKES** 4 servings

- 1 2- to 2¼-pound purchased roasted chicken
- ¾ cup mayonnaise or salad dressing
- 4 tablespoons snipped fresh basil
- ¼ teaspoon salt
- ¼ teaspoon black pepper
- 1½ cups cherry or grape tomatoes, halved
- 1½ cups broccoli florets
- 6 cups shredded romaine lettuce
- ¼ cup finely shredded Parmesan cheese (optional)

❶ Remove skin and bones from chicken and discard. Shred chicken into chunks.

❷ In a large bowl combine mayonnaise, 2 tablespoons of the basil, salt, and pepper. Stir in chicken, tomatoes, and broccoli. Serve over shredded romaine. If desired, top with cheese. Sprinkle with remaining 2 tablespoons basil.

PER SERVING 763 cal., 63 g total fat (14 g sat. fat), 216 mg chol., 1,709 mg sodium, 12 g carbo., 4 g fiber, 46 g pro.

---

quick tip Basil mayonnaise adds fast flavor to sandwiches as well. To make basil mayonnaise, combine the amounts of mayonnaise, basil, salt and pepper mentioned in Step 2 above. Use as a sandwich spread or dip for raw vegetables. Store flavored mayonnaise, tightly covered, in the refrigerator for up to 1 week.

Chicken & Hominy Chili

Gently mashing just half of the beans in this white chili gives it a thick consistency. Top it with green salsa and sour cream, if you like.

PREP 15 minutes **COOK** 15 minutes **MAKES** 4 to 6 servings

- 1 tablespoon cooking oil
- 1 pound skinless, boneless chicken breast halves, cut into 1-inch pieces
- 2 14-ounce cans reduced-sodium chicken broth
- 2 15- to 16-ounce cans navy beans, rinsed and drained
- 1 15.5-ounce can white hominy, rinsed and drained
- 1 4-ounce can diced green chile peppers
- 1 teaspoon ground cumin
- ¼ teaspoon black pepper
- 4 ounces Monterey Jack cheese with jalapeño peppers, shredded

❶ In a 6-quart Dutch oven heat oil on medium heat. Add chicken, half at a time, and cook until no longer pink. Return all chicken to the Dutch oven.

❷ Stir in broth, navy beans, hominy, green chiles, cumin, and pepper. Bring to boiling; reduce heat. Simmer, covered, for 15 minutes.

❸ Using a potato masher, gently mash the mixture to crush about half of the beans. Stir in cheese; heat until cheese melts.

PER SERVING 601 cal., 15 g total fat (7 g sat. fat), 91 mg chol., 1,962 mg sodium, 62 g carbo., 14 g fiber, 53 g pro.

{ If it's a hot summer night, choose the chicken salad; if it's a cold winter night, choose the chili. }

BBQ Chicken Burgers & Waffle Fries

When making burgers of any kind, press down to make a small indentation in the center of the raw patty. This will help the patty stay flat (not rounded) after it's cooked so it can better accommodate toppings and a bun.

START TO FINISH 30 minutes   **OVEN** 425°F   **MAKES** 4 servings

- ⅓   cup bottled barbecue sauce
- ⅓   cup grape jelly or seedless raspberry jam
- 3   cups frozen waffle-cut or thick-cut french-fried potatoes
- 4   slices packaged ready-to-serve cooked bacon, chopped
- 2   tablespoons fine dry bread crumbs
- 2   tablespoons finely chopped honey-roasted walnuts or almonds
- 1   tablespoon bottled barbecue sauce
- ½   teaspoon poultry seasoning
- ¼   teaspoon salt
- ⅛   teaspoon black pepper
- 8   ounces uncooked ground chicken or turkey
- ½   cup shredded Italian-blend cheeses, Monterey Jack cheese with jalapeño peppers, or Gorgonzola cheese
    Snipped fresh chives
- 8   dinner rolls or cocktail-size hamburger buns, split
    Sliced tomato and/or lettuce

❶ Preheat oven to 425°F. Combine the ⅓ cup barbecue sauce and jelly. Mix with a wire whisk until smooth. Set aside.

❷ Arrange potatoes in a single layer on an ungreased baking sheet. Sprinkle with chopped bacon. Bake for 8 minutes.

❸ Meanwhile, in a bowl combine bread crumbs, nuts, 1 tablespoon barbecue sauce, poultry seasoning, salt, and pepper. Add ground chicken; mix well. Shape into 8 balls; place 2 inches apart on greased shallow baking pan. Moisten the bottom of a glass and press each ball to about ¼-inch thickness.

❹ Place pan with burgers in oven. Bake fries and burgers for 5 minutes. Stir fries; turn burgers. Continue baking burgers and fries for 5 more minutes.

❺ Sprinkle cheese over fries. Brush barbecue-jelly mixture over burgers. Bake burgers and fries 2 minutes more or until burgers are no longer pink in centers and cheese is melted on fries.

❻ To serve, sprinkle fries with snipped chives. Place burgers in cocktail buns with additional barbecue-jelly mixture spooned over. Top with tomato slices and/or lettuce.

PER SERVING 537 cal., 21 g total fat (7 g sat. fat), 20 mg chol., 902 mg sodium, 66 g carbo., 4 g fiber, 22 g pro.

Creamy Turkey & Orzo

The tangy flavor in the sauce for this one-dish skillet supper comes from bottled blue cheese salad dressing .

START TO FINISH 25 minutes   **MAKES** 4 servings

- ⅔   cup dried orzo
- 12   ounces turkey breast tenderloin, cut into bite-size strips
- 8   ounces sliced fresh mushrooms
- ¼   cup sliced green onions (2)
- 2   tablespoons olive oil or cooking oil
- 1½   cups milk
- 3   tablespoons all-purpose flour
- ½   cup bottled blue cheese salad dressing
- 1   cup frozen peas
    Salt
    Black pepper

❶ Cook orzo according to package directions; drain.

❷ Meanwhile, in a large skillet cook and stir turkey, mushrooms, and green onions in hot oil on medium heat for 4 to 5 minutes or until turkey is no longer pink.

❸ Combine milk, flour, and salad dressing; add all at once to skillet along with cooked orzo. Cook and stir until thickened and bubbly. Stir in peas. Cook and stir for 2 minutes more. Season to taste with salt and pepper.

PER SERVING 520 cal., 26 g total fat (5 g sat. fat), 65 mg chol., 515 mg sodium, 39 g carbo., 3 g fiber, 33 g pro.

---

quick tip   You may have heard the mantra that when it comes to vegetables, fresh is best—and that is mostly true. However, peas start to get starchy and lose their nutrients almost immediately after being picked, so it's actually best to freeze them right after picking. They're sweeter and more nutritious that way. Keep a bag of peas in your freezer for quick side dishes and stir-ins to main dishes such as this one.

BBQ Chicken Burgers
& Waffle Fries

Cajun Turkey Cutlets
with Melon & Blueberries

Cajun Turkey Cutlets with Melon & Blueberries

A fruit vinaigrette pairs well with this salad.

START TO FINISH 20 minutes **MAKES** 4 servings

- 2 turkey breast tenderloins, cut in half horizontally (about 1 pound)
- 1 tablespoon olive oil
- 1½ teaspoons Cajun seasoning
- 6 cups torn mixed greens
- 1½ cups sliced cantaloupe
- 1 cup fresh blueberries
  Crumbled farmer cheese (optional)
  Purchased salad dressing

❶ Brush turkey with oil. Sprinkle with seasoning. For a charcoal grill, place turkey portions on the rack of an uncovered grill directly over medium coals. Grill for 12 to 15 minutes or until turkey is no longer pink (170°F), turning once. (For a gas grill, preheat grill. Reduce heat to medium. Place turkey on grill rack over heat. Cover; grill as above.) Slice turkey.

❷ Arrange greens on a serving platter along with the turkey, cantaloupe, and blueberries. If desired, top with farmer cheese. Serve with salad dressing.

PER SERVING 359 cal., 22 g total fat (4 g sat. fat), 68 mg chol., 161 mg sodium, 14 g carbo., 3 g fiber, 29 g pro.

Turkey & Sweet Potatoes

The recent popularity of sweet potatoes may owe in part to the discovery that it's one of the most nutritionally dense vegetables on the planet.

START TO FINISH 40 minutes **MAKES** 4 servings

- 1 pound sweet potatoes
- 2 turkey breast tenderloins (1 to 1¼ pounds)
- ½ teaspoon salt
- ¼ teaspoon black pepper
- 1 tablespoon cooking oil
- 1 cup purchased chunky salsa
- ¼ cup orange juice
  Snipped fresh cilantro or parsley (optional)

❶ Peel sweet potatoes; cut into 1-inch pieces. In a saucepan cook sweet potatoes, covered, in enough boiling water to cover for 10 to 12 minutes or until potatoes are just tender; drain.

❷ Meanwhile, cut turkey crosswise into ½-inch slices. Sprinkle with salt and pepper. In a large nonstick skillet cook turkey in hot oil on medium-high heat for 3 to 4 minutes per side or until turkey is no longer pink.

❸ Add salsa, orange juice, and sweet potatoes. Cook until heated through. If desired, sprinkle with snipped fresh cilantro.

PER SERVING 251 cal., 4 g total fat (1 g sat. fat), 70 mg chol., 775 mg sodium, 22 g carbo., 7 g fiber, 30 g pro.

Turkey-Spinach Toss

If you're not a fan of spinach stems, substitute an equal amount of bagged baby spinach for the regular spinach.

START TO FINISH 20 minutes **MAKES** 4 servings

- 2 8-ounce turkey breast tenderloins, halved horizontally
- ¼ teaspoon coarsely ground black pepper
- 2 tablespoons butter
- 2 ounces thinly sliced deli ham
- ½ cup orange juice
- 2 9- to 10-ounce packages fresh spinach
  Salt and black pepper
  Orange wedges (optional)

❶ Season turkey with ¼ teaspoon pepper. In an extra-large skillet heat butter on medium-high heat; add turkey. Cook 12 minutes or until no pink remains, turning once. Meanwhile, cut ham into bite-size strips.

❷ Remove turkey from skillet; cover and keep warm. Add ham to hot skillet; cook and stir for 1 to 2 minutes or until ham is heated through and starting to crisp. With a slotted spoon remove ham from skillet. Add the orange juice to skillet; bring to boiling.

❸ Add spinach, half at a time, to skillet and cook about 1 minute or just until it starts to wilt. Using tongs, remove from skillet and divide among serving plates. Sprinkle with salt and pepper. Top spinach with sliced turkey and ham. Drizzle any remaining orange juice from skillet over turkey. If desired, serve with orange wedges.

PER SERVING 244 cal., 8 g total fat (4 g sat. fat), 94 mg chol., 528 mg sodium, 9 g carbo., 3 g fiber, 34 g pro.

Turkey & Sweet Potatoes

Curry-&-Macadamia-Crusted Turkey

Mango chutney and curry powder are stirred into plain couscous to create a flavorful side to this rich-tasting turkey dish. For even more flavor, cook the couscous in chicken broth instead of water.

START TO FINISH 20 minutes **MAKES** 4 servings

- ½   cup mango chutney
- 1   teaspoon curry powder
- ½   teaspoon salt
- ¼   teaspoon black pepper
- 1½ cups water
- 1   cup quick-cooking couscous
- 2   8-ounce turkey breast tenderloins, halved horizontally
- ½   cup finely chopped macadamia nuts
- 2   tablespoons olive or vegetable oil

❶ Place chutney in a small bowl. Snip any large pieces of fruit in chutney; stir in curry powder, salt, and pepper. Place half of the chutney mixture in a medium saucepan. Add water. Bring to boiling. Stir in couscous. Remove from heat; cover and let stand.

❷ Meanwhile, coat turkey with the remaining chutney mixture. Dip 1 side of each piece in the chopped nuts.

❸ In an extra-large skillet heat oil on medium heat. Add turkey, nut sides down. Cook for 6 minutes. Turn turkey over; cook for 6 to 9 minutes more or until no pink remains (170°F). Spoon any coating remaining in pan onto turkey.

❹ Fluff couscous mixture. Serve couscous with turkey.

PER SERVING 796 cal., 21 g total fat (3 g sat. fat), 105 mg chol., 624 mg sodium, 92 g carbo., 6 g fiber, 55 g pro.

quick tip   If you love macadamia nuts but are skittish about their fat content (or you simply can't find them), almonds make a good substitute here.

Teriyaki-Glazed Turkey Tenderloin Steaks

Glaze a melange of vegetables conveniently cooked in a microwavable steaming bag with some bottled stir-fry sauce and you've trimmed minutes—and mess—off the task of making a traditional stir-fry.

START TO FINISH 30 minutes **MAKES** 4 servings

- 2   turkey breast tenderloins (1 to 1¼ pounds total)
- 1   tablespoon cooking oil
- 1   12-ounce package frozen broccoli, carrots, sugar snap peas, and water chestnuts in microwavable steaming bag
- ½   cup bottled stir-fry sauce
- 1   14.8-ounce pouch cooked long grain white rice
- ¼   cup chopped dry-roasted peanuts

❶ Split each turkey tenderloin in half horizontally to make four ½-inch-thick steaks. In an extra-large skillet cook turkey in hot oil on medium-high heat for 14 to 16 minutes or until no longer pink (170°F), turning once halfway through cooking. Reduce heat to medium if turkey gets too brown. Remove turkey from skillet; keep warm.

❷ Meanwhile, prepare vegetables according to package directions. Transfer vegetables to the skillet used to cook the turkey. Add stir-fry sauce; heat through.

❸ Heat rice according to package directions. Serve turkey and vegetable mixture over rice. Sprinkle with peanuts.

PER SERVING 447 cal., 11 g total fat (1 g sat. fat), 70 mg chol., 1,127 mg sodium, 48 g carbo., 4 g fiber, 35 g pro.

{ Turkey is every bit as versatile as chicken but often gets overlooked in favor of its clucking cousin. }

Turkey Potpies

Parmesan-Crusted Turkey with Mashed Cauliflower

If you're watching your carbohydrate intake (and even if you're not), creamy mashed cauliflower is a great alternative to mashed potatoes.

START TO FINISH 20 minutes   **MAKES** 4 servings

- 3   cups coarsely chopped cauliflower (½ of a head)
- ¼   cup water
- 2   8-ounce turkey breast tenderloins, halved horizontally
       Salt
       Black pepper
- ⅓   cup light mayonnaise or mayonnaise
- ⅓   cup finely shredded Parmesan cheese
- 3   tablespoons fine dry bread crumbs
- 2   tablespoons butter or margarine
       Chopped fresh flat-leaf parsley and/or paprika (optional)

❶ Preheat broiler. In a microwave-safe 1½-quart casserole combine cauliflower and the water. Cover and cook on high for 12 to 15 minutes or until very tender, stirring once.

❷ Meanwhile, sprinkle turkey lightly with salt and pepper. Place on the unheated rack of a broiler pan. Broil 4 inches from heat for 5 minutes. Turn turkey; broil 4 minutes more. Meanwhile, in a small bowl stir together mayonnaise, ¼ cup of the Parmesan cheese, and the bread crumbs. Spread over turkey. Broil for 2 to 3 minutes more or until topping is golden and turkey is no longer pink (170°F).

❸ Add butter and the remaining Parmesan cheese to cauliflower; mash until smooth. Serve mashed cauliflower with turkey. If desired, sprinkle with parsley and/or paprika.

PER SERVING 310 cal., 15 g total fat (6 g sat. fat), 97 mg chol., 574 mg sodium, 10 g carbo., 2 g fiber, 33 g pro.

Turkey Potpies

Although it's nice to share, you don't have to when you serve these individual potpies.

START TO FINISH 30 minutes   **OVEN** 425°F   **MAKES** 6 servings

- ½   of a 15-ounce package rolled refrigerated unbaked piecrust (1 crust)
- 1   2.75-ounce envelope country gravy mix
- 2   6-ounce packages refrigerated cooked turkey breast strips
- 1   10-ounce package frozen mixed vegetables
- 1   cup milk
- 2   teaspoons onion powder

❶ Preheat oven to 425°F. Let piecrust stand at room temperature while preparing filling. In a medium saucepan prepare gravy mix according to package directions. Stir in turkey, vegetables, milk, and onion powder. Cook and stir until heated through. Spoon mixture into six 10-ounce ramekins or individual baking dishes; set aside.

❷ Meanwhile, unroll piecrust. Using a pizza cutter, cut piecrust into 12 wedges. Place 2 wedges over turkey mixture in each ramekin. Place ramekins in a shallow baking pan. Bake for 15 minutes or until crust is golden.

PER SERVING 333 cal., 14 g total fat (6 g sat. fat), 33 mg chol., 975 mg sodium, 34 g carbo., 3 g fiber, 17 g pro.

---

quick tip   If you don't have ramekins, you can make this in a 2-quart round casserole. Spoon the filling into the dish, then roll the piecrust to a circle about ½ inch bigger around than the diameter of the casserole. Roll the crust around a rolling pin, then gently unroll over the top of the dish. Pierce with a fork a few times to allow steam to escape. Bake in a 375°F oven for 20 to 25 minutes or until crust is golden.

{ Leftover turkey is a blessing. Stir it into potpie, turkey and noodles, or turkey chili or soup. }

Turkey Panini with Basil Aïoli

Aïoli is a garlicky French mayonnaise that's often served as a dip for vegetables, fish, and meats. This version is made with purchased mayo and pesto.

START TO FINISH 30 minutes **MAKES** 4 sandwiches

- 2 tablespoons mayonnaise or salad dressing
- 1 tablespoon purchased basil pesto
- 4 ciabatta rolls, split, or 8 slices sourdough bread
- 8 ounces thinly sliced cooked turkey breast
- 1 3.5-ounce package thinly sliced pepperoni
- ½ cup bottled roasted red sweet peppers, sliced
- 4 slices provolone cheese (about 4 ounces)
- 1 to 2 tablespoons olive oil

❶ Preheat an electric sandwich press, covered indoor grill, grill pan, or skillet. In a small bowl combine mayonnaise and pesto. Spread pesto mixture on the cut sides of the rolls. Divide turkey, pepperoni, peppers, and cheese among roll bottoms. Add roll tops. Lightly brush tops and bottoms of sandwiches with olive oil.

❷ Place sandwiches (half at a time, if necessary) in the sandwich press or indoor grill; cook, covered, for 7 to 9 minutes or until bread is toasted and cheese melts. (If using a grill pan or skillet, place sandwiches on grill pan. Weight sandwiches with a heavy skillet and grill about 2 minutes or until bread is lightly toasted. Turn sandwiches over, weight, and grill about 2 minutes or until second side is lightly toasted.)

PER SERVING 506 cal., 30 g total fat (11 g sat. fat), 80 mg chol., 1,534 mg sodium, 30 g carbo., 2 g fiber, 29 g pro.

Turkey-Apple Salad Lettuce Wraps

Serve these wraps in sets of three as a main dish or individually as an appetizer or snack.

START TO FINISH 30 minutes **MAKES** 4 servings

- 12 ounces cooked turkey breast, shredded
- 1 cup chopped green apple (1 medium)
- ½ cup chopped celery (1 stalk)
- ½ cup chopped walnuts, toasted (see note, page 31)
- ½ cup sliced green onions (4)
- ½ cup chopped fresh parsley
- ¼ cup dried tart cherries
- ½ cup light sour cream
- 2 tablespoons lemon juice
- ½ to 1 teaspoon bottled hot pepper sauce
- ¼ teaspoon kosher salt
- ¼ teaspoon freshly ground black pepper
- 12 butterhead (Boston or Bibb) lettuce leaves

❶ In a large bowl combine turkey, apple, celery, walnuts, green onions, parsley, and cherries.

❷ In a small bowl stir together sour cream, lemon juice, hot pepper sauce, kosher salt, and black pepper. Add the sour cream mixture to the turkey mixture; stir until well mixed.

❸ Divide turkey mixture among lettuce leaves, spooning turkey mixture into center of each leaf.* Fold bottom edge of each lettuce leaf up and over filling. Fold opposite sides in and over filling. Roll up from the bottom.

PER SERVING 313 cal., 13 g total fat (3 g sat. fat), 81 mg chol., 205 mg sodium, 19 g carbo., 4 g fiber, 31 g pro.

***NOTE:** If you prefer, serve the turkey mixture over torn lettuce.

quick tip Apples oxidize and begin to turn brown almost immediately after being cut. Be sure you have the turkey shredded and the celery, green onions, and parsley chopped before you chop the apple. Then quickly toss everything with the lemon dressing. The citric acid in the lemon juice will keep the apple from turning brown.

Turkey & Artichoke Toss

Speedy Turkey Wraps

Radish sprouts—if you can find them—add a delightfully spicy crunch to sandwiches and wraps.

START TO FINISH 15 minutes **MAKES** 4 wraps

- ¼ cup cream cheese, softened
- ¼ cup basil pesto
- 4 8- to 10-inch flavored, plain, or whole wheat tortillas
- 8 ounces deli shaved or sliced smoked turkey breast
- 2 cups shredded lettuce or assorted fresh sprouts (such as radish, sunflower, or broccoli sprouts)
- ½ cup chopped tomato and/or ripe avocado

❶ In a small bowl stir together cream cheese and pesto. Spread the cheese mixture over 1 side of each tortilla. Arrange turkey and lettuce on each tortilla. Top with tomato. Roll up.

PER WRAP 313 cal., 18 g total fat (4 g sat. fat), 42 mg chol., 852 mg sodium, 20 g carbo., 1 g fiber, 18 g pro.

Turkey & Artichoke Toss

This cool, crunchy, and colorful salad is a great choice for a night when it's too hot—and you're too busy—to cook.

START TO FINISH 25 minutes **MAKES** 4 servings

- 1 12- to 14-ounce jar quartered marinated artichoke hearts
- ¼ cup bottled roasted garlic vinaigrette salad dressing or creamy Parmesan-basil salad dressing
- 1 tablespoon honey
- 1 5-ounce package baby spinach
- 10 ounces deli roasted turkey, cubed (2 ¼ cups)
- 1 cup cherry tomatoes, halved
- ½ cup packaged coarsely shredded fresh carrots
- ¼ cup sliced almonds, toasted (see note, page 31)

❶ Drain artichokes, reserving ¼ cup of the marinade. For dressing, in a small bowl stir together reserved marinade, salad dressing, and honey; set aside.

❷ In a large salad bowl combine artichokes, spinach, turkey, tomatoes, carrots, and almonds.

❸ Add dressing to spinach mixture; toss to mix. Serve at once.

PER SERVING 342 cal., 20 g total fat (2 g sat. fat), 54 mg chol., 459 mg sodium, 19 g carbo., 3 g fiber, 25 g pro.

Turkey & Sugar Snap Pea Salad

To keep the snap peas crisp-tender and to preserve their bright green color, drain them after cooking and drop them into a bowl of ice-cold water. Drain again before combining with the remaining ingredients.

START TO FINISH 18 minutes **MAKES** 4 servings

- 5 slices bacon
- 2 cups sugar snap peas
- ½ cup light mayonnaise or salad dressing
- 1 tablespoon Dijon mustard
- 1 tablespoon cider vinegar
- 1 tablespoon snipped fresh dill
  Salt
  Black pepper
- 1 small head romaine, coarsely chopped or torn
- 8 ounces smoked turkey breast, cut into bite-size strips

❶ Line a 9-inch microwave-safe pie plate with paper towels. Arrange bacon slices in a single layer on the paper towels. Cover with additional paper towels. Cook on high for 4 to 5 minutes or until bacon is crisp. Carefully remove the pie plate from the microwave. Set cooked bacon slices aside to cool.

❷ Meanwhile, cook the peas, covered, in a small amount of boiling salted water for 2 to 4 minutes or until crisp-tender; drain. Crumble 1 bacon slice; set aside. Break remaining bacon slice into 1-inch pieces.

❸ In a small bowl combine mayonnaise, mustard, vinegar, and dill; season to taste with salt and pepper. Stir in crumbled bacon. Divide chopped romaine among serving plates. Top with sugar snap peas, turkey strips, and bacon pieces. Serve with dressing.

PER SERVING 392 cal., 32 g total fat (9 g sat. fat), 68 mg chol., 1,363 mg sodium, 9 g carbo., 2 g fiber, 17 g pro.

Turkey Cranberry Fried Rice

This one-dish dinner tastes a lot like Thanksgiving—without all the prep and cooking time.

START TO FINISH 25 minutes **MAKES** 4 servings

1	pound uncooked ground turkey
½	cup celery, chopped (1 stalk)
½	cup onion, chopped (1 medium)
1	8.8-ounce package cooked long grain and wild rice
½	cup apple cider
⅓	cup dried cranberries
½	teaspoon dried thyme, crushed
⅓	cup chopped pecans, toasted (see note, page 31)
	Salt
	Black pepper

❶ In an extra-large skillet cook and stir turkey, celery, and onion over medium heat until turkey is no longer pink and vegetables are tender.

❷ Meanwhile, prepare long grain and wild rice according to package directions.

❸ Stir rice, cider, cranberries, and thyme into mixture in skillet. Cook and stir until liquid is absorbed. Stir in pecans. Season to taste with salt and pepper.

PER SERVING 385 cal., 18 g total fat (3 g sat. fat), 90 mg chol., 395 mg sodium, 34 g carbo., 2 g fiber, 23 g pro.

Turkey Cranberry
Fried Rice

Turkey Dinner Burgers

Jalapeño pepper jelly can be red or green. Either type works just fine as a sweet and spicy glaze for these burgers.

PREP 15 minutes **BROIL** 14 minutes **MAKES** 4 servings

1	egg, lightly beaten
½	teaspoon salt
¼	teaspoon black pepper
1	pound uncooked lean ground turkey or ground chicken
¼	cup fine dry bread crumbs
¼	cup jalapeño pepper jelly, melted
	Shredded green cabbage, thinly sliced red onion, and/or other desired toppings
4	ciabatta rolls, potato rolls, kaiser rolls, or hamburger buns, split and toasted

❶ In a large bowl combine egg, salt, and pepper. Add turkey and bread crumbs; mix well. Shape the poultry mixture into four ¾-inch-thick patties.

❷ Place patties on the unheated rack of a broiler pan. Broil 4 to 5 inches from the heat for 12 to 14 minutes or until done (165°F), turning once halfway through cooking time. Brush patties with half of the jalapeño jelly. Broil 1 minute; turn and brush with remaining jelly. Broil 1 minute more.

❸ To assemble, place cabbage, red onion, and/or other toppings on bottoms of rolls and top with patties and roll tops.

PER SERVING 504 cal., 20 g total fat (2 g sat. fat), 55 mg chol., 900 mg sodium, 52 g carbo., 2 g fiber, 28 g pro.

quick tip   To ensure that you get the leanest ground turkey, look for fresh ground turkey made from the breast only. It will be light in color—almost white—rather than dark pink. Regular ground turkey is made with dark and light meat. Frozen ground turkey, which is made from dark meat only, can also contain skin and can be as high in fat and calories as ground beef.

Seafood cooks quickly, so it's a smart choice for quick meals. It's a catch in other ways too. Fresh, light, and healthful, fish and shellfish have a mild taste that pairs with flavors of all kinds.

105   113   129

seafood favorites

Sweet Pepper & Salsa Fish ♥ ▥

If you'd like a little heat in this dish, stir in a seeded, finely chopped jalapeño along with the mushrooms and sweet peppers—or choose a spicy salsa.

START TO FINISH 25 minutes   **MAKES** 4 servings

1	pound fresh or frozen skinless fish fillets, about ¾ inch thick
	Nonstick cooking spray
1½	cups packaged sliced fresh mushrooms
1	cup coarsely chopped green and/or yellow sweet pepper (1 large)
1	small onion, halved lengthwise and sliced
1	cup bottled salsa
	Hot cooked rice (optional)

❶ Thaw fish, if frozen. Rinse fish; pat dry with paper towels. Cut fish into 4 serving-size pieces, if necessary; set aside.

❷ Coat a large nonstick skillet with cooking spray. Heat skillet on medium-high heat. Add mushrooms, sweet pepper, and onion to skillet; cook about 5 minutes or until tender. Remove vegetables with a slotted spoon; set aside.

❸ Reduce heat to medium. Add fish to skillet. Cook, covered, for 6 to 9 minutes or until fish begins to flake when tested with a fork, turning once.

❹ Spoon cooked vegetables on top of fish in skillet; top with salsa. Cook, covered, on low heat about 2 minutes more or until heated through. If desired, serve with hot cooked rice.

PER SERVING 108 cal., 1 g total fat (0 g sat. fat), 22 mg chol., 213 mg sodium, 7 g carbo., 2 g fiber, 18 g pro.

---

quick tip   Cod is a mild-tasting, inexpensive fish that works well in most recipes—like this one—that simply call for fish. It keeps well in the freezer and is good to have on hand for quick, healthful dinners.

Fish with Fresh Tomato Topper ▥

This fish dish has the flavors of snapper Vera Cruz—tomatoes, olives, and cilantro—but with a prep time of less than 20 minutes.

START TO FINISH 18 minutes   **MAKES** 4 servings

½	cup fresh cilantro leaves
4	6-ounce skinless firm-textured fish fillets (such as halibut or cod), ½ to ¾ inch thick
½	teaspoon salt
½	teaspoon black pepper
1¼	cups water
1	cup quick-cooking couscous
2	large tomatoes, coarsely chopped
1	2.25-ounce can sliced pitted ripe olives

❶ Snip half of the cilantro; set aside.

❷ Place fish in a large skillet; sprinkle with the salt, pepper, and snipped cilantro. Add the water. Bring to boiling; reduce heat. Simmer, covered, for 4 minutes. Sprinkle couscous around fish. Top with tomatoes and olives. Cook, covered, about 5 minutes more or until fish begins to flake when tested with a fork. Sprinkle with the remaining cilantro.

PER SERVING 568 cal., 6 g total fat (1 g sat. fat), 54 mg chol., 539 mg sodium, 76 g carbo., 6 g fiber, 48 g pro.

Fish Sandwiches with Spicy Tartar Sauce

Here's a different way to serve up prepared breaded fish sticks—on a bun and slathered with a zippy tartar sauce.

START TO FINISH 20 minutes   **MAKES** 4 or 5 servings

1	11-ounce package frozen baked breaded fish sticks (18)
¼	cup mayonnaise
1	tablespoon dill or sweet pickle relish
1	tablespoon finely chopped onion
1	teaspoon Creole mustard or spicy brown mustard
¼	teaspoon bottled hot pepper sauce
4	or 5 hamburger buns, split and toasted
1	cup purchased shredded iceberg lettuce
¼	cup purchased shredded carrot

❶ Bake fish sticks according to package directions. Meanwhile, in a small bowl combine mayonnaise, pickle relish, onion, mustard, and hot pepper sauce. Divide fish sticks among hamburger buns. Top with mayonnaise mixture, lettuce, and carrot.

PER SERVING 356 cal., 15 g total fat (3 g sat. fat), 24 mg chol., 683 mg sodium, 41 g carbo., 1 g fiber, 12 g pro.

Tilapia Vera Cruz

Tilapia on Melon ♥

Although most of the tilapia eaten in the U.S. comes from China and Taiwan, the best-quality tilapia is U.S. farm-raised. Look for the source before you buy.

START TO FINISH 20 minutes **MAKES** 4 servings

1	pound tilapia fillets
1	tablespoon olive oil
1½	teaspoons lemon-pepper seasoning
½	of a small cantaloupe
1	medium cucumber, thinly sliced
⅓	cup plain low-fat yogurt
1	tablespoon honey

❶ Preheat broiler. Rinse fish; pat dry with paper towels. Cut fish into 4 serving-size pieces, if needed. Measure thickness of fish. Brush fish with the oil; sprinkle with ¾ teaspoon of the lemon-pepper seasoning. Place fish on the rack of an unheated broiler pan.

❷ Broil fish 3 to 4 inches from heat until fish begins to flake when tested with a fork. Allow 4 to 6 minutes per ½-inch thickness.

❸ Meanwhile, peel and seed cantaloupe; cut into thin slices. Arrange cantaloupe and cucumber on a large serving platter. Top with fish. For sauce, in a small bowl combine yogurt, honey, and the remaining ¾ teaspoon lemon-pepper seasoning. Serve sauce over fish and melon mixture.

PER SERVING 204 cal., 6 g total fat (2 g sat. fat), 58 mg chol., 493 mg sodium, 14 g carbo., 1 g fiber, 25 g pro.

Tilapia Vera Cruz

The port of Vera Cruz on the Gulf of Mexico is famous for this dish—usually made with red snapper.

START TO FINISH 25 minutes **MAKES** 4 servings

4	6- to 8-ounce fresh or frozen skinless tilapia, red snapper, mahi mahi, or other fish fillets
1	tablespoon olive oil
1	small onion, cut into thin wedges
1	jalapeño, seeded and finely chopped (see tip, page 19) (optional)
1	clove garlic, minced
1	14.5-ounce can diced tomatoes, undrained
1	cup sliced fresh cremini or button mushrooms
¾	cup pimiento-stuffed olives, coarsely chopped
1	tablespoon snipped fresh oregano or ½ teaspoon dried oregano, crushed
¼	teaspoon salt
⅛	teaspoon black pepper
2	cups hot cooked rice and/or 8 crusty bread slices

❶ Thaw fish, if frozen. Rinse fish; pat dry with paper towels. Set fish aside.

❷ For sauce, in an extra-large skillet heat olive oil on medium heat. Add onion, jalapeño (if desired), and garlic; cook and stir for 2 to 3 minutes or until onion is tender. Add undrained tomatoes, mushrooms, olives, oregano, salt, and black pepper. Bring to boiling.

❸ Place fish in sauce in skillet, spooning sauce over fish. Return to boiling; reduce heat. Simmer, covered, for 8 to 10 minutes or until fish begins to flake when tested with a fork. Serve fish and sauce over rice and/or bread slices.

PER SERVING 363 cal., 10 g total fat (2 g sat. fat), 84 mg chol., 1,111 mg sodium, 31 g carbo., 3 g fiber, 38 g pro.

{ Fish is healthful and simple to prepare. It cooks quickly—a good quality for weeknight dinners. }

Crispy Almond Fish

Serve this crispy fish with steamed green beans, wild rice pilaf, and wedges of lemon for squeezing.

START TO FINISH 30 minutes   **MAKES** 4 servings

- 1 pound fresh or frozen skinless white fish fillets, such as tilapia, cod, or flounder
- ⅓ cup all-purpose flour
- 1 egg, slightly beaten
- 2 tablespoons milk
- ⅓ cup fine dry bread crumbs
- ⅓ cup finely chopped almonds
- ½ teaspoon dried thyme, crushed
- 2 to 3 tablespoons cooking oil

❶ Thaw fish, if frozen. Rinse fish; pat dry with paper towels. Cut into 4 serving-size pieces, if necessary. Measure thickness of fish.

❷ Place flour in a shallow dish. In a second shallow dish whisk together egg and milk. In a third shallow dish combine bread crumbs, almonds, and thyme. Coat both sides of fillets with flour. Dip fillets in the egg mixture; dip in bread crumb mixture to coat.

❸ In a large skillet heat 2 tablespoons oil on medium heat. Add fish fillets (if necessary, cook fish half at a time). Cook until golden and fish begins to flake when tested with a fork, turning once (allow 4 to 6 minutes per ½-inch thickness of fish).

PER SERVING 308 cal., 15 g total fat (3 g sat. fat), 110 mg chol., 145 mg sodium, 16 g carbo., 2 g fiber, 28 g pro.

---

quick tip   Dredging is the process of coating food—such as a fish fillet—in flour and bread crumbs to create a crispy crust. The order in which you dredge is important. Flour comes first to give the egg something to adhere to—then the bread crumbs stick to the egg.

Fish Tostadas with Chili-Lime Cream

Tucking under the thin edges of the fish keeps them from overcooking and drying out so the fish cooks as evenly as possible.

START TO FINISH 20 minutes   **MAKES** 4 servings

- 1 pound fresh tilapia or cod fillets
- ½ teaspoon chili powder
- ¼ teaspoon salt
- 1 lime, halved
- ½ cup sour cream
- ½ teaspoon garlic powder
- 8 6-inch tostada shells
- 2 cups shredded cabbage mix
- 1 avocado, halved, seeded, peeled, and sliced (optional)
- 1 cup cherry tomatoes, quartered (optional)
  Bottled hot pepper sauce (optional)

❶ Preheat broiler. Sprinkle fish with ¼ teaspoon of the chili powder and salt. For chili-lime cream, in a bowl squeeze 2 teaspoons juice from half the lime. Stir in sour cream, garlic powder, and remaining chili powder; set aside. Cut remaining lime half in wedges for serving.

❷ Place fish on unheated greased broiler rack; tuck under thin edges. Place shells on baking sheet on lowest rack. Broil fish 4 inches from heat 4 to 6 minutes per ½-inch thickness until fish flakes with fork. Break in chunks. Serve tostadas with cabbage, chili-lime cream, avocado, remaining lime half, and, if desired, tomatoes and pepper sauce.

PER SERVING 278 cal., 14 g total fat (5 g sat. fat), 67 mg chol., 303 mg sodium, 17 g carbo., 2 g fiber, 25 g pro.

Cornmeal-Crusted
Catfish Rolls

Cornmeal-Crusted Catfish Rolls

These crispy fish fillets are served on cocktail-size rolls so they hang generously over the edges.

START TO FINISH 30 minutes   **MAKES** 4 servings

- 1½ pounds catfish fillets
- ¼ cup cornmeal
- 2 teaspoons Cajun or blackening seasoning
- ¼ cup vegetable oil
- 2 baby sweet peppers or ¼ of a large sweet pepper
- 1 stalk celery
- ¼ of a small red or sweet onion (optional)
- ⅓ cup mayonnaise
- 1 tablespoon ketchup
- ¼ to ½ teaspoon bottled hot pepper sauce (optional)
- 8 cocktail-size rolls, split and toasted

❶ Rinse fish; pat dry. Cut into 8 pieces. In a shallow dish combine cornmeal and 1½ teaspoons of the Cajun seasoning; coat fish with cornmeal mixture.

❷ In a large skillet cook fish in hot oil on medium-high heat for 8 to 10 minutes or until brown and fish flakes when tested with fork.

❸ Meanwhile, thinly slice peppers, celery, and, if using, onion and combine in medium bowl. In small bowl combine mayonnaise, ketchup, the remaining ½ teaspoon Cajun seasoning, and, if desired, hot pepper sauce. Add 1 tablespoon mayonnaise mixture to pepper-celery mixture. Spread some of remaining mayonnaise mixture on cut sides of rolls. Place catfish pieces on roll bottoms. Top with celery mixture and roll tops. Pass any remaining mayonnaise mixture.

PER SERVING 636 cal., 38 g total fat (7 g sat. fat), 88 mg chol., 638 mg sodium, 38 g carbo., 2 g fiber, 34 g pro.

Catfish with Garlic Sauce

Garlic and herb semi-soft cheese warmed and stirred together with milk and fresh oregano makes a quick and creamy sauce for this colorful fish dish.

START TO FINISH 20 minutes   **MAKES** 4 servings

- 12 baby zucchini and/or yellow summer squash, trimmed and halved lengthwise
- 2 tablespoons cooking oil
- 4 6-ounce skinless catfish fillets
  Salt
  Black pepper
- ⅓ cup fine dry bread crumbs
- 8 cherry tomatoes, halved
- 2 tablespoons snipped fresh oregano
- ½ 5- to 6.5- ounce (⅓ cup) semisoft cheese with garlic and herb
- ¼ cup milk

❶ In an extra-large skillet cook zucchini in 1 tablespoon of the hot oil for 3 minutes or until crisp-tender. Remove and set aside.

❷ Brush catfish with remaining oil. Sprinkle with salt and pepper and coat with bread crumbs. Cook fish in same skillet on medium-high heat for 8 to 10 minutes or until fish flakes, turning once. Remove fish from skillet and place on serving platter; keep warm.

❸ Add zucchini back to the skillet along with the cherry tomatoes and 1 tablespoon of the oregano. Cook and stir until heated through. Meanwhile, in a small saucepan combine cheese, remaining oregano, and milk; heat through. Serve vegetables with fish and spoon sauce over fish.

PER SERVING 413 cal., 27 g total fat (8 g sat. fat), 98 mg chol., 310 mg sodium, 11 g carbo., 1 g fiber, 31 g pro.

{ Monterey Bay Aquarium's Seafood Watch rates U.S.-raised catfish as a "Best Choice" fish. }

Bacon, Egg, Spinach & Tuna Salad

Tuna is a lean fish. The lack of fat makes it a healthful choice, but it also means it easily dries out if overcooked. Be sure there is still some pink in the center.

START TO FINISH 25 minutes   **MAKES** 4 servings

- 4   eggs
- 6   slices bacon
- 12 ounces tuna steaks
- ½   cup white wine vinegar
- 2   to 3 tablespoons honey
- 1   tablespoon Dijon mustard
- 1   6-ounce package fresh baby spinach
     Freshly ground black pepper

❶ Place eggs in a saucepan; cover with water. Bring to a rapid boil. Remove from heat; cover. Let stand 10 to 15 minutes (yolks will be soft-set at 10 minutes). Drain. Rinse with cold water and let cool. Peel and halve.

❷ Meanwhile, in a large skillet cook bacon on medium heat until crisp. Remove bacon from skillet; crumble bacon and set aside. Remove 2 tablespoons drippings from skillet for dressing. Add tuna to skillet; cook on medium-high heat 3 minutes per side or until slightly pink in center. Transfer to cutting board; cover and keep warm.

❸ Wipe skillet clean. Whisk in reserved drippings, vinegar, honey, and mustard to skillet. Bring to boiling.

❹ Slice tuna. Line plates with spinach. Top with sliced tuna, crumbled bacon, and eggs. Drizzle with dressing. Season to taste with pepper.

PER SERVING 481 cal., 32 g total fat (10 g sat. fat), 289 mg chol., 702 mg sodium, 11 g carbo., 1 g fiber, 34 g pro.

quick tip   The method of cooking eggs in the recipe above—bringing them to boil and then removing them from the heat to finish cooking to the desired doneness—prevents them from getting the green ring that sometimes appears on a hard-cooked egg yolk.

Curried Tuna on Biscuits

With peas, carrot, and tuna in a creamy curried sauce, this is a one-dish meal.

START TO FINISH 20 minutes   **MAKES** 4 servings

- 3   tablespoons butter
- 3   tablespoons all-purpose flour
- 2   to 3 teaspoons curry powder
- ¼   teaspoon salt
- 2   cups milk
- 1   12-ounce can chunk white tuna, drained
- 1   cup frozen peas
- ½   cup purchased coarsely shredded fresh carrot
- 4   frozen baked biscuits for microwave

❶ In a large saucepan melt butter on medium heat. Stir in flour, curry powder, and salt. Cook and stir for 30 seconds. Add milk all at once. Cook and stir until thick and bubbly; cook and stir 1 minute more. Stir in tuna, peas, and carrot; cook and stir until heated through.

❷ Meanwhile, heat biscuits according to package directions. Serve tuna mixture over split biscuits.

PER SERVING 494 cal., 23 g total fat (10 g sat. fat), 68 mg chol., 1,208 mg sodium, 39 g carbo., 3 g fiber, 31 g pro.

Tuna Salad with Capers

The dressed tuna would make a delicious sandwich filling as well as a topping for this crunchy green salad.

START TO FINISH 25 minutes   **MAKES** 6 servings

- ½   cup mayonnaise or salad dressing
- 2   tablespoons capers, drained
- 2   tablespoons lemon juice
- 1   tablespoon snipped fresh tarragon
- 1   teaspoon Cajun seasoning
- 1   12-ounce can solid white tuna
- 2   tablespoons milk
- 1   10-ounce package torn mixed greens (romaine blend) or 8 cups torn romaine
- 2   cups shredded cabbage with carrot (coleslaw mix)
- 2   small tomatoes, cut into wedges

❶ In a small bowl combine mayonnaise, capers, lemon juice, tarragon, and Cajun seasoning. Set aside. In a large bowl flake tuna into large chunks; toss with 3 tablespoons of the mayonnaise mixture. Stir milk into remaining mayonnaise mixture.

❷ Divide greens among 6 plates; top with shredded cabbage, tuna, and tomato wedges. Serve with remaining mayonnaise mixture.

PER SERVING 228 cal., 17 g total fat (3 g sat. fat), 38 mg chol., 455 mg sodium, 5 g carbo., 2 g fiber, 15 g pro.

Bacon, Egg, Spinach & Tuna Salad

Fast Niçoise Salad

Tuna & Twisty Noodles

This superfast version of tuna and noodles goes from stovetop to tabletop in 15 minutes.

START TO FINISH 15 minutes   **MAKES** 4 servings

- 1 10-ounce container refrigerated light Alfredo pasta sauce
- 1 cup water
- 2 3-ounce packages ramen noodles (any flavor)
- 2 6-ounce cans 50%-less-salt chunk light tuna, drained
- 2 cups yellow summer squash, halved lengthwise and sliced (2 small)
- 1 cup sugar snap peas, halved diagonally
   Black pepper

❶ In a large skillet combine Alfredo sauce and the water; bring to boiling. Break up noodles (discard seasoning packet). Stir noodles, tuna, squash, and sugar snap peas into skillet. Return to boiling; reduce heat. Simmer, covered, for 5 minutes. Season to taste with pepper.

PER SERVING 396 cal., 14 g total fat (8 g sat. fat), 70 mg chol., 751 mg sodium, 35 g carbo., 2 g fiber, 31 g pro.

Tuna with Chipotle-Raspberry Sauce

You can save the remaining chipotle peppers for another use. Transfer them to a tightly sealed container and freeze. You may want to divide them among several small containers so you can thaw just what you need.

START TO FINISH 25 minutes   **MAKES** 4 servings

- 4 5- to 6-ounce fresh or frozen tuna steaks, cut 1 inch thick
- 1 tablespoon olive oil
- ¼ teaspoon salt
- ¼ teaspoon black pepper
- ½ cup raspberry preserves
- 1 tablespoon chopped chipotle pepper in adobo sauce (see note, page 19)
- 2 tablespoons orange juice

❶ Preheat broiler. Thaw tuna, if frozen. Rinse tuna; pat dry with paper towels. Brush tuna with oil; season with salt and pepper. Place tuna on the rack of an unheated broiler pan or a foil-lined baking sheet. Broil 4 to 5 inches from the heat for 8 to 12 minutes or until fish flakes when tested with a fork, turning once.

❷ Meanwhile, in small bowl combine raspberry preserves, chipotle pepper, and orange juice. About 1 minute before fish is done, spoon a small amount of the preserves on each steak. Serve with additional sauce.

PER SERVING 300 cal., 5 g total fat (1 g sat. fat), 64 mg chol., 228 mg sodium, 29 g carbo., 1 g fiber, 33 g pro.

Fast Niçoise Salad ♥

True Niçoise has tuna, hard-cooked eggs, green beans, potatoes, and meaty Niçoise olives, and this version goes together in 20 minutes. Serve this speedy "salade Niçoise" with crusty French bread and a glass of chilled white wine.

START TO FINISH 20 minutes   **MAKES** 4 servings

- 2 cups refrigerated red potato wedges
- 1 tablespoon butter
- 6 cups packaged mixed salad greens
- 2 5-ounce pouches or cans lemon-pepper chunk light tuna
- 1 cup cherry tomatoes
- ⅓ cup bottled roasted garlic vinaigrette salad dressing
   Salt
   Freshly ground black pepper

❶ In a large skillet cook potatoes in melted butter on medium heat for 15 minutes or until golden, stirring occasionally.

❷ Divide greens among 4 plates. Top with tuna, tomatoes, and potatoes. Drizzle vinaigrette. Season to taste with salt and pepper.

PER SERVING 269 cal., 11 g total fat (1 g sat. fat), 31 mg chol., 426 mg sodium, 15 g carbo., 4 g fiber, 26 g pro.

quick tip   If you can't find lemon-pepper tuna, you can use any herb-seasoned tuna—or season plain tuna with a little bit of lemon-pepper seasoning.

Hawaiian Tuna Toss 🎬

Crunchy and spicy-sweet, this salad will transport you to the tropics. Swap the pineapple for slices of fresh mango, if you'd like.

START TO FINISH 15 minutes   **MAKES** 4 servings

5	cups packaged shredded broccoli (broccoli slaw mix)
2	5-ounce pouches sweet and spicy marinated chunk light tuna
½	cup bottled honey-dijon salad dressing
½	small fresh pineapple, cut into 4 slices
½	cup macadamia nuts, chopped

① In a large bowl toss together broccoli slaw, tuna, and salad dressing.

② Arrange a quartered pineapple slice on each of 4 plates. Spoon broccoli mixture over pineapple. Sprinkle with nuts.

PER SERVING 399 cal., 25 g total fat (3 g sat. fat), 31 mg chol., 480 mg sodium, 27 g carbo., 5 g fiber, 18 g pro.

---

quick tip   If you don't have honey-dijon salad dressing, any salad dressing that's on the sweet side, including balsamic vinaigrette, Asian-ginger vinaigrette, or poppy seed dressing, works on this salad.

Hawaiian Tuna Toss

Fresh Feta Salmon Pasta

This healthful pasta dish is a fresh way to use leftover grilled, poached, or baked salmon. If you don't have leftover salmon, you can use canned.

START TO FINISH 35 minutes   **MAKES** 4 servings

6	ounces whole wheat penne or rotini pasta
	Nonstick cooking spray
2	cloves garlic, minced
4	large roma tomatoes, chopped
½	cup sliced green onions
12	ounces cooked salmon, broken into chunks, or two 6-ounce cans water-pack, skinless, boneless salmon, drained
⅛	teaspoon salt
3	tablespoons snipped fresh basil
½	teaspoon black pepper
2	teaspoons olive oil
¾	cup crumbled feta cheese (3 ounces)
	Fresh basil sprigs

① In a 4-quart Dutch oven cook pasta according to package directions. Drain well. Return pasta to Dutch oven; cover to keep warm.

② Lightly coat an unheated large nonstick skillet with cooking spray. Heat skillet on medium-high heat. Add garlic; cook and stir for 15 seconds. Add tomatoes and green onions to skillet; cook and stir just until tender. Sprinkle salmon with salt. Add salmon, snipped basil, and pepper to skillet. Heat through.

③ Add oil to drained pasta; toss to mix. Add salmon mixture and feta cheese to pasta; toss gently. Garnish with basil sprigs.

PER SERVING 442 cal., 20 g total fat (6 g sat. fat), 86 mg chol., 384 mg sodium, 37 g carbo., 6 g fiber, 31 g pro.

Fish with Pesto
& Wine Pasta

Fish with Pesto & Wine Pasta

Make this elegant dish with a dry white wine you'd like to drink. Any white wine works fine, including Pinot Grigio, Chardonnay, or Sauvignon Blanc.

START TO FINISH 30 minutes   **MAKES** 4 servings

- 2 cups dried penne (6 ounces)
- 2 cups packaged sliced fresh mushrooms
- ½ cup dry white wine
- ⅓ cup purchased basil pesto
- 2 tablespoons lemon juice
- 1 tablespoon drained capers
- 4 fresh or frozen salmon or swordfish steaks, cut ¾ inch thick (1¼ pounds)
- ¼ teaspoon salt
- ¼ teaspoon black pepper
- 2 tablespoons olive oil or cooking oil

1 In a large saucepan cook the pasta in lightly salted boiling water for 4 minutes; drain and set aside. (Pasta will not be tender.) In a large bowl combine the partially cooked pasta, mushrooms, wine, pesto, lemon juice, and capers; set aside.

2 Meanwhile, sprinkle both sides of the fish steaks with the salt and pepper. In an extra-large skillet cook the fish steaks in hot oil on medium-high heat for 1 minute; turn and cook 1 minute more. Reduce heat to medium.

3 Spoon the pasta mixture around the fish in skillet. Bring to boiling; reduce heat. Simmer, covered, on medium heat for 6 to 9 minutes or until fish flakes easily with a fork and pasta is tender.

PER SERVING 597 cal., 31 g total fat (3 g sat. fat), 78 mg chol., 464 mg sodium, 38 g carbo., 2 g fiber, 39 g pro.

Salmon with Pepper Relish

If you like sweet-sour flavors, you'll like this salmon with a side of sweet-sour pepper and mango relish.

START TO FINISH 20 minutes   **MAKES** 4 servings

- 4 4- to 5-ounce skinless salmon fillets
  Salt
  Black pepper
- ½ cup mango chutney (cut up any large pieces)
- ¾ cup chopped yellow sweet pepper (1 medium)
- ½ cup chopped red onion (1 medium)
- ½ cup shredded carrot (1)
- 2 tablespoons cider vinegar
  Salt
  Black pepper

1 Preheat broiler. Rinse fish; pat dry with paper towels. Measure thickness of fish. Sprinkle fish lightly with salt and pepper. Place fish on the lightly greased rack of a broiler pan. Broil 4 inches from heat until fish begins to flake when tested with a fork, turning once halfway through broiling. (Allow 4 to 6 minutes per ½-inch thickness of fish.) Brush with ¼ cup of the chutney during the last 2 minutes of broiling time.

2 Meanwhile, for pepper relish, in a medium bowl combine the remaining ¼ cup chutney, sweet pepper, red onion, carrot, and vinegar. Season to taste with salt and black pepper. Serve pepper relish with fish.

PER SERVING 314 cal., 12 g total fat (3 g sat. fat), 67 mg chol., 484 mg sodium, 24 g carbo., 1 g fiber, 23 g pro.

{ The American Heart Association recommends eating fatty fish such as salmon twice a week. }

Poached Salmon with Citrus Salad

The peppery taste of watercress or arugula is a delicious contrast to the sweetness of the citrus in this salad. Cara Cara oranges are an especially juicy and low-acid variety.

START TO FINISH 25 minutes   **MAKES** 4 servings

- 4 **4-ounce fresh or frozen skinless salmon, cod, or haddock fillets, about 1 inch thick**
- 1 **lime**
- 6 **oranges (navel, blood, Cara Cara, and/or tangerines)**
- ½ **cup water**
- ¼ **cup olive oil**
- 1 **teaspoon sugar**
-    **Salt**
-    **Black pepper**
- 2 **tablespoons vegetable oil**
- 6 **wonton wrappers, cut into ½-inch strips**
- 1 **7-ounce bunch watercress, trimmed, or 4 cups arugula or baby spinach**

❶ Thaw fish, if frozen. Rinse fish; pat dry with paper towels. Finely shred 1 teaspoon peel from lime; set aside. Squeeze juice from the lime and 2 of the oranges; combine juices. Measure ¼ cup juice for dressing and set aside. Pour the remaining juice into a large nonstick skillet; add water and the lime peel. Bring to boiling. Add salmon; reduce heat to medium. Simmer, covered, for 8 to 12 minutes or until fish begins to flake when tested with a fork.

❷ Meanwhile, for dressing, in a small bowl whisk together the reserved ¼ cup juice, olive oil, and sugar; season to taste with salt and pepper.

❸ For wonton strips, in another large skillet heat oil on medium-high heat. Add wonton strips; cook about 1 to 2 minutes or until crisp, stirring often.

❹ Peel and section or slice remaining oranges; arrange oranges, watercress, and salmon on dinner plates. Drizzle with dressing. Pass wonton strips.

PER SERVING 553 cal., 36 g total fat (6 g sat. fat), 63 mg chol., 303 mg sodium, 32 g carbo., 5 g fiber, 27 g pro.

Peppered Salmon with Quick Ratatouille

Ratatouille is a vegetable melange from the south of France that always includes eggplant, tomatoes, and some kind of squash—usually zucchini.

START TO FINISH 20 minutes   **OVEN** 450°F   **MAKES** 4 servings

- 4 **6-ounce skinless salmon fillets**
-    **Salt**
-    **Freshly ground black pepper**
- 2 **tablespoons cooking oil**
- 1 **large red sweet onion, cut into thin wedges**
- 2 **medium zucchini, halved lengthwise and cut into 1-inch pieces**
- 1 **small eggplant, peeled and cubed**
- 1 **14.5-ounce can Italian-style stewed tomatoes, undrained**

❶ Preheat oven to 450°F. Measure thickness of fish. Sprinkle fish lightly with salt; sprinkle generously with pepper. Place fish on a baking sheet. Bake until fish begins to flake when tested with a fork. (Allow 4 to 6 minutes per ½-inch thickness of fish.)

❷ Meanwhile, in an extra-large skillet heat oil on medium-high heat. Add onion to skillet; cook for 2 minutes. Add zucchini, eggplant, and undrained tomatoes. Bring to boiling; reduce heat. Simmer, covered, for 5 minutes. Serve vegetable mixture with fish.

PER SERVING 450 cal., 26 g total fat (5 g sat. fat), 100 mg chol., 601 mg sodium, 19 g carbo., 7 g fiber, 37 g pro.

quick tip   When the fish counter doesn't have skinless salmon fillets, just ask the butcher to skin them for you. It's easy to destroy a perfect piece of fish trying to do it yourself.

Barbecued Salmon with
Fresh Nectarine Salsa

Mediterranean Salmon & Noodle Bowl

Use any variety of refrigerated fettuccine in this dish—plain, spinach, lemon-pepper, or tomato.

START TO FINISH 20 minutes **MAKES** 4 servings

- 1 9-ounce package refrigerated fettuccine
- 2 tablespoons olive oil
- 1 pound skinless, boneless 1-inch-thick salmon, cut in 8 pieces
   Salt
   Black pepper
- 6 cups packaged fresh baby spinach
- ½ cup bottled roasted red or yellow sweet peppers
- ½ cup reduced-calorie balsamic vinaigrette salad dressing

① Prepare pasta according to package directions.

② Meanwhile, brush 1 tablespoon of the olive oil on salmon. Sprinkle with salt and black pepper. Heat an extra-large skillet on medium heat; add salmon. Cook 8 to 12 minutes or until salmon flakes, turning once. Remove salmon; cover and keep warm.

③ Add spinach, sweet peppers, and remaining oil to skillet. Cook and stir 1 to 2 minutes until spinach is wilted. Drain pasta; add to skillet. Add dressing; toss to coat. Season with salt and black pepper.

④ To serve, divide spinach-pasta mixture among 4 bowls. Top with salmon.

PER SERVING 508 cal., 25 g total fat (5 g sat. fat), 108 mg chol., 733 mg sodium, 39 g carbo., 3 g fiber, 31 g pro.

Barbecued Salmon with Fresh Nectarine Salsa

Barbecue sauce is surprisingly delicious on salmon. Because fish cooks so quickly, you can brush the sauce on before you begin cooking and it won't burn.

START TO FINISH 20 minutes **MAKES** 4 servings

- 4 4- to 5-ounces fresh skinless salmon fillets, about 1 inch thick
- 3 tablespoons bottled barbecue sauce
- 2 nectarines, pitted and chopped
- ¾ cup fresh blueberries
- ¼ cup coarsely chopped pecans, toasted (see note, page 31)
   Lemon wedges

① Rinse fish; pat dry with paper towels. Lightly sprinkle salmon with salt and pepper. Place 2 tablespoons of the barbecue sauce in a small bowl; brush sauce on both sides of the salmon.

② For charcoal grill, cook salmon on greased grill rack directly over medium coals for 8 to 12 minutes or until salmon flakes when tested with a fork, turning once halfway through grilling. (For gas grill, preheat grill. Reduce heat to medium. Place salmon on greased grill rack over medium heat. Cover and grill as above.)

③ For nectarine salsa, in a medium bowl combine nectarines, blueberries, pecans, and the remaining 1 tablespoon barbecue sauce. Season with salt. Serve salmon with salsa and lemon wedges.

PER SERVING 318 cal., 17 g total fat (3 g sat. fat), 66 mg chol., 344 mg sodium, 17 g carbo., 3 g fiber, 24 g pro.

{ The mild flavor of salmon lends itself well to both sweet and savory preparations. }

Sesame-Teriyaki Sea Bass

Sea bass is a great choice for introducing people who claim not to like fish to the wonders of eating fish. It has a buttery texture and a mild flavor that is simply delicious.

START TO FINISH 25 minutes   **MAKES** 4 servings

4	4-ounce fresh or frozen sea bass, rockfish, or other fish fillets, ½ to ¾ inch thick
¼	teaspoon black pepper
3	tablespoons soy sauce
¼	cup sweet rice wine (mirin)
2	teaspoons honey
2	teaspoons cooking oil
2	teaspoons sesame seeds and/or black sesame seeds, toasted (see note, page 31)

1 Thaw fish, if frozen. Rinse fish; pat dry with paper towels. Sprinkle fish with pepper; set aside.

2 For glaze, in a small saucepan combine soy sauce, rice wine, and honey. Bring to boiling; reduce heat. Simmer, uncovered, about 10 minutes or until glaze is slightly thickened and reduced to ⅓ cup; set aside.

3 Meanwhile, in a large nonstick skillet cook fish fillets in hot oil on medium heat until fish is golden and begins to flake when tested with a fork, turning once. (Allow 4 to 6 minutes per ½-inch thickness.) Drain fish on paper towels.

4 To serve, transfer fish to a serving platter. Drizzle glaze over fish. Sprinkle with sesame seeds.

PER FILLET 196 cal., 5 g total fat (1 g sat. fat), 46 mg chol., 783 mg sodium, 13 g carbo., 0 g fiber, 23 g pro.

---

quick tip   The Monterey Bay Aquarium keeps a running list of which varieties of fish are safe to eat, abundant, well-managed, and caught or farmed in environmentally friendly ways. If something is on the "Avoid" list, the aquarium offers up good options. Learn more at seafoodwatch.org.

Seared Scallops with Ginger Sauce ♥

If you can find them, look for dry-packed scallops. They are not soaked in a phosphate solution that—although it prevents them from drying out—also prevents them from getting a nice crust when seared, as they are in this recipe.

START TO FINISH 15 minutes   **MAKES** 4 servings

1	pound fresh or frozen sea scallops
4	teaspoons butter or margarine
⅓	cup chicken broth
¼	cup frozen pineapple-orange juice concentrate, thawed
1	teaspoon grated fresh ginger

1 Thaw scallops, if frozen. Rinse scallops; pat dry with paper towels. Heat butter in a large skillet on medium-high heat. Add scallops to skillet. Cook, stirring frequently, for 2 to 3 minutes or until scallops turn opaque. Remove scallops from skillet; keep warm.

2 For sauce, add chicken broth, juice concentrate, and ginger to skillet. Bring to boiling. Boil, uncovered, until sauce is reduced by about half. Spoon sauce over scallops.

PER SERVING 168 cal., 5 g total fat (3 g sat. fat), 48 mg chol., 311 mg sodium, 10 g carbo., 0 g fiber, 19 g pro.

Seared Scallops with Ginger Sauce

Tea-Sauced Scallops
with Orange & Honey

Tea-Sauced Scallops with Orange & Honey

Black tea leaves impart a fruity flavor to this unusual dish.

START TO FINISH 30 minutes　**MAKES** 4 servings

- 2　tablespoons olive oil
- 1　large clove garlic, minced
- 1　pound sea scallops
- ¾　cup orange juice
- 4　teaspoons Keemun tea leaves or other Chinese black tea leaves
- 4　teaspoons honey
- 2　teaspoons reduced-sodium soy sauce
- 6　ounces Chinese egg noodles, rice noodles, or angel hair pasta
- 1　medium orange sweet pepper, cut into bite-size strips
- 1　medium green onion, cut into thin strips
- 　Cilantro sprigs (optional)

① Heat olive oil in a large nonstick skillet on medium-high heat. Add minced garlic; cook and stir for 30 seconds. Add scallops. Cook and stir for 4 to 6 minutes or just until the scallops turn opaque. Transfer scallops to a small bowl; cover and keep warm.

② Carefully pour orange juice into skillet, stirring to dislodge any particles adhering to pan. Add tea leaves; cook and stir mixture for 30 seconds. Add honey, soy sauce, and any scallop liquid from the bowl. Reduce heat; simmer, uncovered, for 3 minutes or until sauce thickens slightly.

③ Cook Chinese noodles or pasta according to package directions, adding the sweet pepper the last 3 minutes of cooking. Drain; set aside.

④ Strain tea mixture through a fine-mesh sieve; return liquid to the pan, discarding solids. Transfer scallops from bowl to pan with a slotted spoon; toss gently to coat with the sauce. To serve, arrange noodles onto 4 warm dinner plates. Top with scallops and sauce. Garnish with green onion and, if desired, cilantro sprigs.

PER SERVING 383 cal., 10 g total fat (2 g sat. fat), 73 mg chol., 286 mg sodium, 48 g carbo., 2 g fiber, 26 g pro.

Scallop Stir-Fry Salad ♥

Sea scallops are large, like the sea—and bay scallops are small, like a bay.

START TO FINISH 30 minutes　**MAKES** 2 servings

- 6　ounces fresh or frozen bay scallops
- 1　tablespoon orange juice
- 1　tablespoon reduced-sodium soy sauce
- 1½　teaspoons rice vinegar or white wine vinegar
- ½　teaspoon toasted sesame oil
- 1　tablespoon cooking oil
- ½　cup fresh pea pods, strings and tips removed and halved if desired
- ½　medium red sweet pepper, coarsely chopped
- ¼　cup sliced green onions (2)
- ½　12-ounce jar baby corn, rinsed and drained
- 1　cup shredded napa cabbage
- 1　cup shredded fresh spinach or romaine

① Thaw scallops, if frozen. Rinse scallops; pat dry with paper towels. In a small bowl stir together orange juice, soy sauce, vinegar, and sesame oil. Set aside.

② In a medium skillet cook and stir scallops in 2 teaspoons hot oil on medium-high heat for 2 minutes or until scallops are opaque. Remove scallops from skillet.

③ Add remaining 1 teaspoon cooking oil to the skillet. Add pea pods, sweet pepper, and green onions; cook and stir for 2 to 3 minutes or until crisp-tender. Add cooked scallops, baby corn, and orange juice mixture to skillet; cook and stir about 1 minute or until heated through. Remove from heat.

④ In a large salad bowl combine napa cabbage and spinach. Top with scallop mixture; toss gently to combine.

PER SERVING 203 cal., 9 g total fat (1 g sat. fat), 28 mg chol., 633 mg sodium, 12 g carbo., 4 g fiber, 18 g pro.

Scallop Stir-Fry Salad

Scallops with Dill Sauce

The flavor of dill is a natural with many kinds of fish and seafood, including scallops.

PREP 20 minutes   **BROIL** 8 minutes   **MAKES** 4 kabobs

- 1   pound fresh or frozen sea scallops
- 3   tablespoons butter, melted
- ¼   teaspoon black pepper
- ⅛   teaspoon paprika
- ⅔   cup mayonnaise
- 1   tablespoon finely chopped onion
- 2   teaspoons lemon juice
- 1½ teaspoons snipped fresh dill or ½ teaspoon dried dill
     Romaine lettuce leaves (optional)
     Lemon wedges (optional)

❶ Thaw scallops, if frozen. Rinse scallops; pat dry with paper towels. Halve any large scallops. Thread scallops onto four 8- to 10-inch skewers, leaving a ¼-inch space between pieces. Preheat broiler. Place skewers on the greased unheated rack of a broiler pan.

❷ In a small bowl stir together butter, pepper, and paprika. Brush half of the mixture over scallops. Broil about 4 inches from the heat for 8 to 10 minutes or until scallops are opaque, turning and brushing with the remaining melted butter mixture halfway through broiling.

❸ Meanwhile, for dill sauce, in a small bowl stir together mayonnaise, onion, lemon juice, and dill. If desired, line 4 plates with lettuce leaves. Serve scallops on plates with dill sauce and, if desired, lemon wedges.

PER KABOB 451 cal., 39 g total fat (9 g sat. fat), 88 mg chol., 475 mg sodium, 3 g carbo., 0 g fiber, 19 g pro.

---

quick tip   If using bamboo skewers, soak them in enough water to cover for at least 30 minutes before using.

Spicy Shrimp Pasta

The oil from oil-packed sun-dried tomatoes infuses this dish with rich flavor. Vary the amount of crushed red pepper to suit your taste.

START TO FINISH 20 minutes   **MAKES** 4 servings

- 8   ounce dried angel hair pasta
- 3   cups fresh broccoli florets
- 1   6.5-ounce jar sun-dried tomato strips with Italian herb packed in oil
- 2   shallots, finely chopped
- 1   pound frozen peeled and deveined shrimp with tails, thawed and drained
- ¼   to ½ teaspoon crushed red pepper
     Salt
     Black pepper
- ¼   cup snipped fresh basil

❶ In a 4-quart Dutch oven cook pasta with broccoli according to pasta package directions. Drain; return to Dutch oven. Cover to keep warm.

❷ Meanwhile, drain tomatoes, reserving oil. If necessary, add olive oil to equal ¼ cup. In an extra-large skillet heat oil on medium-high heat. Add shallots; cook and stir 1 to 2 minutes or until tender. Add shrimp and crushed red pepper; cook and stir 4 minutes. Add sun-dried tomatoes; cook and stir 1 minute more or until shrimp are opaque.

❸ Toss shrimp mixture with cooked pasta. Season with salt and pepper. Drizzle with additional olive oil. Transfer to serving bowls. Sprinkle with snipped fresh basil.

PER SERVING 526 cal., 19 g total fat (3 g sat. fat), 172 mg chol., 394 mg sodium, 55 g carbo., 5 g fiber, 34 g pro.

Lemon Shrimp Salad

Shrimp with Vermicelli ♥

If you forgot to take the shrimp out of the freezer and put them in the refrigerator to thaw, you can gently thaw them by placing the bag in cool water or by placing the shrimp in a colander and running cool water over them.

START TO FINISH 30 minutes   **MAKES** 4 servings

- 12   ounces fresh or frozen medium shrimp, peeled and deveined
- 4   ounces dried multigrain angel hair pasta
- 1   large onion, halved and thinly sliced
- 2   tablespoons butter
- ¼   to ½ teaspoon crushed red pepper
- 1   8-ounce can tomato sauce with basil, garlic, and oregano
- 1   medium yellow summer squash or zucchini, halved lengthwise and thinly sliced
- ⅛   teaspoon salt
- 4   cups prewashed baby spinach
- 1   cup cherry tomatoes, halved
- 2   tablespoons finely shredded Parmesan cheese

① Thaw shrimp if frozen. Cook pasta according to package directions; drain.

② Meanwhile, in an extra-large skillet cook onion in hot butter until tender. Add shrimp and crushed red pepper; cook and stir for 1 minute. Add tomato sauce, squash, and salt. Bring to boiling; reduce heat. Simmer, covered, for 5 minutes.

③ Stir drained pasta, spinach, and cherry tomatoes into skillet. Toss gently on medium heat until heated through. Sprinkle with Parmesan cheese.

PER SERVING 279 cal., 8 g total fat (4 g sat. fat), 114 mg chol., 588 mg sodium, 31 g carbo., 5 g fiber, 21 g pro.

Lemon Shrimp Salad ♥

If you like pepper, sprinkle this salad with coarsely ground or cracked black pepper before serving.

PREP 20 minutes   **MAKES** 4 servings

- 1   pound cooked shrimp in shells
- ¼   cup light mayonnaise dressing or salad dressing
- 2   tablespoons lemon juice
- 1   tablespoon water
- ¼   to ½ teaspoon Cajun seasoning
- ½   small red onion, thinly sliced
- 1   5-ounce package mixed baby salad greens (6 cups)

① Peel and devein shrimp, leaving tails intact if desired. For dressing, in a small bowl stir together mayonnaise dressing, lemon juice, water, and Cajun seasoning.

② In a large bowl combine shrimp and red onion. Add dressing; toss gently to coat. To serve, divide salad greens among 4 serving plates; top with shrimp mixture.

PER SERVING 148 cal., 6 g total fat (1 g sat. fat), 171 mg chol., 310 mg sodium, 5 g carbo., 0 g fiber, 19 g pro.

---

quick tip   Shrimp are classified as small, medium, large, or jumbo, depending on how many of them it takes to equal a pound. For instance, if you see a number on the package that reads "12/15," that means there are between 12 and 15 shrimp per pound. (Those are considered jumbo shrimp.) Generally there are 36 to 45 small shrimp per pound; 30 to 35 medium shrimp per pound; 24 to 30 large shrimp per pound; and 14 to 20 extra-large shrimp per pound.

{ Even in its simplest preparations, shrimp is inherently elegant. }

Shortcut Shrimp Risotto 🎬

This streamlined risotto won't have quite the creamy texture that traditional risotto does, but it doesn't require 30 to 45 minutes of near-constant stirring either. The shrimp is added right at the end of cooking time to ensure that it doesn't get overcooked and rubbery.

START TO FINISH 30 minutes **MAKES** 4 servings

2	14-ounce cans reduced-sodium chicken broth
1⅓	cups Arborio rice or short grain white rice
½	cup onion, finely chopped (1 medium)
1	tablespoon snipped fresh basil or ¾ teaspoon dried basil, crushed
1	10- to 12-ounce package frozen peeled cooked shrimp, thawed
1½	cups frozen peas
¼	cup grated Parmesan cheese

1 In a large saucepan combine broth, rice, onion, and dried basil (if using). Bring mixture to boiling; reduce heat. Cover and simmer for 18 minutes.

2 Stir in shrimp and peas. Cover and cook for 3 minutes more (do not lift lid). Stir in fresh basil (if using). Divide among 4 plates. Sprinkle each serving with cheese.

PER SERVING 305 cal., 3 g total fat (1 g sat. fat), 143 mg chol., 767 mg sodium, 45 g carbo., 3 g fiber, 25 g pro.

---

quick tip Arborio rice is specified for risotto because its high starch content is what gives risotto its classically creamy and luxurious texture. Although it's the most common rice used for risotto, it is not the only one. You can also use Vialone Nano or Carnaroli.

Greek Leeks & Shrimp Stir-Fry ♥

Bouquet garni is a dried herb blend that includes parsley, thyme, and bay leaf.

START TO FINISH 30 minutes **MAKES** 4 servings

1¼	pounds fresh or frozen peeled, deveined medium shrimp
⅔	cup water
⅓	cup lemon juice
1	tablespoon cornstarch
¼	teaspoon bouquet garni seasoning or dried oregano, crushed
1	cup couscous
¼	teaspoon salt
1½	cups boiling water
1	tablespoon olive oil
1⅓	cups thinly sliced leeks
½	cup crumbled feta cheese (2 ounces)
	Pita wedges (optional)

1 Thaw shrimp, if frozen. Rinse shrimp and pat dry with paper towels; set aside.

2 In a small bowl combine ⅔ cup water, lemon juice, cornstarch, and ¼ teaspoon bouquet garni seasoning. Set aside.

3 In a small bowl combine couscous, ½ teaspoon bouquet garni, and salt. Pour boiling water over couscous. Cover and let stand for 5 minutes.

4 Meanwhile, heat oil in wok or extra-large skillet on medium-high heat. Cook and stir leeks in hot oil for 2 to 3 minutes or until leeks are tender. Remove leeks from wok; set aside. Stir lemon juice mixture. Add to wok and bring to boiling. Add shrimp and cook 2 to 3 minutes or until opaque. Stir in cooked leeks and half of the feta cheese.

5 To serve, fluff couscous with a fork. Transfer couscous to a serving platter. Spoon shrimp over couscous and sprinkle with remaining feta cheese. If desired, serve with pita wedges.

PER SERVING 424 cal., 9 g total fat (3 g sat. fat), 228 mg chol., 527 mg sodium, 45 g carbo., 3 g fiber, 37 g pro.

Peanut-Sauced Shrimp & Pasta

Peanut-Sauced Shrimp & Pasta

Bottled peanut sauce makes it so simple to stir up Thai-style food at home, you don't need takeout.

START TO FINISH 20 minutes   **MAKES** 4 servings

- 12 ounces fresh or frozen peeled, deveined medium shrimp with tails
- ½ 14-ounce package dried medium rice noodles
- 4 cups boiling water
- 1 tablespoon vegetable oil
- 12 ounces fresh asparagus spears, trimmed, cut into 2-inch pieces (3 cups)
- 1 cup ¾-inch pieces red and/or yellow sweet pepper
- ½ cup bottled peanut sauce

① Thaw shrimp, if frozen. Rinse shrimp; pat dry with paper towels. Place noodles in a large bowl. Pour boiling water over noodles; let stand for 10 minutes.

② Meanwhile, in a large skillet heat oil on medium-high heat. Add shrimp, asparagus, and sweet pepper. Cook and stir for 3 to 5 minutes or until shrimp are opaque. Add peanut sauce; heat through.

③ Drain noodles; divide among 4 shallow bowls. Using a fork, twist noodles into nests. Top with shrimp-vegetable mixture.

PER SERVING 396 cal., 9 g total fat (2 g sat. fat), 129 mg chol., 642 mg sodium, 55 g carbo., 5 g fiber, 21 g pro.

Seafood Curry

Packaged precooked flavored rice provides the foundation for this quick-to-fix curry that features imitation crabmeat.

START TO FINISH 20 minutes   **MAKES** 4 servings

- 1 tablespoon vegetable oil
- 1 medium sweet onion, cut into thin wedges
- 2 teaspoons curry powder
- 2 8.8-ounce pouches cooked garden vegetable-flavor rice
- ½ cup orange juice
- 1 8-ounce package flake-style imitation crabmeat
- ½ peeled and cored pineapple, cut into bite-size pieces

① In a large skillet heat oil on medium heat. Add onion; cook and stir until tender. Add curry powder; cook and stir for 1 more minute. Carefully stir in rice and orange juice; heat through. Add imitation crabmeat and pineapple. Cook, covered, about 4 minutes or until heated through.

PER SERVING 331 cal., 7 g total fat (1 g sat. fat), 11 mg chol., 1,141 mg sodium, 60 g carbo., 2 g fiber, 9 g pro.

Crab Louis

Who's Louis? No one knows for sure, but his classic salad that dates back to the early 1900s usually features crabmeat, lettuce, avocado, lemon, and its trademark creamy, spicy pink dressing.

START TO FINISH 20 minutes   **MAKES** 6 servings

- ½ cup mayonnaise
- ¼ cup chili sauce
- 1 tablespoon finely chopped green sweet pepper
- 1 tablespoon finely chopped fresh parsley
- 1 tablespoon prepared horseradish
- 1 tablespoon minced green onion
- ¼ teaspoon salt
- ⅛ teaspoon cayenne pepper
- ⅛ teaspoon Worcestershire sauce
- 6 cups torn lettuce
- 3 ripe avocados, halved, seeded, peeled, and sliced
- 1 tablespoon lemon juice
- 1 pound fresh cooked crabmeat, picked over, rinsed, and patted dry, or canned lump crabmeat

  Sliced lemon

  Cherry tomatoes

① In a medium bowl whisk together mayonnaise, chili sauce, green pepper, parsley, horseradish, green onion, salt, cayenne pepper, and Worcestershire sauce until smooth.

② Arrange lettuce on 6 serving plates. Brush avocado slices with lemon juice; divide among plates. Divide crabmeat and arrange on centers of plates; spoon about 2 tablespoons of dressing over each serving. Garnish with lemon slices and cherry tomatoes.

PER SERVING 290 cal., 18 g total fat (3 g sat. fat), 81 mg chol., 604 mg sodium, 16 g carbo., 6 g fiber, 18 g pro.

quick tip   If you use canned crabmeat, be sure to buy lump crabmeat. These are the largest pieces of meat from the body of the crab. It's also the most expensive type of canned crabmeat, but in a salad that features crab as its main ingredient, it's worth the price.

Even the most enthusiastic meat eaters won't miss the meat in these dishes based on vegetables, grains, cheeses, eggs, and pasta. Cutting back on meat doesn't mean cutting back on flavor.

132 **140** **148**

meatless main dishes

139

Bow Tie Pasta with Fresh Mozzarella

The cubes of fresh mozzarella are only warmed—not melted—in this dish, so they retain their wonderful chewy, toothsome texture.

START TO FINISH 30 minutes **MAKES** 6 servings

1	16-ounce package dried bow tie pasta
3	tablespoons olive oil
4	large roma tomatoes, seeded and chopped, or 2 cups cherry tomatoes, halved
1	15-ounce can cannellini beans (white kidney beans), rinsed and drained
8	ounces fresh mozzarella cheese, cubed
¼	cup finely shredded Parmesan cheese
¼	cup snipped fresh basil or 1 teaspoon dried basil, crushed
2	cloves garlic, minced
¼	teaspoon salt

❶ In a 5- to 6-quart Dutch oven cook pasta according to package directions; drain and return to pan. Add olive oil and toss with pasta to coat. Add tomatoes, cannellini beans, mozzarella and Parmesan cheeses, basil, garlic, and salt; toss gently to coat.

PER SERVING 513 cal., 17 g total fat (7 g sat. fat), 29 mg chol., 385 mg sodium, 69 g carbo., 6 g fiber, 24 g pro.

quick tip If you can find the tiny fresh mozzarella balls called *bocconcini* in Italian, they're a perfect fit for this dish. There's no cubing needed if they're smaller than 1 inch. If they're slightly larger than that, just cut them in half.

Fusilli with Garlic Pesto & Aged Pecorino

Pecorino Romano cheese is a hard Italian grating cheese made from sheep's milk. Aged pecorino has a wonderfully sharp, pungent flavor.

START TO FINISH 35 minutes **MAKES** 6 to 8 servings

15	cloves garlic, peeled
½	cup packed fresh basil leaves
1	pound dried fusilli, gemelli, or tagliatelle pasta
½	cup olive oil
⅓	cup pine nuts, toasted (see note, page 31)
2	tablespoons finely shredded Pecorino Romano cheese (½ ounce)
¾	teaspoon sea salt
⅛	teaspoon freshly ground black pepper
1	cup small fresh basil leaves
¼	cup finely shredded Pecorino Romano cheese (1 ounce)

❶ In a 5- to 6-quart Dutch oven cook garlic cloves in a large amount of boiling salted water for 8 minutes. Using a slotted spoon, transfer garlic to a blender. Add ⅓ cup basil leaves to the boiling water and cook for 5 seconds; remove with slotted spoon and drain well on paper towels. (Do not drain boiling water.) Add basil to blender.

❷ Add pasta to the boiling water and cook according to package directions. Before draining pasta, remove ½ cup of the hot cooking water and set aside. Drain pasta; return to Dutch oven.

❸ Meanwhile, for pesto, add oil, 2 tablespoons of the pine nuts, 2 tablespoons cheese, salt, and pepper to blender. Cover and blend until nearly smooth (pesto will be thin).

❹ Add pesto to cooked pasta; toss gently to coat. If necessary, toss in enough of the reserved cooking water to help coat the pasta evenly with pesto. Transfer pasta mixture to a serving bowl. Sprinkle with 1 cup basil leaves, ¼ cup cheese, and remaining pine nuts. Serve immediately.

PER SERVING 524 cal., 26 g total fat (4 g sat. fat), 5 mg chol., 264 mg sodium, 61 g carbo., 3 g fiber, 13 g pro.

quick tip The fresh basil leaves will darken if left on top of the hot pasta very long. To avoid this, serve the pasta right after adding the basil.

Fusilli with Garlic Pesto
& Aged Pecorino

Smoky Mushroom Stroganoff

Italian Pasta Primavera

"Primavera" means spring in Italian. The term refers to the generous dose of vegetables in this creamy, saucy dish.

START TO FINISH 30 minutes **MAKES** 6 servings

- 1 16-ounce package dried fusilli
- 8 ounces broccoli, rinsed, trimmed, and cut into florets (about 2 cups)
- 8 ounces cauliflower, rinsed, trimmed, and cut into florets (about 2 cups)
- 1½ cups milk
- 3 tablespoons all-purpose flour
- 1 teaspoon salt
- ¼ teaspoon black pepper
- 1 cup grated Parmesan cheese
- ¼ cup oil-packed dried tomatoes, well drained and chopped

❶ In a 4- to 6-quart Dutch oven cook pasta according to package directions, adding broccoli and cauliflower the last 4 to 5 minutes of cooking time. Drain and return to Dutch oven.

❷ Meanwhile, in a medium microwave-safe mixing bowl whisk together milk, flour, salt, and pepper. Microwave, covered, on high for 3 to 4 minutes, stirring every 30 seconds or until thickened. Add milk mixture, Parmesan cheese, and dried tomatoes to cooked pasta in Dutch oven. Stir gently to combine.

PER SERVING 415 cal., 7 g total fat (3 g sat. fat), 17 mg chol., 657 mg sodium, 68 g carbo., 5 g fiber, 19 g pro.

quick tip Reserve the oil from oil-packed dried tomatoes and use it to flavor a homemade salad dressing—or to liven up hot cooked pasta.

Smoky Mushroom Stroganoff

You won't miss the meat in this meatless version of the classic dish. Try it with a variety of mushrooms instead of just one kind.

START TO FINISH 18 minutes **MAKES** 4 servings

- 1 8.8-ounce package dried pappardelle (wide egg noodles)
- 1½ pound package sliced mushrooms, such as button, cremini, and/or shiitake
- 2 cloves garlic, minced
- 1 tablespoon olive oil
- 1 8-ounce carton light sour cream
- 2 tablespoon all-purpose flour
- 1½ teaspoons smoked paprika
- ¼ teaspoon black pepper
- 1 cup vegetable broth
   Snipped fresh parsley (optional)

❶ Cook noodles according to package directions. Drain; keep warm.

❷ In an extra-large skillet cook mushrooms and garlic in hot oil on medium-high heat 5 to 8 minutes or until tender, stirring occasionally. Remove mushrooms with a slotted spoon; cover to keep warm.

❸ For sauce, in a bowl combine sour cream, flour, paprika, and pepper. Stir in broth until smooth. Add to skillet. Cook and stir until thickened and bubbly; cook and stir 1 minute more. Serve mushroom mixture and sauce over noodles. If desired, sprinkle with parsley.

PER SERVING 407 cal., 13 g total fat (5 g sat. fat), 72 mg chol., 443 mg sodium, 59 g carbo., 4 g fiber, 17 g pro.

Eating meatless even once a week is good for your health— and for your pocketbook.

Pasta with Swiss Chard 🎬

If you can find it, use rainbow chard in this dish. It's fabulously colorful, with dark green leaves and stems and veins of bright pink, orange, and yellow.

START TO FINISH 35 minutes   **MAKES** 4 servings

8	ounces dried whole grain bow tie or mostaccioli pasta
12	ounces fresh Swiss chard or spinach
1	tablespoon olive oil
4	cloves garlic, minced
⅔	cup light ricotta cheese
¼	cup fat-free milk
¼	cup snipped fresh basil or 1 teaspoon dried basil, crushed
¼	teaspoon salt
¼	teaspoon black pepper
⅛	teaspoon ground nutmeg
2	medium tomatoes, seeded and chopped
¼	cup shredded Parmesan cheese

❶ Cook pasta according to package directions, except omit any oil or salt. Drain well. Return pasta to hot saucepan. Cover and keep warm.

❷ Meanwhile, cut out and discard center ribs from Swiss chard or remove stems from spinach. Coarsely chop greens; set aside. In a large nonstick skillet heat oil on medium heat. Add garlic; cook for 15 seconds. Add Swiss chard or spinach. Cook on medium-low heat about 3 minutes or until greens are wilted and tender, stirring frequently. Stir in ricotta cheese, milk, basil, salt, pepper, and nutmeg. Cook and stir for 3 to 5 minutes more or until heated through.

❸ Add the ricotta mixture and tomatoes to cooked pasta; toss gently to combine. Sprinkle individual servings with Parmesan cheese.

PER SERVING 307 cal., 8 g total fat (2 g sat. fat), 14 mg chol., 435 mg sodium, 51 g carbo., 8 g fiber, 14 g pro.

Peach & Edamame Soba Salad

Flavorful soba noodles are a type of Japanese noodle made from buckwheat and wheat flour. They are available in both fresh and dried forms.

START TO FINISH 30 minutes   **MAKES** 4 servings

6	ounces dried soba (buckwheat noodles) or multigrain spaghetti
2	cups frozen shelled sweet soybeans (edamame), thawed, or one 15-ounce can black beans, rinsed and drained
3	medium peaches or nectarines, halved, pitted, and coarsely chopped
1	large red sweet pepper, seeded and cut into bite-size strips
¼	cup sliced green onions (2)
¼	cup rice vinegar
2	tablespoons reduced-sodium soy sauce
1	tablespoon toasted sesame oil
2	teaspoons grated fresh ginger
¼	cup sliced almonds, toasted (see note, page 31)

❶ In a large saucepan cook soba according to package directions. Drain and rinse with cold water; drain well. In a large bowl toss together soba, edamame, peaches, sweet pepper, and green onions.

❷ In a small screw-top jar combine vinegar, soy sauce, sesame oil, and ginger; cover and shake well. Pour over soba mixture. Toss to coat. Sprinkle each serving with almonds.

PER SERVING 368 cal., 11 g total fat (1 g sat. fat), 0 mg chol., 632 mg sodium, 55 g carbo., 9 g fiber, 18 g pro.

quick tip Sesame oil is sold two ways. The light-color oil is made from untoasted seeds. It has a light, nutty flavor and is used primarily in salad dressings and for sauteing. Darker Asian-style sesame oil is made from toasted seeds and has more intense flavor. It's used in salad dressings and to add flavor to stir-fries. A little goes a long way!

Red Lentil Rice

Red Lentil Rice

Red lentils are smaller than brown lentils and tend to break down faster than brown lentils when cooked. If you want them to retain their shape, don't overcook them. If you can't find them in your supermarket, look for them at an Indian grocery or health food store.

START TO FINISH 35 minutes **MAKES** 6 servings

1	tablespoon olive oil
½	cup chopped onion (1 medium)
2	cloves garlic, minced
1	teaspoon cumin seeds, crushed
½	teaspoon salt
⅛	teaspoon cayenne pepper
1⅓	cups basmati rice or long grain rice
2	14-ounce cans vegetable broth or chicken broth
½	cup water
1	cup frozen peas
½	cup dry red lentils, rinsed
¼	cup snipped fresh mint
1	teaspoon garam masala
1	recipe Yogurt Raita

❶ In a 4-quart Dutch oven heat olive oil on medium heat. Add onion, garlic, cumin seeds, salt, and cayenne pepper. Cook and stir for 2 minutes. Add rice; cook and stir 1 minute more. Remove from heat. Carefully add broth and water; bring to boiling. Reduce heat and simmer, covered, for 10 minutes.

❷ Stir in peas and lentils; return to boiling. Reduce heat; simmer, covered, for 8 to 10 minutes or just until lentils are tender. Remove from heat; stir in mint and garam masala. Let stand, covered, for 5 minutes before serving. Serve with Yogurt Raita.

YOGURT RAITA: In a medium bowl combine one 6-ounce carton plain yogurt; ¾ cup seeded, chopped cucumber; 1 medium tomato, seeded and chopped; 1 tablespoon snipped fresh mint; ⅛ teaspoon salt; and a dash of black pepper.

PER SERVING 274 cal., 3 g total fat (1 g sat. fat), 3 mg chol., 827 mg sodium, 50 g carbo., 4 g fiber, 10 g pro.

Quick Rice & Black Beans

This brown rice and black bean dish is loaded with healthful fiber and tastes hearty.

START TO FINISH 25 minutes **MAKES** 4 servings

1¼	cups uncooked instant brown rice
1	14-ounce can reduced-sodium chicken broth
1	15-ounce can black beans, rinsed and drained
1½	cups frozen whole kernel corn
1	cup salsa
2	tablespoons snipped fresh cilantro
1	cup shredded Monterey Jack or cheddar cheese (4 ounces)
	Thinly sliced jalapeños (optional) (see note, page 19)

❶ In a large saucepan combine rice, broth, beans, corn, and salsa. Bring to boiling; reduce heat. Simmer, covered, for 10 minutes.

❷ Remove from heat. Stir in cilantro and half of the cheese. Let stand, covered, for 5 minutes.

❸ Top with remaining cheese and, if desired, jalapeño slices.

PER SERVING 411 cal., 12 g total fat (6 g sat. fat), 25 mg chol., 1,188 mg sodium, 62 g carbo., 10 g fiber, 22 g pro.

Quick Rice & Black Beans

Spicy Vegetable Fried Rice ♥

Always use chilled cooked rice to make fried rice so the grains separate nicely when stir-fried with the other ingredients. If you use hot cooked rice, you'll wind up with a gloppy, sticky mess.

START TO FINISH 30 minutes **MAKES** 4 servings

- 4 eggs
- 2 tablespoons water
  Nonstick cooking spray
- 1 tablespoon olive oil
- 1 tablespoon finely chopped, peeled fresh ginger
- 2 cloves garlic, minced
- 2 cups chopped Chinese cabbage
- 1 cup coarsely shredded carrot
- 1 cup fresh pea pods, trimmed
- 2 cups cooked brown rice
- ⅓ cup sliced green onions (3)
- 2 tablespoons reduced-sodium soy sauce
- 1 to 2 teaspoons Sriracha chile sauce
- 2 tablespoons snipped fresh cilantro
  Lime slices or wedges

❶ In a small bowl whisk together eggs and water. Coat an unheated very large nonstick skillet with cooking spray. Preheat skillet on medium heat. Pour in egg mixture. Cook, without stirring, until mixture begins to set on the bottom and around edges. With a spatula or large spoon, lift and fold the partially cooked eggs so the uncooked portion flows underneath. Continue cooking for 2 to 3 minutes or until egg mixture is cooked through but is still glossy and moist, keeping eggs in large pieces. Carefully transfer eggs to a medium bowl; set aside.

❷ In the same skillet heat oil on medium-high heat. Add ginger and garlic; cook for 30 seconds. Add cabbage, carrot, and pea pods; cook and stir for 2 minutes. Stir in cooked eggs, brown rice, green onions, soy sauce, and chile sauce; cook and stir about 2 minutes or until heated through. Top with cilantro. Serve with lime slices.

PER SERVING 250 cal., 9 g total fat (2 g sat. fat), 212 mg chol., 367 mg sodium, 31 g carbo., 4 g fiber, 11 g pro.

Open-Face Veggie Burgers

Steak-sauced onions add oomph to these knife-and-fork vegetarian burgers.

START TO FINISH 20 minutes **MAKES** 4 sandwiches

- 2 tablespoons olive oil
- 1 large sweet onion, halved and thinly sliced (about 3 cups)
- 1 10-ounce package refrigerated or frozen meatless burger patties
- 2 tablespoons mayonnaise or salad dressing
- 1 teaspoon yellow mustard
- 4 ½-inch-thick slices ciabatta, toasted
- 1 cup fresh baby spinach
- 2 tablespoons steak sauce

❶ In a large skillet heat olive oil on medium-high heat. Add onion; cook for 8 to 10 minutes or until very tender, stirring frequently.

❷ Meanwhile, prepare patties according to package microwave directions.

❸ In a small bowl combine mayonnaise and mustard; spread on 1 side of each bread slice. Top with spinach and a patty. Stir steak sauce into cooked onion. Spoon onion mixture over patties.

PER SANDWICH 329 cal., 20 g total fat (3 g sat. fat), 3 mg chol., 688 mg sodium, 21 g carbo., 5 g fiber, 18 g pro.

---

quick tip Types of sweet onions include Vidalia, Maui, and Walla Walla—any of them work beautifully in this recipe. As sweet onions cook, their sugars condense and caramelize, and they get even sweeter!

Vegetarian Cream Cheese & Bagels

Caprese Salad Sandwiches

Caprese salad is the classic Italian salad made with fresh mozzarella, slices of ripe tomato, and fresh basil—the colors of the Italian flag. Sandwiches with the same ingredients are sold at Italian train stations to hungry commuters.

START TO FINISH 30 minutes   **MAKES** 4 sandwiches

- 1   10-ounce loaf baguette-style French bread
- ½   cup yellow or red pear tomatoes, cherry tomatoes, and/or grape tomatoes, quartered
- ¼   cup coarsely chopped cucumber
- ¼   of a red, yellow, or green sweet pepper, seeded and cut into thin strips
- 1   ounce fresh mozzarella cheese, cubed
- 2   tablespoons chopped green onion (1)
- 2   tablespoons snipped fresh basil
- 1   tablespoon red wine vinegar or cider vinegar
- 1   teaspoon olive oil
- ⅛   teaspoon black pepper
- ¾   cup mixed spring greens

❶ Cut baguette crosswise into 4 equal portions to create 4 mini baguettes. Cut a thin horizontal slice from the top of each portion. Using a knife, carefully remove bread from the centers of the mini baguettes, leaving ¼-inch-thick shells. Set aside. (Reserve the center baguette pieces for another use.)

❷ In a small bowl combine tomatoes, cucumber, sweet pepper, mozzarella cheese, green onion, basil, vinegar, oil, and black pepper. Line bottoms of the baguette pieces with mixed spring greens. Fill baguette pieces with the tomato mixture. Replace tops. If desired, wrap each sandwich in plastic wrap and chill for up to 2 hours before serving.

PER SANDWICH 244 cal., 4 g total fat (2 g sat. fat), 5 mg chol., 489 mg sodium, 42 g carbo., 2 g fiber, 10 g pro.

Vegetarian Cream Cheese & Bagels ♥ 🎬

Who needs lox when you have a flavorful combination of cucumber, onion, avocado, and roasted red peppers?

START TO FINISH 30 minutes   **MAKES** 4 servings

- ½   8-ounce tub light cream cheese (½ cup)
- 1   tablespoon snipped fresh dill or 1 teaspoon dried dill
- ¼   teaspoon salt
- ⅛   teaspoon black pepper
- 4   whole wheat bagel halves, toasted, or 4 slices whole wheat bread, toasted
- ½   medium cucumber, thinly sliced
- ½   medium red onion, thinly sliced
- ½   medium avocado, halved, seeded, peeled, and thinly sliced
- ¾   cup bottled roasted red sweet peppers, drained and cut into thin strips
  Fresh dill sprigs (optional)

❶ In a small bowl stir together cream cheese, snipped or dried dill, salt, and black pepper. Spread bagel halves with the cream cheese mixture. Top with cucumber slices, onion slices, avocado slices, and red pepper strips. If desired, top with fresh dill sprigs.

PER SERVING 222 cal., 8 g total fat (3 g sat. fat), 13 mg chol., 301 mg sodium, 31 g carbo., 5 g fiber, 9 g pro.

quick tip   Instead of making your own flavored cream cheese, you can use prepared herb-garlic or chive cream cheese on this bagel sandwich.

{ Many meatless dishes feature cheese—a nice excuse to indulge. }

Garden Sliders

These diminutive sandwiches can be served as a main dish (two per person) or as a fresh vegetarian option on an appetizer buffet.

START TO FINISH 30 minutes   **MAKES** 6 servings

- 1   15- to 16-ounce can Great Northern or cannellini beans, rinsed and drained
- 2   tablespoons olive oil
- 2   cloves garlic, minced
- ½   teaspoon Italian seasoning, crushed
       Salt
       Black pepper
- 1   medium yellow summer squash, cut into ¼-inch slices
- 24   ¼-inch slices baguette-style French bread
- 2   medium roma tomatoes, cut into ¼-inch slices
- 1   small cucumber, cut into ¼-inch slices
       Small celery top sprigs, small tomato wedges, and/or pickle slices (optional)

❶ For bean spread, in a blender or food processor combine drained beans, 1 tablespoon of the oil, garlic, and Italian seasoning. Cover; blend or process until smooth. Season with salt and pepper.

❷ To grill squash, toss squash slices with the remaining 1 tablespoon olive oil. Place in a grill basket. Place basket directly over medium coals for about 5 minutes or just until squash is tender, turning once halfway through grilling.

❸ Spread 1 side of each bread slice with bean spread. Top half of the bread with tomato, squash, and cucumber slices. Top with remaining bread slices, spread sides down. Secure sandwiches with wooden picks. If desired, top with celery sprigs, tomato wedges, and/or pickle slices.

PER SERVING 240 cal., 4 g total fat (0 g sat. fat), 0 mg chol., 578 mg sodium, 46 g carbo., 6 g fiber, 12 g pro.

Zucchini-Carrot Burgers ♥

You don't have to miss the pleasure of biting into a thick burger if you're going meatless. This veggie-packed patty contains crushed stone-ground wheat crackers to give it heartiness and heft.

START TO FINISH 25 minutes   **MAKES** 4 servings

- ¼   cup refrigerated or frozen egg product, thawed
- 1   tablespoon olive oil
- 1   teaspoon dried oregano, crushed
- 1   cup crushed stone-ground wheat crackers (about 22)
- 1   cup finely shredded zucchini
- 1   cup finely shredded carrot
- ¼   cup chopped green onions
- ½   cup plain low-fat yogurt
- 2   small cloves garlic, minced
- 1   teaspoon finely shredded lemon peel
- 2   large whole wheat pita bread rounds, halved crosswise
- 1   cup shredded leaf lettuce
- 1   small tomato, thinly sliced
- ½   small cucumber, thinly sliced

❶ In a medium bowl combine egg product, 1 teaspoon of the oil, and oregano. Add the crushed crackers, zucchini, carrot, and green onions; mix well. Form the vegetable mixture into four 3½-inch-diameter patties.

❷ In a large nonstick skillet heat the remaining oil on medium heat. Add patties to skillet. Cook for 5 to 7 minutes or until patties are golden brown, turning once. Meanwhile, for sauce, in a small bowl combine the yogurt, garlic, and lemon peel.

❸ To serve, fill the pita bread halves with vegetable patties. Add the lettuce, tomato slices, cucumber slices, and sauce.

PER SERVING 253 cal., 8 g total fat (2 g sat. fat), 2 mg chol., 364 mg sodium, 38 g carbo., 5 g fiber, 9 g pro.

{ Veggie burgers can be based on beans, grains, or—obviously— shredded veggies. }

Tomato-Basil Panini

Tomato-Basil Panini

Make this grilled tomato and feta cheese sandwich at the peak of tomato season for the sweetest, juiciest flavor.

PREP 20 minutes **COOK** 2 minutes per batch **MAKES** 4 servings

Olive oil nonstick cooking spray

8 slices whole wheat bread; four 6-inch whole wheat hoagie rolls, split; or 2 whole wheat pita bread rounds, halved crosswise and split horizontally

4 cups fresh baby spinach leaves

1 medium tomato, cut in 8 slices

⅛ teaspoon salt

⅛ teaspoon black pepper

¼ cup thinly sliced red onion

2 tablespoons shredded fresh basil

½ cup crumbled reduced-fat feta cheese (2 ounces)

❶ Lightly coat an unheated electric sandwich press, panini griddle, covered indoor grill, grill pan, or large nonstick skillet with nonstick cooking spray; set aside.

❷ Place 4 of the bread slices, roll bottoms, or pita pieces on a work surface; divide half of the spinach leaves among these bread slices, roll bottoms, or pita pieces. Top spinach with a tomato slice; sprinkle lightly with salt and pepper. Add red onion and basil. Top with feta and the remaining spinach. Top with the remaining bread slices, roll tops, or pita pieces. Press down firmly.

❸ Preheat sandwich press, panini griddle, or covered indoor grill according to manufacturer's directions. (Or heat grill pan or skillet on medium heat.) Add sandwiches, in batches if necessary. If using sandwich press, panini griddle, or covered indoor grill, close lid and grill for 2 to 3 minutes or until bread is toasted. (If using grill pan or skillet, place a heavy skillet on top of sandwiches. Cook on medium heat for 1 to 2 minutes or until bottoms are toasted. Carefully remove top skillet, which may be hot. Turn sandwiches and top again with the skillet. Cook for 1 to 2 minutes more or until bread is toasted.)

PER SERVING 174 cal., 5 g total fat (2 g sat. fat), 5 mg chol., 597 mg sodium, 27 g carbo., 5 g fiber, 10 g pro.

White Beans & Goat Cheese Wraps 🥘

These no-cook bean and cheese wraps are perfect picnic food. Roll them tightly in plastic wrap or foil and keep them cool until it's time to eat.

START TO FINISH 20 minutes **MAKES** 6 servings

1 19-ounce can cannellini beans (white kidney beans), rinsed and drained

1 4-ounce package soft goat cheese (chèvre)

1 tablespoon chopped fresh oregano

1 tablespoon chopped fresh parsley

6 8-inch whole wheat flour tortillas, warmed, if desired

6 cups fresh baby spinach leaves

1 12-ounce jar roasted red sweet peppers, drained and thinly sliced

❶ In a medium bowl mash beans lightly with a fork. Add goat cheese, oregano, and parsley; stir until well mixed.

❷ Divide bean mixture among tortillas, spreading evenly. Top bean mixture with spinach and roasted peppers. Roll up tortillas; cut in half to serve.

PER SERVING 248 cal., 8 g total fat (4 g sat. fat), 9 mg chol., 552 mg sodium, 31 g carbo., 16 g fiber, 18 g pro.

White Bean & Sweet Potato Chili

It's easy to have the ingredients for this colorful chili on hand. Everything comes in a can—with the exception of fresh pantry staples onion and garlic.

START TO FINISH 30 minutes **MAKES** 6 servings

1 tablespoon cooking oil

1 large onion, chopped (1 cup)

3 cloves garlic, minced

2 15- to 19-ounce cans cannellini beans (white kidney beans), rinsed and drained

2 14.5-ounce cans Mexican-style stewed tomatoes, cut up, undrained

1 14-ounce can vegetable or chicken broth

1 4-ounce can diced green chile peppers

1 15-ounce can cut sweet potatoes, drained and cut in bite-size pieces

❶ In a 4-quart Dutch oven heat oil on medium heat. Add onion and garlic; cook until tender. Stir in beans, undrained tomatoes, broth, and green chiles. Bring to boiling, reduce heat.

❷ Stir in sweet potatoes. Simmer, uncovered, for 15 minutes.

PER SERVING 162 cal., 3 g total fat (0 g sat. fat), 1 mg chol., 1,007 mg sodium, 33 g carbo., 7 g fiber, 10 g pro.

Kale-Goat Cheese Frittata

Kale is incredibly good for you. It's loaded with vitamins A, K, and C, and—like most dark green, leafy greens—it's also rich in iron and calcium.

START TO FINISH 25 minutes   **MAKES** 6 servings

- 2 cups coarsely torn fresh kale
- 1 medium onion, halved and thinly sliced
- 2 teaspoons olive oil
- 6 eggs
- 4 egg whites
- ¼ teaspoon salt
- ⅛ teaspoon black pepper
- ¼ cup drained oil-packed dried tomatoes, thinly sliced
- 1 ounce goat cheese, crumbled

❶ Preheat broiler. In a large ovenproof nonstick skillet cook and stir kale and onion in oil on medium heat for 10 minutes or until onion is tender.

❷ Meanwhile, in a medium bowl whisk together eggs, egg whites, salt, and pepper. Pour over kale mixture in skillet. Cook on medium-low heat. As egg mixture sets, run a spatula around the edge of the skillet, lifting egg mixture so the uncooked portion flows underneath. Continue cooking and lifting edge until egg mixture is almost set but still glossy and moist.

❸ Sprinkle egg mixture with dried tomatoes and goat cheese. Broil 4 to 5 inches from the heat for 1 to 2 minutes or until eggs are set. Cut into wedges to serve.

PER SERVING 145 cal., 9 g total fat (3 g sat. fat), 216 mg chol., 242 mg sodium, 6 g carbo., 1 g fiber, 11 g pro.

quick tip   If you drop a bit of shell into the bowl when cracking eggs, use one half of an empty shell to scoop it out. The shell acts to attract the piece of broken shell.

Mediterranean Beans & Greens Salad

Purchased balsamic vinaigrette gets a flavor boost from freshly grated orange peel in this crunchy salad. It's served with a yummy slice of toasted bread spread with soft goat cheese and sprinkled with fresh basil.

MAKES 6 servings

- 8 cups mixed salad greens, such as torn or small whole leaves romaine lettuce, baby spinach, and/or arugula
- ¼ cup small fresh basil leaves
- ½ medium cucumber, thinly sliced
- 1 15-ounce can cannellini beans (white kidney beans), rinsed and drained
- 1 15-ounce can black beans, rinsed and drained
- 3 medium roma tomatoes, cored and cut into wedges
- ½ cup reduced-calorie balsamic vinaigrette salad dressing
- 1 teaspoon finely shredded orange peel
- 6 slices baguette-style sourdough bread, toasted
- 2 ounces soft goat cheese (chèvre)
- 1 tablespoon snipped fresh basil

❶ Arrange salad greens and ¼ cup basil on a large serving platter. Arrange cucumber and beans over greens. Top with tomato wedges.

❷ In a small bowl combine salad dressing and orange peel. Drizzle over salad. Spread toasted bread with goat cheese and sprinkle with snipped basil. Serve with salad.

PER SERVING 238 cal., 6 g total fat (2 g sat. fat), 4 mg chol., 809 mg sodium, 40 g carbo., 9 g fiber, 15 g pro.

{ Frittatas are so versatile. You can toss in almost anything you find in the fridge that goes with eggs. }

Edamame Bread Salad

Layered Southwestern Salad with Tortilla Strips ♥

Add the tortilla strips right before serving so they stay crisp.

PREP 15 minutes **BAKE** 15 minutes **OVEN** 350°F
MAKES 6 servings

2	6-inch corn tortillas
	Nonstick cooking spray
½	cup light sour cream
¼	cup snipped fresh cilantro
2	tablespoons fat-free milk
1	teaspoon olive oil
1	large clove garlic, minced
½	teaspoon chili powder
½	teaspoon finely shredded lime peel
¼	teaspoon salt
¼	teaspoon black pepper
6	cups torn romaine lettuce
4	roma tomatoes, chopped (2 cups)
1	15-ounce can black beans, rinsed and drained
1	cup fresh corn kernels
½	cup shredded reduced-fat cheddar cheese (2 ounces)
1	avocado, halved, seeded, peeled, and chopped
	Snipped fresh cilantro (optional)

❶ Preheat oven to 350°F. Cut tortillas into ½-inch-wide strips; place in a 15×10×1-inch baking pan. Coat tortillas lightly with cooking spray. Bake for 15 to 18 minutes or until crisp, stirring once. Cool on wire rack.

❷ For dressing, in a small bowl stir together sour cream, the ¼ cup cilantro, milk, oil, garlic, chili power, lime peel, salt, and pepper.

❸ Place lettuce in a large glass serving bowl. Top with tomatoes, beans, corn, cheese, and avocado. Add dressing and sprinkle with tortilla strips. If desired, garnish with additional cilantro.

PER SERVING 227 cal., 11 g total fat (3 g sat. fat), 12 mg chol., 386 mg sodium, 29 g carbo., 9 g fiber, 11 g pro.

---

quick tip It isn't necessary to cook the corn. However, for a roasted flavor and softer texture, try baking it with the tortilla strips. Place the strips at one end of the baking pan and the corn at the other end.

Edamame Bread Salad

This two-bean take on bread salad features both green beans and nutty-tasting green soybeans.

PREP 30 minutes **COOK** 6 minutes **MAKES** 6 servings

¾	cup feta cheese
½	cup Greek yogurt or plain low-fat yogurt
2	tablespoons snipped fresh basil
1	small clove garlic, minced
2	12-ounce packages frozen soybeans (edamame)
1½	pounds fresh green beans, trimmed
1	recipe Balsamic Dressing
2	cups yellow cherry tomatoes, halved
12	slices crusty country bread, toasted
	Fresh basil leaves

❶ In a bowl combine feta cheese and yogurt. Using a fork, mash into paste. Add basil and garlic; mash to blend. Season with salt and pepper. Refrigerate, covered, up to 8 hours.

❷ In a saucepan bring 8 cups lightly salted water to boiling. Add soybeans and green beans; return to boiling. Reduce heat and cook, covered, 6 to 8 minutes or until tender. Drain; cool. Prepare Balsamic Dressing.

❸ Add tomatoes to bean mixture. Drizzle with half of the dressing; toss to coat. Refrigerate, covered, up to 8 hours. Toss before serving.

❹ Spread feta mixture on bread slices; place slices on serving plate; mound bean mixture on top. Drizzle remaining dressing and sprinkle with basil leaves.

BALSAMIC DRESSING: In a blender combine ¼ cup extra virgin olive oil, 2 tablespoons balsamic vinegar, 2 tablespoons red wine vinegar, and ¼ cup lightly packed fresh basil leaves; blend until smooth. Add 2 tablespoons whipping cream and blend to mix. Season to taste with salt and pepper.

PER SERVING 474 cal., 24 g total fat (7 g sat. fat), 27 mg chol., 679 mg sodium, 46 g carbo., 10 g fiber, 22 g pro.

In any season, soups and stews offer up comfort, cheer, and nourishment. This collection of savory soups and stews is proof that the pot doesn't have to simmer all day to produce delicious results.

157
162
169

soups & stews

Beef-Vegetable Stew 🍲

It may taste as if it's simmered all day, but it takes only 20 minutes, start to finish, to get this hearty stew on the table.

START TO FINISH 20 minutes   **MAKES** 5 servings

2	cups water
1	10.75-ounce can condensed golden mushroom soup
1	10.75-ounce can condensed tomato soup
½	cup dry red wine or beef broth
2	cups chopped cooked roast beef
1	16-ounce package frozen sugar snap stir-fry vegetables or one 16-ounce package frozen cut broccoli
½	teaspoon dried thyme, crushed

❶ In a 4-quart Dutch oven combine water, mushroom soup, tomato soup, and wine. Stir in beef, frozen vegetables, and thyme.

❷ Cook on medium heat until bubbly, stirring frequently. Continue cooking, uncovered, for 4 to 5 minutes or until vegetables are crisp-tender, stirring occasionally.

PER SERVING 304 cal., 10 g total fat (4 g sat. fat), 56 mg chol., 852 mg sodium, 24 g carbo., 4 g fiber, 23 g pro.

Beef-Vegetable Stew

Corn Bread-Crusted Chili

A quick trip under the broiler gives this corn bread-topped chili a crisp, buttery crust.

START TO FINISH 20 minutes   **MAKES** 4 servings

1	pound ground beef
1	15-ounce can chili beans in chili gravy, undrained
1	16-ounce jar salsa
1	cup frozen whole kernel corn
1¼	cups packaged corn bread stuffing mix
3	tablespoons butter, melted
1	to 2 tablespoons snipped fresh parsley (optional)

❶ Preheat broiler. In a large broilerproof skillet cook beef until brown, stirring occasionally. Drain off fat. Stir in undrained chili beans, salsa, and corn; heat through. Spread beef mixture into an even layer.

❷ Meanwhile, in a small bowl combine stuffing mix, butter, and, if desired, parsley. Sprinkle evenly over beef mixture. Broil 3 to 4 inches from the heat about 2 minutes or until top is golden brown.

PER SERVING 588 cal., 28 g total fat (12 g sat. fat), 100 mg chol., 1,249 mg sodium, 53 g carbo., 9 g fiber, 33 g pro.

quick tip This recipe requires a broilerproof skillet. Stainless steel works fine, but cast iron is even better. A cast-iron skillet is a terrific tool for all kinds of cooking. You can saute, roast, bake, and broil in it and, over time if it's cared for properly it develops a natural nonstick coating. You can buy cast-iron skillets preseasoned. Wash only in hot water—no soap—to preserve the nonstick coating.

Fresh Corn &
Chicken Chowder

Hearty Chicken & Barley Soup 🍲

There are so many delicious ways to take advantage of purchased roasted chicken from the supermarket deli. This homey soup is one of them.

START TO FINISH 20 minutes   **MAKES** 4 servings

2	14-ounce cans chicken broth with roasted garlic
1	cup water
½	cup quick-cooking barley
1	2 ¼- to 2 ½-pound purchased roasted chicken
1	cup packaged julienne or shredded fresh carrots
1	cup fresh pea pods, halved
	Black pepper

❶ In a large saucepan combine broth, water, and barley. Bring to boiling; reduce heat. Simmer, covered, for 10 minutes.

❷ Meanwhile, remove skin and bones from chicken and discard. Coarsely shred 2 cups of the chicken. Reserve remaining chicken for another use. Stir the 2 cups chicken, the carrots, and pea pods into the barley mixture in the saucepan. Cook on medium heat until heated through. Season to taste with pepper.

PER SERVING 280 cal., 12 g total fat (4 g sat. fat), 77 mg chol., 1,301 mg sodium, 25 g carbo., 5 g fiber, 21 g pro.

---

quick tip   In very simple recipes such as this soup, the quality of every ingredient counts. Simply using good quality salt and pepper can make a noticeable difference in the taste of your food. Fresh-ground pepper—like fresh-ground coffee—has the most flavor and aroma. The whole peppercorns available in bottles fitted with grinders makes it easy to incorporate fresh-ground pepper into your cooking.

Fresh Corn & Chicken Chowder

Make this soup at the height of sweet corn season—July and August—for the best and freshest flavor. If you don't want to add crushed red pepper, try a garnish of chopped fresh basil—or both.

START TO FINISH 30 minutes   **MAKES** 4 servings

12	ounces skinless, boneless chicken breast halves or chicken thighs
4	fresh ears of sweet corn
1	32-ounce container reduced-sodium chicken broth
½	cup green sweet pepper, chopped (1 small)
1	cup milk
1¼	cups instant mashed potato flakes
	Salt
	Black pepper
	Crushed red pepper (optional)

❶ In a 6-quart Dutch oven combine chicken, corn, and broth. Cover; bring to boiling on high heat. Reduce heat. Simmer 12 minutes or until chicken is no longer pink. Remove chicken and corn to cutting board.

❷ Add half the sweet pepper to broth in Dutch oven. Stir in milk and potato flakes. Shred chicken using 2 forks. Return chicken to Dutch oven. Using a kitchen towel to hold hot corn, cut kernels from cobs. Place corn in Dutch oven; heat through. Season to taste with salt and black pepper. Ladle soup into 4 bowls. Sprinkle each serving with remaining sweet pepper and crushed red pepper.

PER SERVING 269 cal., 3 g total fat (1 g sat. fat), 54 mg chol., 721 mg sodium, 33 g carbo., 3 g fiber, 29 g pro.

---

quick tip   Use a clean kitchen towel to help hold hot corn when cutting off kernels from cob.

{ Fresh corn chowder, with its sunny yellow color and sweet taste, is a bit of summer in a bowl. }

Simply Ramen Chicken Soup 🍲

This soup is so fast to fix (just 15 minutes!), you can make it for lunch. It hits the spot on a cold day when a cold sandwich just doesn't hit the spot.

START TO FINISH 15 minutes   **MAKES** 4 servings

2	14-ounce cans reduced-sodium chicken broth
2	3-ounce packages chicken-flavor ramen noodles
½	teaspoon dried oregano or basil, crushed
1	10-ounce package frozen cut broccoli
2	cups shredded cooked chicken or turkey
¼	cup sliced almonds, toasted (see note, page 31)

1 In a large saucepan bring chicken broth, the seasoning packet from the ramen noodles, and oregano to boiling. Break up noodles. Add noodles and broccoli to mixture in saucepan; return to boiling. Reduce heat; simmer, uncovered, for 3 minutes. Stir in chicken; heat through.

2 Ladle soup into 4 bowls. Sprinkle with almonds.

PER SERVING 316 cal., 14 g total fat (2 g sat. fat), 62 mg chol., 965 mg sodium, 19 g carbo., 3 g fiber, 29 g pro.

Easy Oriental Chicken Soup

This Asian-inspired soup is easily doubled to feed a large crowd. Stir in a little crushed red pepper or chili sauce, such as Sriracha, if you like your food fiery.

START TO FINISH 15 minutes   **MAKES** 3 servings

1	tablespoon cooking oil
8	ounces skinless, boneless chicken thighs or breast halves, cut into thin bite-size strips
3	cups water
½	16-ounce package frozen broccoli, carrots, and water chestnuts (2 cups)
1	3-ounce package chicken-flavor ramen noodles
2	tablespoons reduced-sodium soy sauce

1 In a large saucepan heat oil over medium-high heat. Add chicken; cook and stir for 2 to 3 minutes or until no longer pink. Remove from heat. Drain off fat.

2 Carefully add water, frozen vegetables, and seasoning packet from ramen noodles to chicken in saucepan. Bring to boiling. Break up noodles; add to saucepan. Reduce heat. Cover and simmer about 3 minutes or until noodles are tender. Stir in soy sauce. Skim off fat, if necessary.

PER SERVING 288 cal., 13 g total fat (1 g sat. fat), 65 mg chol., 1,046 mg sodium, 21 g carbo., 2 g fiber, 19 g pro.

Smoked Turkey Chuckwagon Soup 🍲

Although this recipe calls for white hominy, you could certainly use yellow or golden hominy as well. The color of the hominy simply reflects the color of the corn from which it was made.

START TO FINISH 20 minutes   **MAKES** 4 servings

2	14-ounce cans reduced-sodium chicken broth
1	15-ounce can white hominy, drained
1	11-ounce can condensed tomato rice soup
2	cups chopped smoked turkey (about 10 ounces)
½	cup chopped yellow sweet pepper (1 small)
⅓	cup bottled salsa
1	teaspoon ground cumin
1½	cups crushed tortilla chips (2 ½ ounces)
	Sour cream (optional)

1 In a large saucepan combine chicken broth, hominy, tomato rice soup, turkey, sweet pepper, salsa, and cumin. Bring to boiling; reduce heat. Simmer, uncovered, about 5 minutes or until sweet pepper is tender.

2 Ladle into 4 soup bowls. Top each serving with tortilla chips and, if desired, sour cream.

PER SERVING 318 cal., 10 g total fat (2 g sat. fat), 38 mg chol., 2,013 mg sodium, 39 g carbo., 5 g fiber, 20 g pro.

quick tip   Bottled salsa is a quick flavor booster—all in one jar. Keep a selection of salsas—chunky, smooth, red, green, hot, and mild—in your pantry for all kinds of purposes.

White Bean-Turkey Chili
with Corn Bread Dumplings

Corn Chowder 🍲

Serve this one-step, five-ingredient chowder with a crisp green salad and crusty sourdough rolls. A few grinds of freshly ground pepper will give it a bit of zing, if you like.

START TO FINISH 20 minutes   **MAKES** 4 servings

1	8-ounce tub cream cheese with chives and onions
1	14.75-ounce can cream-style corn
2	cups milk
8	ounces smoked turkey breast, chopped
1	cup frozen peas
	Black pepper

❶ In a medium saucepan heat cream cheese over medium heat to soften; blend in corn and milk. Add turkey and peas; heat through. Season to taste with black pepper.

PER SERVING 397 cal., 23 g total fat (15 g sat. fat), 88 mg chol., 1,159 mg sodium, 27 g carbo., 3 g fiber, 19 g pro.

Smoky Corn & Chicken Noodle Soup

The smoky flavor in this creamy corn soup comes from a sprinkle of smoked Gouda cheese.

START TO FINISH 30 minutes   **MAKES** 6 servings

4	14-ounce cans chicken broth
1	8-ounce package frozen egg noodles
1	cup frozen whole kernel corn, thawed
1	tablespoon olive oil
2	cups chopped cooked chicken
1	14.75-ounce can cream-style corn
	Black pepper
	Shredded smoked Gouda cheese or mozzarella cheese

❶ In a 4- 6-quart Dutch oven bring chicken broth to boiling. Add noodles and cook, uncovered, for 20 minutes.

❷ Meanwhile, pat whole kernel corn dry with paper towels. Line a 15×10×1-inch baking pan with foil. Spread corn in the baking pan and drizzle with olive oil; toss to coat. Broil 4 to 5 inches from the heat for 5 to 8 minutes or until light brown, stirring once; set aside.

❸ Add chicken, cream-style corn, and whole kernel corn to Dutch oven. Heat through. Season to taste with pepper. Ladle into 6 bowls. Top each serving with shredded smoked Gouda cheese.

PER SERVING 307 cal., 8 g total fat (2 g sat. fat), 88 mg chol., 1,304 mg sodium, 40 g carbo., 2 g fiber, 20 g pro.

White Bean-Turkey Chili with Corn Bread Dumplings

This healthful chili is crowned with dumplings made from a quick-to-fix corn bread mix.

START TO FINISH 22 minutes   **MAKES** 4 servings

1	pound cooked turkey
1	16-ounce jar chunky salsa
1	15-ounce can cannellini beans, rinsed and drained
1	teaspoon chili powder
1	8.5-ounce package corn bread mix
1	egg
¼	cup shredded cheddar cheese (1 ounce) (optional)
	Slivered green onions (optional)
	Chili powder (optional)

❶ Chop turkey. In a 4-quart Dutch oven combine turkey, salsa, beans, chili powder, and ⅔ cup water. Bring to boiling.

❷ Meanwhile, for dumplings, in a medium bowl mix together corn bread mix, egg, and ¼ cup water. Drop batter by large spoonfuls into boiling turkey chili.

❸ Cover; reduce heat and simmer for 10 to 15 minutes or until a wooden pick inserted into a dumpling comes out clean. Ladle into 4 bowls. If desired, top each serving with cheese, green onions, and chili powder.

PER SERVING 555 cal., 15 g total fat (4 g sat. fat), 140 mg chol., 1,618 mg sodium, 64 g carbo., 11 g fiber, 47 g pro.

---

quick tip   If you can't find cannellini beans, any white bean works fine in this chili, including Great Northern and navy beans.

Curried Turkey Soup

With turkey breast, fresh vegetables, and noodles, this simple soup is a light and healthful, yet satisfying one-dish meal.

START TO FINISH 20 minutes   **MAKES** 4 servings

12	ounces turkey breast tenderloin, cut into ½-inch cubes
2	teaspoons curry powder
1	tablespoon vegetable oil
5	cups water
1	3-ounce package chicken-flavor ramen noodles
1	cup broccoli florets
1	cup packaged shredded fresh carrots
	Salt
	Black pepper
	Fresh cilantro leaves (optional)

❶ In a large bowl combine turkey and curry powder; toss to coat. In a large saucepan heat oil on medium-high heat; add turkey. Cook and stir about 2 minutes or until brown. Carefully stir in the water, seasoning packet from the ramen noodles, broccoli, and carrots. Cook, covered, on high heat just until boiling.

❷ Break up noodles; add to soup. Cook, uncovered, for 3 minutes, stirring once or twice. Season to taste with salt and pepper. If desired, top with cilantro.

PER SERVING 241 cal., 8 g total fat (2 g sat. fat), 53 mg chol., 520 mg sodium, 19 g carbo., 2 g fiber, 24 g pro.

---

quick tip   Curry powder is a blend of up to 20 spices that most often includes cardamom, chiles, cumin, fennel, fenugreek, cinnamon, cloves, coriander, and turmeric (which gives it the distinctive yellow color). It comes in both mild and hot varieties—choose according to your taste. Buy it in small quantities, because it quickly loses its flavor.

Turkey Ravioli Soup

If you don't have dried Italian seasoning, use ¾ teaspoon dried oregano and ¾ teaspoon dried basil.

START TO FINISH 25 minutes   **MAKES** 6 servings

6	cups reduced-sodium chicken broth
¾	cup chopped red sweet pepper (1 medium)
½	cup chopped onion (1 medium)
1½	teaspoons dried Italian seasoning, crushed
1½	cups cooked turkey cut into bite-size pieces (about 8 ounces)
1	9-ounce package refrigerated light cheese ravioli
2	cups shredded fresh spinach
	Finely shredded Parmesan cheese (optional)

❶ In a 6-quart Dutch oven combine chicken broth, sweet pepper, onion, and Italian seasoning. Bring to boiling; reduce heat. Simmer, covered, for 5 minutes. Add turkey and ravioli. Return to boiling; reduce heat. Simmer, uncovered, about 6 minutes or just until ravioli is tender. Stir in spinach.

❷ Ladle soup into 4 bowls. If desired, sprinkle each serving with Parmesan cheese.

PER SERVING 246 cal., 7 g total fat (3 g sat. fat), 48 mg chol., 879 mg sodium, 24 g carbo., 2 g fiber, 22 g pro.

Turkey Tortilla Soup

Look for a fire-roasted salsa to add a smoky twist to this Mexican-style soup. Fire-roasted salsas come in both green and red varieties, as well as in mild, medium, and hot styles.

START TO FINISH 20 minutes   **MAKES** 4 servings

3	6-inch corn tortillas, cut in strips
2	tablespoons cooking oil
1	cup purchased red or green salsa
2	14-ounce cans reduced-sodium chicken broth
2	cups cubed cooked turkey (12 ounces)
1	large zucchini, coarsely chopped
	Sour cream (optional)
	Fresh cilantro leaves (optional)
	Lime wedges (optional)

❶ In a large skillet cook tortilla strips in hot oil until crisp; remove with slotted spoon and drain on paper towels.

❷ In a large saucepan combine salsa and chicken broth; bring to boiling over medium-high heat. Add turkey and zucchini; heat through.

❸ Ladle soup into 4 bowls; sprinkle with tortilla strips. If desired, serve with sour cream, cilantro, and lime wedges.

PER SERVING 262 cal., 11 g total fat (2 g sat. fat), 53 mg chol., 920 mg sodium, 16 g carbo., 3 g fiber, 26 g pro.

Sausage Posole

Sausage Posole 🍲

Posole is a thick, hearty Mexican soup that always contains hominy—white or yellow corn that has been hulled and degermed. It adds a chewy, toothsome texture to this dish.

START TO FINISH 20 minutes   **MAKES** 4 servings

- 1   tablespoon vegetable oil
- 1   pound cooked light smoked sausage, cut into 1-inch pieces
- 1   large sweet onion, cut into wedges
- 2   14.5-ounce cans Mexican-style stewed tomatoes, undrained
- 1   15-ounce can golden hominy, drained
- 1   large green sweet pepper, cut into bite-size pieces

1 In a 4-quart Dutch oven heat oil on medium heat. Add sausage and onion; cook for 5 minutes, stirring occasionally. Drain off fat. Add undrained tomatoes, hominy, and pepper. Bring to boiling; reduce heat. Simmer, covered, for 5 minutes.

PER SERVING 406 cal., 20 g total fat (8 g sat. fat), 70 mg chol., 1,943 mg sodium, 39 g carbo., 7 g fiber, 22 g pro.

Sweet Sausage & Asparagus Soup

The best way to trim the woody bottom off an asparagus stalk is to snap off the end where it naturally bends toward the top of the spear.

START TO FINISH 20 minutes   **MAKES** 4 servings

- 2   14-ounce cans chicken broth with roasted garlic
- 2   cups water
- 1   cup dried small shell macaroni
- 8   ounces frozen cooked mild Italian sausage links, thawed and thinly sliced (3 links)
- 8   ounces asparagus spears, trimmed and cut into 1-inch pieces
     Black pepper
- ¼   cup shredded fresh basil

1 In a 4-quart Dutch oven combine broth and water; bring to boiling. Add macaroni; boil gently, uncovered, for 5 minutes. Add sausage and asparagus; boil gently, uncovered, about 5 minutes more or until macaroni is tender. Season to taste with pepper. Stir in basil just before serving.

PER SERVING 177 cal., 6 g total fat (2 g sat. fat), 19 mg chol., 1,114 mg sodium, 19 g carbo., 1 g fiber, 13 g pro.

Pork & Potato Stew 🍲

Using refrigerated diced potatoes, purchased shredded carrots, and refrigerated cooked pork makes super-quick work of this hearty stew.

START TO FINISH 20 minutes   **MAKES** 4 servings

- 1   cup water
- 3   cups packaged refrigerated diced potatoes with onions
- 1   cup packaged shredded fresh carrots
- 1   teaspoon dried Italian seasoning, crushed
- 1   17-ounce package refrigerated cooked pork roast au jus
- 1   14.5-ounce can Italian-style stewed tomatoes, undrained
- 2   medium zucchini, halved lengthwise and cut into ½-inch slices
     Salt
     Black pepper

1 In a large skillet combine the water, potatoes, carrots, and Italian seasoning. Bring to boiling; reduce heat. Simmer, covered, for 5 minutes.

2 Cut pork roast into chunks; add pork and juices from package to skillet. Stir in undrained tomatoes and zucchini. Bring to boiling; reduce heat. Simmer, covered, for 2 to 3 minutes more or until zucchini is crisp-tender. Season to taste with salt and pepper.

PER SERVING 296 cal., 6 g total fat (2 g sat. fat), 72 mg chol., 1,123 mg sodium, 33 g carbo., 6 g fiber, 29 g pro.

---

quick tip   Crushing dried herbs before adding them to the pot releases their flavorful oils.

Chilly Ham & Cucumber Bisque

This creamy bisque is based on buttermilk, which gives it a refreshingly tart flavor. English cucumbers are long and slender and are usually wrapped in plastic rather than being waxed, so there's no need to peel them. They are often referred to as seedless because the tiny seeds are nearly undetectable.

START TO FINISH 17 minutes   **MAKES** 4 servings

- 8   ounces cubed cooked ham
- 1   English cucumber, cut up
- 3   cups buttermilk
      Salt and black pepper
- 1   cup packaged shredded fresh carrots
- 1   small red sweet pepper, chopped

❶ In a large nonstick skillet cook ham on medium-high heat for 4 to 5 minutes or until light brown. Set aside.

❷ In a blender combine cucumber and buttermilk; blend until smooth. Season to taste with salt and pepper. Ladle cucumber mixture into 4 soup bowls. Divide ham, carrots, and sweet pepper evenly among the bowls.

PER SERVING 196 cal., 7 g total fat (3 g sat. fat), 40 mg chol., 1,099 mg sodium, 18 g carbo., 2 g fiber, 17 g pro.

Chilly Ham & Cucumber Bisque

Spicy Red Beans & Sausage Soup 🍲

Substitute a can of fire-roasted tomatoes for the plain diced tomatoes to add a touch of warm, smoky flavor to this soup.

START TO FINISH 30 minutes   **MAKES** 6 servings

- 6   ounces uncooked chorizo sausage or uncooked turkey Italian sausage links, casings removed
- ¾   chopped green sweet pepper (1 medium)
- ½   cup thinly sliced green onions (4)
- 1   clove garlic, minced
- 2   15- to 16-ounce cans kidney beans, rinsed and drained
- 1   14.5-ounce can diced tomatoes, undrained
- 1   14-ounce can reduced-sodium chicken broth
- 1   cup water
- 3   cups coarsely chopped fresh kale or spinach
- ⅓   cup no-salt-added tomato paste
- ½   teaspoon dried thyme, crushed

❶ In a 4- to 6-quart Dutch oven cook chorizo sausage until brown, stirring to break up sausage as it cooks. Drain off fat. Add sweet pepper, green onions, and garlic to sausage. Cook for 3 to 5 minutes or just until sweet pepper is tender, stirring occasionally.

❷ Add kidney beans, undrained tomatoes, broth, water, kale (if using), tomato paste, and thyme to Dutch oven. Bring to boiling; reduce heat. Simmer, covered, for 10 minutes. Stir in spinach (if using); heat through.

PER SERVING 295 cal., 12 g total fat (4g sat. fat), 25 mg chol., 900 mg sodium, 35 g carbo., 11 g fiber, 20 g pro.

quick tip   If you are watching fat intake, you can reduce the amount of fat in your food by cooking and then rinsing ground meats such as sausage in a colander under hot running tap water. Just be sure it has completely drained before proceeding with your recipe.

Veggie Fish Chowder

Veggie Fish Chowder

Choose a firm-texture fish—such as cod, salmon, halibut, or black sea bass for this potato-based chowder.

PREP 20 minutes   **COOK** 10 minutes   **MAKES** 4 servings

- 1   pound cod, salmon, or other firm-textured fish, cut into 4 pieces
       Black pepper
- 1   32-ounce package reduced-sodium chicken broth
- 1   cup water
- 1   cup thinly sliced carrots (2 medium)
- 1   cup sugar snap peas, halved diagonally
- 1   4-ounce package (or half a 7.2-ounce package) butter-and-herb-flavor instant mashed potatoes
- ¼   cup finely shredded Parmesan cheese

❶ Season fish lightly with pepper; set aside. In a 4-quart saucepan bring broth and water to boiling. Add carrots; cover and cook for 5 minutes. Add fish and peas. Return to boiling. Reduce heat. Simmer, covered, for 3 minutes or until fish flakes easily when tested with a fork.

❷ Stir in mashed potatoes and simmer for 2 minutes.

❸ Break fish into bite-size pieces. Ladle chowder into 4 bowls. Sprinkle with Parmesan cheese.

PER SERVING 269 cal., 5 g total fat (2 g sat. fat), 52 mg chol., 1,269 mg sodium, 28 g carbo., 3 g fiber, 28 g pro.

---

quick tip   Flavored instant mashed potatoes act as a tasty thickener for this chowder. They're a handy item to have in your pantry because they have a long shelf life and they have other uses, too. Try them as a breading for fried foods or use them in place of bread crumbs, rice, or oatmeal in your favorite meat loaf recipe.

Tuna Tortellini Soup 🎬

For the richest flavor, use whole milk to make this soup. If you want to save on fat and calories a bit, use 2% instead. Using 1% or skim will make the consistency of the soup too thin.

START TO FINISH 20 minutes   **MAKES** 6 servings

- 3   cups milk
- 2   10.75-ounce cans condensed cream of potato soup
- 1   cup frozen loose-pack peas
- 1   teaspoon dried basil, crushed
- 1   9-ounce package refrigerated cheese tortellini
- 1   12-ounce can tuna, drained and flaked
- ⅓   cup dry white wine

❶ In a large saucepan combine milk, cream of potato soup, peas, and basil; bring just to boiling. Add tortellini. Simmer, uncovered, for 6 to 8 minutes or until tortellini is tender, stirring frequently to prevent sticking. Stir in tuna and wine. Heat through.

PER SERVING 351 cal., 9 g total fat (4 g sat. fat), 59 mg chol., 1,267 mg sodium, 38 g carbo., 2 g fiber, 27 g pro.

---

quick tip   If you're watching fat and calories, water-pack tuna is the best choice. However, tuna packed in oil has the best flavor. Either works well in this recipe.

{ With a well-stocked pantry, you can whip up a pot of warm, comforting soup in no time. }

Crab & Corn Chowder 🍲

Cream-style corn is the base for this silky fast-fix chowder. Semisoft cheese flavored with garlic and herbs provides the flavor.

START TO FINISH 15 minutes **MAKES** 4 servings

- 1 **14.75-ounce can cream-style corn**
- 1 **4- to 6-ounce container semisoft cheese with garlic and herbs, cut up**
- 1½ **cups milk**
- 1 **8-ounce package flake-style imitation crabmeat**
- 1 **cup grape tomatoes, halved**
- 2 **tablespoons snipped fresh parsley**

❶ In a large saucepan combine corn and cheese; heat and stir until cheese melts. Gradually stir in milk; cook and stir until heated through.

❷ Stir in crabmeat and tomatoes. Sprinkle with parsley.

PER SERVING 289 cal., 12 g total fat (8 g sat. fat), 45 mg chol., 816 mg sodium, 35 g carbo., 2 g fiber, 12 g pro.

Pepper & Basil Tortellini Soup

Looking for a meatless meal? This Italian-style three-cheese tortellini soup fills the bill.

START TO FINISH 20 minutes **MAKES** 4 servings

- 1 **14.5-ounce can Italian-style stewed tomatoes, undrained**
- 1 **14-ounce can reduced-sodium chicken broth**
- 1¼ **cups water**
- 1 **9-ounce package refrigerated three-cheese tortellini**
- 2 **small red and/or yellow sweet peppers, chopped**
- ⅓ **cup snipped fresh basil**
  Grated Parmesan cheese (optional)

❶ In a large saucepan combine undrained tomatoes, chicken broth, and water; bring to boiling. Add tortellini and sweet pepper. Return to boiling; reduce heat. Simmer, covered, about 7 minutes or until tortellini is tender. Stir in basil. If desired, serve with Parmesan cheese.

PER SERVING 245 cal., 5 g total fat (2 g sat. fat), 30 mg chol., 816 mg sodium, 40 g carbo., 3 g fiber, 13 g pro.

Chilled Cucumber-Chickpea Soup

When it's too hot for hot food, serve this cooling soup packed with such Middle Eastern flavors as sesame, coriander, and paprika.

START TO FINISH 25 minutes **MAKES** 4 servings

- 1 **recipe Coriander-Paprika Spice Rub**
- ½ **pound peeled and deveined cooked cocktail shrimp, chopped**
- 2 **medium cucumbers**
- 1 **15-ounce can chickpeas (garbanzo beans), rinsed and drained**
- ¼ **cup tahini (sesame seed paste)**
- ¼ **cup packed fresh mint leaves**
- 2 **tablespoons lemon juice**
- 1 **tablespoon olive oil**
- 1 **tablespoon honey**
- 2 **cloves garlic, smashed**
- 1½ **teaspoons ground coriander**
- ¼ **teaspoon cayenne pepper**
- ¼ **teaspoon salt**
- ¼ **teaspoon black pepper**
- 3 **cups ice cubes**
- ⅓ **cup cherry tomatoes, quartered**
- 2 **green onions, cut in 1-inch slivers**

❶ Prepare Coriander-Paprika Spice Rub. In a medium bowl toss shrimp with spice rub; set aside. Thinly slice enough cucumber to measure ⅓ cup; set aside. Peel, seed, and cut up remaining cucumbers.

❷ In a blender combine cut-up cucumbers, chickpeas, tahini, mint, lemon juice, olive oil, honey, garlic, coriander, cayenne, salt, and black pepper. Cover; blend until smooth, scraping sides as needed.

❸ Just before serving, with motor running, add ice cubes, a few at a time, through lid opening until smooth and thickened (blender will be full). Pour into 4 bowls. Top each serving with shrimp, sliced cucumber, tomatoes, and green onions.

CORIANDER-PAPRIKA SPICE RUB: In a small bowl combine 1 teaspoon ground coriander, ½ teaspoon paprika, ¼ teaspoon salt, and ¼ teaspoon black pepper.

PER SERVING 357 cal., 14 g total fat (2 g sat. fat), 111 mg chol., 752 mg sodium, 41 g carbo., 7 g fiber, 22 g pro.

Curried Vegetable Soup

Curried Vegetable Soup

Cut the fat and calories a bit in this soup by using light coconut milk, if you like. The body of the soup will be a bit thinner, but it will taste just as good.

START TO FINISH 20 minutes   **MAKES** 4 servings

3	cups cauliflower florets
1	14-ounce can unsweetened coconut milk
1	14-ounce can vegetable or chicken broth
1	tablespoon curry powder
¼	cup chopped fresh cilantro
2	cups frozen baby peas-vegetable blend
¼	teaspoon salt
2	pita bread rounds, cut into wedges (optional)
1	tablespoon olive oil
¼	teaspoon curry powder
	Fresh cilantro leaves (optional)
	Crushed red pepper (optional)

❶ Heat broiler. In a 6-quart Dutch oven combine cauliflower, coconut milk, broth, curry powder, and the ¼ cup cilantro. Bring to boiling on high heat. Reduce heat to medium-low. Simmer, covered, 10 minutes or until cauliflower is tender. Stir in frozen vegetable blend. Cook, uncovered, until heated through. Stir in salt.

❷ Meanwhile, if desired, place pita wedges on baking sheet. Brush both sides with oil. Sprinkle with ¼ teaspoon curry powder. Broil 3 to 4 inches from heat for 4 minutes, turning once, until golden. Serve soup with pita wedges. If desired, sprinkle each serving with cilantro and red pepper.

PER SERVING 138 cal., 6 g total fat (4 g sat. fat), 0 mg chol., 620 mg sodium, 19 g carbo., 4 g fiber, 3 g pro.

quick tip   If you make this curried soup with vegetable broth, it is not only a vegetarian but a vegan soup, meaning no animal products at all.

Minestrone 🎬

All this veggie-packed, low-sodium soup needs to make a full meal is some chewy European-style bread. Serve it with a light Italian wine, such as a Valipocella or Bardolino.

START TO FINISH 30 minutes   **MAKES** 6 servings

1	medium onion, chopped
1	tablespoon olive oil
2	14-ounce cans reduced-sodium chicken broth
1½	cups water
1	15-ounce can cannellini beans, rinsed and drained
1	medium zucchini, coarsely chopped
1	cup sliced carrots
3	cloves garlic, minced
¾	cup dried multigrain elbow macaroni
1	tablespoon snipped fresh oregano or 1 teaspoon dried oregano, crushed
6	cups coarsely torn, trimmed Swiss chard or 8 cups packaged fresh baby spinach leaves
1	14.5-ounce can no-salt-added diced tomatoes
	Fresh oregano

❶ In a 5- to 6-quart Dutch oven cook onion in hot oil on medium heat until tender, stirring occasionally. Add broth, water, beans, zucchini, carrots, and garlic. Bring to boiling. Add pasta and dried oregano, if using. Return to boiling; reduce heat. Simmer, covered, 5 minutes. Stir in Swiss chard. (If using spinach, stir in with tomatoes.) Simmer, uncovered, 5 to 7 minutes more or until pasta is tender, stirring occasionally.

❷ Stir in tomatoes and fresh (if using) oregano, and, if using, spinach. Remove from heat. Season with salt and pepper. Sprinkle with additional fresh oregano.

PER SERVING 162 cal., 3 g total fat (0 g sat. fat), 0 mg chol., 554 mg sodium, 30 g carbo., 7 g fiber, 10 g pro.

Soup is much-loved the world over, whether it's curry from India or minestrone from Italy.

Broccoli-Potato Soup with Greens

The greens in this soup stay flavorful and have bright color because they're not cooked, just slightly wilted when added to the hot soup after it's ladled into the bowls.

START TO FINISH 20 minutes **MAKES** 4 servings

- 2 medium red potatoes, chopped
- 1 14-ounce can reduced-sodium chicken broth
- 3 cups small broccoli florets
- 2 cups milk
- 3 tablespoons all-purpose flour
- 2 cups smoked Gouda cheese, shredded (8 ounces)
- 2 cups torn winter greens (such as curly endive, chicory, romaine, escarole, or spinach)
   Smoked Gouda cheese, shredded (optional)

❶ In a large saucepan combine potatoes and broth. Bring to boiling; reduce heat. Simmer, covered, 8 minutes. Mash slightly. Add broccoli and milk; bring just to simmering.

❷ In a medium bowl toss flour with cheese; gradually add to soup, stirring cheese until melted. Season to taste with black pepper. Ladle soup into 4 bowls. Divide the greens evenly among the bowls. If desired, sprinkle with additional smoked Gouda cheese.

PER SERVING 365 cal., 18 g total fat (11 g sat. fat), 74 mg chol., 782 mg sodium, 28 g carbo., 4 g fiber, 23 g pro.

Pumpkin Soup with Spiced Croutons ♥

Both the rich, creamy soup and the crisp croutons on top are flavored with pumpkin pie spice.

START TO FINISH 30 minutes **MAKES** 8 side-dish servings

- 2 medium carrots, sliced
- 2 tablespoons butter
- 1 medium onion, finely chopped
- 1 stalk celery, finely chopped
- 1 clove garlic, minced
- 2 15-ounce cans pumpkin
- 1 32-ounce package reduced-sodium chicken broth
- ½ cup half-and-half or light cream
- ½ cup water
- 3 tablespoons maple syrup
- 1 teaspoon pumpkin pie spice
- 1 recipe Spiced Croutons
   Celery leaves (optional)

❶ In a large saucepan cook carrots in hot butter on medium heat for 2 minutes; add onion, celery, and garlic. Cook 8 to 10 minutes or until vegetables are tender.

❷ Stir in pumpkin, broth, half-and-half, water, maple syrup, and pumpkin pie spice. Heat through. Season with salt and black pepper.

❸ To serve, top soup with Spiced Croutons and celery leaves.

SPICED CROUTONS: In a bowl toss 3 cups of 1-inch bread cubes with 2 teaspoons pumpkin pie spice. In a large skillet cook bread cubes in 2 tablespoons hot butter for 8 minutes or until toasted, turning occasionally.

PER SERVING 200 cal., 9 g total fat (5 g sat. fat), 21 mg chol., 537 mg sodium, 28 g carbo., 4 g fiber, 5 g pro.

quick tip If you don't have 1 teaspoon of pumpkin pie spice, stir together ½ teaspoon ground cinnamon, ¼ teaspoon ground ginger, ¼ teaspoon ground allspice, and ⅛ teaspoon ground nutmeg.

Pumpkin Soup with Spiced Croutons

Smoke, fire, and hot coals bring out so much flavor in foods, few extra ingredients are needed. No wonder so many home cooks claim grilling as their favorite way to cook.

189

190

209

from the grill

BLT Steak

How do you improve upon a juicy grilled steak? Top it with fresh tomato, greens, dressing—and bacon.

START TO FINISH 30 minutes   **MAKES** 4 servings

- 2 boneless beef top loin steaks, cut 1¼ inches thick
- 2 slices bacon
- ½ cup bottled balsamic vinaigrette salad dressing
- 8 slices red and/or yellow tomato
- 2 cups mixed baby salad greens

1 Trim fat from steaks. For a charcoal grill, grill steaks on the rack of an uncovered grill directly over medium coals for 13 to 17 minutes for medium rare (145°F) or 17 to 21 minutes for medium (160°F), turning once halfway through grilling. (For a gas grill, preheat grill. Reduce heat to medium. Place steaks on grill rack over heat. Cover and grill as above.)

2 Meanwhile, in a large skillet cook bacon on medium heat until crisp. Remove bacon and drain on paper towels. Crumble bacon and set aside. Drain fat, reserving 1 tablespoon drippings in skillet. Add the salad dressing to the skillet. Cook and stir over high heat about 1 minute, scraping up brown bits. Remove from heat.

3 To serve, halve the steaks. Place a piece of steak on each of 4 dinner plates. Top each steak with 2 tomato slices, some of the cooked bacon, and some of the mixed greens. Pour some of the sauce over each steak.

PER SERVING 556 cal., 42 g total fat (14 g sat. fat), 122 mg chol., 636 mg sodium, 5 g carbo., 1 g fiber, 38 g pro.

Ocho Rios Coffee-Pepper Beef

Ocho Rios Coffee-Pepper Beef

Ground coffee is the surprise element in the rub for this steak named for a port town on the island of Jamaica.

PREP 15 minutes   **GRILL** 15 minutes   **MAKES** 4 servings

- 4 6-ounce center-cut beef tenderloin steaks, cut 1½ to 2 inches thick
- 2 tablespoons olive oil
- 1 clove garlic, minced
- 3 tablespoons finely ground coffee beans
- 2 teaspoons coarsely ground black pepper
- ½ teaspoon kosher salt
- ½ teaspoon ground cumin
  Roasted Sweet Potato Fries (optional)

1 Trim fat from steaks. In a small bowl combine oil and garlic. Brush steaks with oil mixture.

2 In a plastic bag combine ground coffee, pepper, salt, and cumin. Add steaks, one at a time, shaking to coat steaks with coffee mixture.

3 For a charcoal grill, grill steaks on the rack of an uncovered grill directly over medium coals for 15 to 19 minutes for medium rare (145°F) or 18 to 23 minutes for medium (160°F), turning once halfway through grilling. (For a gas grill, preheat grill. Reduce heat to medium. Place steaks on grill rack over heat. Cover and grill as above.) Slice steaks.

4 If desired, serve meat with Roasted Sweet Potato Fries.

PER SERVING 333 cal., 18 g total fat (5 g sat. fat), 114 mg chol., 339 mg sodium, 3 g carbo., 0 g fiber, 38 g pro.

ROASTED SWEET POTATO FRIES: Preheat oven to 425°F. Lightly grease a 15×10×1-inch baking pan; set aside. Cut each of 2 medium sweet potatoes lengthwise into 8 wedges; cut large wedges in half crosswise. In a medium bowl combine 1 to 2 tablespoons olive oil, 1 to 2 teaspoons coarse salt, and ½ teaspoon coarsely ground black pepper. Add potato wedges; toss gently to coat. Transfer potato wedges to the prepared baking pan. Bake for 30 to 35 minutes or until potatoes are tender and brown, turning once.

Jalapeño Beef Kabobs

Beef Tenderloin with Lemon-Dijon Cream

Using mostly cottage cheese and just a little bit of whipping cream keeps the creamy sauce for the beef medallions light and low fat.

PREP 15 minutes   **GRILL** 4 minutes   **MAKES** 4 to 6 servings

- 1   cup low-fat cottage cheese
- ¼   cup whipping cream
- 1   tablespoon lemon juice
- 1   tablespoon Dijon mustard
- 1   teaspoon snipped fresh thyme or oregano
- 1   to 1½ pounds beef tenderloin
      Salt
      Black pepper
      Snipped fresh watercress or chives (optional)

1. For lemon-Dijon cream, in a food processor or blender combine cottage cheese, whipping cream, lemon juice, mustard, and thyme. Cover and process or blend until smooth. Cover and set aside until ready to serve (up to 30 minutes).

2. Trim fat and silverskin from meat. Using a very sharp knife, cut tenderloin* across the grain into ¼- to ½-inch slices. Sprinkle meat slices with salt and pepper.

3. For a charcoal grill, grill beef slices on the rack of an uncovered grill directly over hot coals for 4 minutes for medium rare (145°F), turning once halfway through grilling. (For a gas grill, preheat grill. Place beef on grill rack over high heat. Cover and grill as above.)

4. Serve meat with lemon-Dijon cream. If desired, garnish with watercress.

PER SERVING 282 cal., 15 g total fat (7 g sat. fat), 92 mg chol., 523 mg sodium, 3 g carbo., 0 g fiber, 32 g pro.

*****NOTE:** Partially freeze beef for easier slicing.

Jalapeño Beef Kabobs

The lemony-herb flavor of grilled tomatillos adds an interesting element to these spicy kabobs.

PREP 15 minutes   **GRILL** 12 minutes   **MAKES** 4 servings

- 1   10-ounce jar jalapeño pepper jelly
- 2   tablespoons lime juice
- 1   clove garlic, minced
- 4   small purple or white boiling onions or 8 very small red onions
- 4   baby pattypan squash, halved crosswise, if large
- 1   pound boneless beef sirloin steak, cut 1 inch thick
- 4   fresh tomatillos, husked and cut into quarters
- ½   medium red and/or green sweet pepper, cut into 1-inch squares
      Hot cooked polenta (optional)

1. For glaze, in a small saucepan combine the jalapeño jelly, lime juice, and garlic. Cook and stir over medium heat until jelly is melted. Remove from heat.

2. In a small covered saucepan cook onions in a small amount of boiling water for 3 minutes. Add squash; cook for 1 minute more; drain. Trim fat from steak. Cut steak into 1-inch cubes. On eight 6- to 8-inch metal skewers alternately thread onions, squash, steak, tomatillos, and sweet pepper, leaving ¼-inch space between pieces.

3. For a charcoal grill, grill kabobs on the rack of an uncovered grill directly over medium coals for 12 to 14 minutes for medium (160°F), turning once and brushing occasionally with glaze during the last 5 minutes of grilling. (For a gas grill, preheat grill. Reduce heat to medium. Place kabobs on grill rack over heat. Cover and grill as above.)

4. Serve kabobs with hot polenta, if desired, and any remaining glaze.

PER SERVING 444 cal., 11 g total fat (4 g sat. fat), 76 mg chol., 71 mg sodium, 61 g carbo., 2 g fiber, 27 g pro.

{ The rich taste of beef takes beautifully to the smoke and fire of the grill. }

Beef Steaks with Tomato-Garlic Butter

The flavored butter can be made a day ahead, covered, and chilled. Just take it out of the refrigerator to allow it to soften for an hour or so before using.

PREP 12 minutes   **GRILL** 8 minutes   **MAKES** 4 servings

- ½ cup butter, softened
- 1 tablespoon snipped oil-packed dried tomatoes
- 1 tablespoon chopped kalamata olives
- 1 tablespoon finely chopped green onion
- 1 clove garlic, minced
- 4 boneless beef top loin steaks, cut 1 inch thick (1½ pounds)
  Salt (optional)
  Black pepper (optional)

1 For tomato-garlic butter, in a small bowl combine butter, tomatoes, kalamata olives, green onion, and garlic. Set aside.

2 Trim fat from steaks. For a charcoal grill, grill steaks on the rack of an uncovered grill directly over medium coals for 10 to 12 minutes for medium rare (145°F) or 12 to 15 minutes for medium (160°F), turning once halfway through grilling. (For a gas grill, preheat grill. Reduce heat to medium. Place steaks on grill rack over heat. Cover; grill as above). If desired, sprinkle steaks with salt and pepper.

3 To serve, spread 1 tablespoon of the butter mixture over each steak. Cover and chill remaining butter mixture.

PER SERVING 383 cal., 22 g total fat (11 g sat. fat), 161 mg chol., 227 mg sodium, 0 g carbo., 0 g fiber, 45 g pro.

quick tip Use any leftover flavored butter as a tasty spread for bread, stir into hot cooked polenta or rice, or toss hot cooked vegetables or noodles with it.

Ribeyes with Chipotle Butter

These juicy ribeyes get a double dose of flavor. Before they're grilled, they're rubbed with cumin, paprika, salt, pepper, and adobo sauce. After they come off the grill, they're topped with a dab of smoky chipotle butter.

PREP 15 minutes   **GRILL** 14 minutes   **MAKES** 4 servings

- ¼ cup butter, softened
- 1 tablespoon finely chopped shallot
- 2 teaspoons snipped fresh basil or cilantro
- 1½ teaspoons lime juice
- 1 teaspoon finely chopped chipotle pepper in adobo sauce (see note, page 19)
- 2 teaspoons ground cumin
- 1 teaspoon paprika
- ½ teaspoon salt
- ½ teaspoon ground white pepper
- 1 tablespoon olive oil
- ¼ teaspoon adobo sauce (from canned chipotle pepper in adobo sauce)
- 4 8- to 10-ounce beef ribeye steaks, cut 1 inch thick
  Lime wedges
  Vinaigrette coleslaw (optional)

1 For chipotle butter, in a small bowl stir together butter, shallot, snipped basil or cilantro, lime juice, and chipotle pepper until combined; set aside.

2 In another small bowl stir together cumin, paprika, salt, and pepper. Stir in oil and adobo sauce until a paste forms. Spread mixture over both sides of steaks.

3 For a charcoal grill, grill steaks on the rack of an uncovered grill directly over medium coals until desired doneness, turning once halfway through grilling. Allow 14 to 18 minutes for medium (160°F). (For a gas grill, preheat grill. Reduce heat to medium. Place steaks on grill rack over heat. Grill as above). Serve steaks with chipotle butter, lime wedges, and, if desired, coleslaw.

PER SERVING 416 cal., 27 g total fat (12 g sat. fat), 118 mg chol., 519 mg sodium, 2 g carbo., 1 g fiber, 40 g pro.

Barbecue-Sauced
Burgers

Barbecue-Sauced Burgers

Horseradish mustard mixed into the raw ground beef spikes the burgers with flavor.

PREP 6 minutes **GRILL** 14 minutes **MAKES** 4 sandwiches

- 1 pound lean ground beef
- 1 to 2 tablespoons horseradish mustard
- ¼ teaspoon salt
- ¼ teaspoon black pepper
- 3 to 4 ounces white cheddar cheese or cheddar cheese, sliced
- 4 hamburger buns, split and toasted
- ¼ cup barbecue sauce
   Arugula, tomato slices, and/or red onion slices

❶ In a large mixing bowl combine beef, horseradish mustard, salt, and pepper; mix well. Shape into four ¾-inch thick patties.

❷ For a charcoal grill, grill patties on the rack of an uncovered grill directly over medium coals for 14 to 18 minutes or until done (160°F), turning once halfway through grilling. Top burgers with cheese during the last 1 minute of grilling. (For a gas grill, preheat grill. Reduce heat to medium. Place patties on grill rack over heat. Cover and grill as above.) Serve on buns with barbecue sauce, arugula, tomato, and/or onions.

PER SANDWICH 476 cal., 27 g total fat (12 g sat. fat), 99 mg chol., 722 mg sodium, 26 g carbo., 2 g fiber, 31 g pro.

Asian Burgers

Asian Burgers ♥

These delicious burgers are a blend of super-lean ground beef and ground pork flavored with hoisin sauce and five-spice powder.

PREP 25 minutes **GRILL** 10 minutes **MAKES** 6 sandwiches

- 3 tablespoons bottled hoisin sauce
- 1 tablespoon finely chopped onion
- 1 teaspoon five-spice powder
- ¼ teaspoon crushed red pepper
- 1 pound 95% lean ground beef
- 8 ounces ground pork
- 6 ½- to ¾-inch-thick slices peeled and cored fresh or canned pineapple
- 6 ½-inch-thick slices red onion
- ½ cup snow pea pods, strings and tips removed
- 6 whole wheat hamburger buns, split and toasted

❶ In a very large bowl combine hoisin sauce, finely chopped onion, five-spice powder, and crushed red pepper. Add beef and pork; mix well. Shape into six ½-inch-thick patties.

❷ For a charcoal grill, place patties, pineapple, and red onion on the rack of an uncovered grill directly over medium coals. Grill pineapple and onion for 4 to 6 minutes or until lightly brown, turning once. Grill patties for 10 to 13 minutes or until done (160°F), turning once halfway through grilling. (For a gas grill, preheat grill. Reduce heat to medium. Place patties, pineapple, and red onion on grill rack over heat. Cover and grill as above.)

❸ Halve pea pods lengthwise. Place pineapple on bun bottoms. Top with patties, red onion, pea pods, and bun tops.

PER SANDWICH 382 cal., 13 g total fat (5 g sat. fat), 74 mg chol., 412 mg sodium, 38 g carbo., 4 g fiber, 28 g pro.

quick tip Although you may see some grillers pressing down on burgers with a spatula as they cook (theoretically, to flatten them), don't do it. Every time the burgers are pressed, they lose precious juices.

Double-Beef Burgers

The double beef in these savory beef burgers is chopped corned beef stirred into the mix, along with chopped cabbage, caraway seeds, and soft rye bread crumbs.

PREP 15 minutes   **GRILL** 14 minutes   **MAKES** 4 sandwiches

- 1   egg, lightly beaten
- 1   2½-ounce package very thinly sliced corned beef, chopped
- ⅓   cup finely chopped cabbage
- ¼   cup soft rye bread crumbs (about ½ slice)
- ½   teaspoon caraway seeds
- ¼   teaspoon salt
- 1   pound lean ground beef
- 1   large red onion, sliced
- 4   kaiser rolls, split
- 3   tablespoons horseradish mustard

1 In a medium bowl combine egg, corned beef, cabbage, bread crumbs, caraway seeds, and salt. Add ground beef; mix well. Shape mixture into four ¾-inch-thick patties.

2 For a charcoal grill, place patties on the rack of an uncovered grill directly over medium coals. Grill for 14 to 18 minutes or until done (160°F), turning once halfway through grilling. Add onion slices to the grill during the last 10 to 12 minutes or until tender, turning once halfway through grilling. Toast kaiser rolls on the grill. (For a gas grill, preheat grill. Reduce heat to medium. Place patties, then onion slices and kaiser rolls on grill rack over heat. Cover and grill as above.)

3 Spread kaiser rolls with horseradish mustard. Serve burgers in rolls with onion slices.

PER SANDWICH 479 cal., 22 g total fat (7 g sat. fat), 138 mg chol., 861 mg sodium, 36 g carbo., 2 g fiber, 33 g pro.

quick tip   To make your own soft bread crumbs, simply whirl bread in a food processor. For finer crumbs, remove the crust first.

Grilled Chili Burgers

Chimichurri sauce—a savory blend of herbs, vinegar, olive oil, garlic, and hot chiles—is as common in Argentina as ketchup or salsa is in this country. It's a must with Argentina's famous grilled beef.

PREP 20 minutes   **GRILL** 10 minutes   **MAKES** 6 sandwiches

- 1   recipe Chimichurri
- 1   pound 95% lean ground beef
- 8   ounces ground pork
- 1   tablespoon chili powder
- ½   teaspoon onion powder
- ¼   teaspoon ground cumin
- ⅛   teaspoon salt
- 3   whole wheat pita bread rounds, quartered and toasted
- ¾   cup bottled roasted red sweet peppers, drained and cut into strips

1 Prepare Chimichurri; set aside. In a large bowl combine beef, pork, chili powder, onion powder, cumin, and salt. Mix well. Shape into six ½-inch-thick patties.

2 For a charcoal grill, grill patties on the rack of an uncovered grill for 10 to 13 minutes or until done (160°F), turning once halfway through grilling. (For a gas grill, preheat grill. Reduce heat to medium. Place patties on grill rack over heat. Cover and grill as above.)

3 Place each patty on top of two of the pita quarters. Top with roasted peppers and Chimichurri.

CHIMICHURRI: In a small bowl combine ½ cup finely snipped fresh flat-leaf parsley; ½ cup finely snipped fresh cilantro; 2 tablespoons red wine vinegar; 1 tablespoon olive oil; 2 cloves garlic, minced; ¼ teaspoon salt; ¼ teaspoon black pepper; and ⅛ teaspoon cayenne pepper.

PER SANDWICH 325 cal., 15 g total fat (5 g sat. fat), 74 mg chol., 407 mg sodium, 21 g carbo., 4 g fiber, 26 g pro.

Old-World Veal Burgers

Grilled Herb Burgers

Combining different meats in burgers—such as the ground turkey and lean ground beef here—gives the finished burgers a more interesting taste and texture than if just one meat is used.

PREP 20 minutes   **GRILL** 14 minutes   **MAKES** 8 sandwiches

- 1 egg, lightly beaten
- ⅔ cup chopped onion
- ½ cup grated Parmesan cheese
- ¼ cup snipped fresh oregano and/or basil or 2 teaspoons dried oregano and/or basil, crushed
- ¼ cup ketchup
- 2 cloves garlic, minced
- ¼ teaspoon salt
- ¼ teaspoon black pepper
- 1 pound lean ground beef
- 1 pound uncooked ground turkey
- 8 ciabatta rolls, split
- 16 tomato slices
  Fresh oregano and/or basil sprigs (optional)

❶ In a large bowl combine egg, onion, Parmesan cheese, snipped fresh or dried oregano and/or basil, ketchup, garlic, salt, and pepper. Add ground beef and ground turkey; mix well. Shape mixture into eight ¾-inch-thick patties.

❷ For a charcoal grill, place patties on the rack of an uncovered grill directly over medium coals. Grill for 14 to 18 minutes or until no longer pink (165°F), turning once halfway through grilling. Toast ciabatta rolls on the grill. (For a gas grill, preheat grill. Reduce to medium. Place patties, then ciabatta rolls on grill rack over heat. Cover and grill as above.)

❸ Serve burgers on toasted ciabatta rolls with tomato slices and, if desired, additional fresh oregano and/or basil sprigs.

PER SANDWICH 381 cal., 16 g total fat (6 g sat. fat), 114 mg chol., 611 mg sodium, 29 g carbo., 2 g fiber, 31 g pro.

Old-World Veal Burgers

These German-style burgers are delicious with a side of sauerkraut and a good German beer.

PREP 20 minutes   **GRILL** 14 minutes   **MAKES** 4 sandwiches

- 1 egg, lightly beaten
- 2 tablespoons beer or water
- ¾ cup soft rye bread crumbs (1 slice)
- ½ teaspoon caraway seeds
- ½ teaspoon dried marjoram, crushed
- 1 clove garlic, minced
- ¼ teaspoon salt
- ¼ teaspoon black pepper
- 1 pound ground veal or lean ground beef
- 8 slices rye bread
- 4 slices Swiss cheese (4 ounces)
- 3 tablespoons German-style mustard, creamy Dijon mustard blend, or stone-ground mustard

❶ In a large bowl combine egg and beer. Stir in bread crumbs, caraway seeds, marjoram, garlic, salt, and pepper. Add ground veal; mix well. Shape mixture into four ¾-inch-thick patties.

❷ For a charcoal grill, place patties on the rack of an uncovered grill directly over medium coals. Grill for 14 to 18 minutes or until done (160°F), turning once halfway through grilling. (For a gas grill, preheat grill. Reduce heat to medium. Place patties on grill rack over heat. Cover and grill as above.)

❸ When patties are nearly done, add rye bread slices to the grill. Grill for 1 to 2 minutes or until bottoms are light brown. Turn bread slices; place cheese on 4 bread slices. Grill for 1 to 2 minutes more or until bottoms are light brown.

❹ Place patties on the cheese-topped bread slices. Spread the plain bread slices with mustard; place on top of patties.

PER SERVING 492 cal., 19 g total fat (9 g sat. fat), 172 mg chol., 1,056 mg sodium, 37 g carbo., 4 g fiber, 37 g pro.

{ *Burgers are an infinitely versatile mix of meats, herbs, seasonings, cheeses, and breads.* }

Feta-Stuffed Pita Burgers

Be sure to seal the edges of the stuffed patties tightly so that the yummy filling doesn't leak out during grilling.

PREP 20 minutes   **GRILL** 12 minutes   **MAKES** 4 sandwiches

2	tablespoons cornmeal
2	tablespoons milk
1	tablespoon finely chopped onion
1	clove garlic, minced
¼	teaspoon salt
¼	teaspoon dried oregano, crushed
⅛	teaspoon lemon-pepper seasoning
8	ounces lean ground lamb
8	ounces lean ground beef
⅓	cup finely crumbled feta cheese
1	tablespoon milk
¼	teaspoon ground cumin
¼	teaspoon cayenne pepper
2	large pita bread rounds
2	cups arugula and/or watercress

1 In a medium bowl combine cornmeal, 2 tablespoons milk, onion, garlic, salt, oregano, and lemon-pepper seasoning. Add ground lamb and ground beef; mix well. Shape mixture into eight ¼-inch-thick patties.

2 For filling, in a small bowl combine feta cheese and 1 tablespoon milk. Divide filling among 4 patties. Top with the remaining patties; press edges to seal.

3 In a small bowl combine cumin and cayenne pepper. Sprinkle mixture over patties.

4 For a charcoal grill, place patties on the rack of an uncovered grill directly over medium coals. Grill for 12 to 16 minutes or until done (160°F), turning once halfway through grilling. (For a gas grill, preheat grill. Reduce heat to medium. Place patties on grill rack over heat. Cover and grill as above.)

5 To serve, cut pita bread rounds in half crosswise. Serve burgers in pita halves with arugula.

PER SANDWICH 422 cal., 25 g total fat (11 g sat. fat), 92 mg chol., 568 mg sodium, 22 g carbo., 1 g fiber, 25 g pro.

Chimichurri Chicken ♥

Serve this grilled chicken with crusty bread to soak up the remains of any delicious chimichurri sauce.

START TO FINISH 20 minutes   **MAKES** 4 servings

4	skinless, boneless chicken breast halves
3	tablespoons cooking oil
½	teaspoon salt
¼	teaspoon black pepper
12	ounces fresh young green beans
¾	cup packed fresh flat-leaf parsley
1	tablespoon cider vinegar
2	cloves garlic, halved
¼	teaspoon crushed red pepper
1	lemon, zested and juiced
	Lemon wedges (optional)

1 Brush chicken with 1 tablespoon of the oil; sprinkle with ¼ teaspoon of the salt and the black pepper. On charcoal grill, cook chicken on rack directly over medium coals for 12 to 15 minutes or until no longer pink, turning once halfway through grilling time.

2 Place beans in a microwave-safe 1½-quart dish. Add 1 tablespoon water. Cover with vented plastic wrap. Cook on high 3 minutes; drain.

3 For chimichurri sauce, in a small food processor combine parsley, the remaining oil, the vinegar, garlic, ¼ teaspoon salt, and red pepper. Process until nearly smooth. Serve chicken and beans topped with chimichurri sauce, lemon peel, and juice. If desired, serve with lemon wedges.

PER SERVING 281 cal., 12 g total fat (2 g sat. fat), 82 mg chol., 376 mg sodium, 8 g carbo., 3 g fiber, 35 g pro.

Chimichurri Chicken

Grilled Chicken
& Creamy Corn

Grilled Chicken & Creamy Corn ♥

Smoked paprika—also called pimenton—comes in both sweet and hot varieties. Use the "dolce," or sweet, here.

START TO FINISH 20 minutes   **MAKES** 4 servings

2	tablespoons olive oil
1	teaspoon smoked paprika
3	fresh ears of sweet corn
4	skinless, boneless chicken breast halves
	Salt
	Black pepper
⅓	cup sour cream
	Milk
¼	cup shredded fresh basil

❶ In small bowl combine olive oil and paprika. Brush corn and chicken with oil mixture. Lightly season with salt and pepper.

❷ For a charcoal grill, grill chicken directly over medium coals for 12 to 15 minutes or until chicken is no longer pink (170°F), turning once halfway through grilling. (For a gas grill, preheat grill. Reduce heat to medium. Place chicken on grill rack over heat. Cover and grill as above.)

❸ Carefully cut kernels from cob by firmly holding the corn at the top (using a kitchen towel to grip, if necessary) and slicing downward with a sharp knife. Transfer to a bowl; stir in sour cream. Season with additional salt and pepper. Stir in milk to desired creaminess. Slice chicken breasts. Serve with corn; sprinkle shredded basil.

PER SERVING 309 cal., 13 g total fat (4 g sat. fat), 89 mg chol., 238 mg sodium, 14 g carbo., 2 g fiber, 36 g pro.

Grilled Chicken Fettuccine

Grilled Chicken Fettuccine

This creamy pesto-sauced dish tastes like something you'd order at your favorite Italian-style restaurant.

PREP 20 minutes   **GRILL** 12 minutes   **MAKES** 6 servings

1	cup whipping cream
⅓	cup butter
¾	cup grated Parmesan cheese
4	skinless, boneless chicken breast halves
	Salt
	Black pepper
12	ounces dried fettuccine
¼	cup purchased basil pesto
1	cup cherry tomatoes, halved
¼	cup snipped fresh basil
	Cracked black pepper
	Toasted pine nuts (optional)

❶ In a small saucepan heat whipping cream and butter until butter melts. Gradually add Parmesan cheese, stirring until combined. Cover and keep warm over low heat.

❷ Season chicken lightly with salt and pepper. For a charcoal grill, grill chicken on the rack of an uncovered grill directly over medium coals for 12 to 15 minutes or until chicken is no longer pink (170°F), turning once halfway through grilling. (For a gas grill, preheat grill. Reduce heat to medium. Place chicken on grill rack over heat. Cover and grill as above.)

❸ Meanwhile, cook fettuccine according to package directions. Drain and keep warm.

❹ Cut grilled chicken into bite-size pieces. In a medium bowl toss chicken with 1 tablespoon of the pesto. Add remaining pesto and Parmesan mixture to the hot cooked fettuccine. Add tomatoes and toss to coat. Arrange fettuccine on a serving platter; sprinkle with basil and pepper. Top with grilled chicken. If desired, garnish with pine nuts.

PER SERVING 673 cal., 38 g total fat (17 g sat. fat), 148 mg chol., 389 mg sodium, 47 g carbo., 2 g fiber, 36 g pro.

quick tip   Purchased pesto comes in both jars in the condiment section and in tubs in the refrigerated section. If it's available, try to buy the refrigerated type. Generally it's fresher, has better and brighter color and better flavor than the jarred pesto.

Lamb Burgers with Feta & Mint

Here's a fresh, casual take on lamb with mint jelly.

PREP 15 minutes   **GRILL** 14 minutes   **MAKES** 4 sandwiches

1½   pounds lean ground lamb or beef
2   teaspoons black pepper
4   kaiser rolls, split
4   lettuce leaves
½   cup crumbled feta cheese (2 ounces)
4   tomato slices
1   tablespoon snipped fresh mint

❶ Shape lamb into four ¾-inch-thick patties. Season to taste with pepper. For a charcoal grill, grill patties on the greased rack of an uncovered grill directly over medium coals for 14 to 18 minutes or until done (160°F), turning once halfway through grilling. (For a gas grill, preheat grill. Reduce heat to medium. Place patties on grill rack over heat. Cover and grill as above).

❷ Serve patties on kaiser rolls. Top each with lettuce, feta cheese, tomatoes, and mint.

PER SANDWICH 544 cal., 29 g total fat (12 g sat. fat), 126 mg chol., 564 mg sodium, 32 g carbo., 2 g fiber, 37 g pro.

Basil-Chicken Burgers

Look for ground chicken made from breast meat only.

PREP 15 minutes   **GRILL** 10 minutes   **MAKES** 4 sandwiches

¼   cup snipped fresh basil
¼   cup fine dry bread crumbs
4   teaspoons Worcestershire sauce
⅛   teaspoon salt
⅛   teaspoon black pepper
1   pound ground chicken
8   slices French bread, toasted, or 4 kaiser rolls or hamburger buns, split and toasted
    Assorted condiments (such as lettuce leaves, sliced tomato, and/or sliced onion) (optional)

❶ In a large bowl combine basil, bread crumbs, Worcestershire sauce, salt, and pepper. Add ground chicken; mix well. Shape chicken mixture into four ½-inch-thick patties.

❷ For a charcoal grill, grill patties on the rack of an uncovered grill directly over medium coals for 10 to 13 minutes or until no longer pink (170°F), turning once halfway through grilling. (For a gas grill, preheat grill. Reduce heat to medium. Place patties on grill rack over heat. Cover and grill as above.)

❸ Serve patties on French bread. If desired, serve with assorted condiments.

PER SANDWICH 334 cal., 11 g total fat (0 g sat. fat), 0 mg chol., 678 mg sodium, 32 g carbo., 2 g fiber, 25 g pro.

Tandoori Chicken Burgers

The crunchy, refreshing Minty Cucumbers cool the (relatively mild) fire of the cayenne-spiced burgers.

PREP 15 minutes   **GRILL** 14 minutes   **MAKES** 4 sandwiches

¼   cup fine dry bread crumbs
2   teaspoons garam masala or curry powder
¼   teaspoon salt
¼   teaspoon cayenne pepper
1   pound uncooked ground chicken
2   tablespoons plain yogurt
4   seeded hamburger buns or kaiser rolls, split and toasted
1   recipe Minty Cucumbers
    Lettuce

❶ In a large bowl combine bread crumbs, garam masala, salt, and cayenne pepper. Add ground chicken and yogurt; mix well. Shape mixture into four ¾-inch-thick patties.

❷ For a charcoal grill, grill patties on the rack of an uncovered grill directly over medium coals for 14 to 18 minutes or until no longer pink (170°F), turning once halfway through grilling. (For a gas grill, preheat grill. Reduce heat to medium. Place patties on grill rack over heat. Cover and grill as above.)

❸ Serve patties on toasted buns with Minty Cucumbers and lettuce.

MINTY CUCUMBERS: Combine 1 cucumber, thinly sliced; ½ cup thinly sliced red onion; ¼ cup snipped fresh mint; 1 tablespoon bottled sesame vinaigrette; and ¼ teaspoon salt.

PER SANDWICH 383 cal., 13 g total fat (1 g sat. fat), 0 mg chol., 841 mg sodium, 37 g carbo., 2 g fiber, 27 g pro.

quick tip   Garam masala is quite different from curry powder—but both are Indian spice blends. Although "garam" means "warm" or "hot," garam masala is generally not hot. It can contain up to 12 spices—usually black pepper, cinnamon, cloves, coriander, cumin, cardamom, dried chiles, fennel, mace, and nutmeg. If you can't find it in your supermarket, look at an Indian market. Buy it in small quantities so it's more likely to get used up before it loses its freshness and flavor.

Turkey-Cranberry Burgers

Turkey-Cranberry Burgers ♥

Who says turkey and cranberry sauce is just for Thanksgiving? The classic combo tastes every bit as good on a toasted bun as it does accompanied by stuffing and mashed potatoes.

PREP 20 minutes **GRILL** 12 minutes **MAKES** 4 sandwiches

- ½ cup finely shredded carrot
- ¼ cup thinly sliced green onions (2)
- 2 tablespoons fine dry bread crumbs
- 2 tablespoons fat-free milk
- ¼ teaspoon dried Italian seasoning, crushed
- ⅛ teaspoon salt
- ⅛ teaspoon black pepper
- 12 ounces uncooked ground turkey breast or chicken breast
- 4 whole wheat hamburger buns, split and toasted
- 1 cup mixed baby greens
- ¼ cup whole cranberry sauce

1 In a medium bowl stir together carrot, green onions, bread crumbs, milk, Italian seasoning, salt, and pepper. Add ground turkey; mix well. Shape the turkey mixture into four ½-inch-thick patties.

2 For a charcoal grill, grill patties on a greased rack of an uncovered grill directly over medium coals for 12 to 15 minutes or until patties are done (165°F), turning once halfway through grilling. (For a gas grill, preheat grill. Reduce heat to medium. Place patties on grill rack over heat. Cover and grill as above).

3 Arrange mixed greens on bottoms of buns. Top with patties and cranberry sauce; replace top halves of buns.

PER SANDWICH 254 cal., 2 g total fat (0 g sat. fat), 34 mg chol., 386 mg sodium, 33 g carbo., 3 g fiber, 25 g pro.

Asian-Apricot Glazed Chops

The most famous brand of chili-garlic sauce is Sriracha. You might want to taste a bit of it before you stir it into the preserves—it's pretty powerful stuff! The sweetness of the preserves does temper the heat a bit, however.

PREP 15 minutes **GRILL** 11 minutes **MAKES** 4 servings

- ⅓ cup apricot preserves
- 1 tablespoon Oriental chili-garlic sauce
- 2 teaspoons soy sauce
- ¼ teaspoon ground ginger
- 4 boneless pork sirloin chops, cut ¾ inch thick
  Salt
  Black pepper

1 For glaze, place apricot preserves in a small bowl; snip any large pieces of fruit. Stir in chili-garlic sauce, soy sauce, and ginger. Set glaze aside. Sprinkle both sides of chops with salt and pepper.

2 For a charcoal grill, grill chops on the rack of an uncovered grill directly over medium coals for 11 to 13 minutes or until chops are slightly pink in center and juices run clear (160°F), turning once halfway through grilling and brushing with glaze during the last 2 to 3 minutes of grilling. (For a gas grill, preheat grill. Reduce heat to medium. Place chops on grill rack over heat. Cover and grill as above.)

PER SERVING 317 cal., 9 g total fat (3 g sat. fat), 106 mg chol., 515 mg sodium, 20 g carbo., 0 g fiber, 36 g pro.

quick tip   While apricot preserves are the first choice for this glaze, you could also use peach or pineapple preserves—or even orange marmalade.

{ Translated for the grill, familiar flavors like turkey and cranberry sauce take on a fun freshness. }

Margarita-Glazed Pork Chops ♥

A splash of tequila infuses the orange and jalapeño glaze with a woody, smoky flavor.

PREP 10 minutes   **GRILL** 7 minutes   **MAKES** 4 servings

- **4**   boneless pork top loin chops, cut ¾ inch thick (1 to 1½ pounds total)
- **⅓**   cup low-sugar orange marmalade
- **1**   jalapeño, seeded and finely chopped (see note, page 19)
- **2**   tablespoons tequila or lime juice
- **½**   teaspoon grated fresh ginger or ¼ teaspoon ground ginger
- **¼**   cup snipped fresh cilantro

1 Trim fat from pork. For glaze, in a small bowl stir together orange marmalade, jalapeño pepper, tequila, and ginger.

2 For a charcoal grill, place chops on the rack of an uncovered grill directly over medium coals. Grill for 7 to 9 minutes or until no pink remains (160°F) and juices run clear, turning once halfway through grilling and spooning glaze over chops frequently during the last 2 minutes of grilling. (For a gas grill, preheat grill. Reduce heat to medium. Place chops on grill rack over heat. Cover and grill as above.)

3 To serve, sprinkle pork chops with cilantro.

PER SERVING 184 cal., 3 g total fat (1 g sat. fat), 62 mg chol., 211 mg sodium, 8 g carbo., 0 g fiber, 26 g pro.

Margarita-Glazed
Pork Chops

Pork Chops with Hot Pineapple Salsa

Most recipes that contain jalapeños call for them to be seeded because that is where most of the heat is stored. If you like fiery food, allow a few of the seeds to be stirred into the salsa.

PREP 20 minutes   **GRILL** 7 minutes   **MAKES** 4 servings

- **1**   20-ounce can crushed pineapple (juice pack), undrained
- **1**   15-ounce can black-eyed peas, rinsed and drained
- **½**   cup finely chopped red onion (1 medium)
- **⅓**   cup finely chopped red sweet pepper
- **¼**   cup snipped fresh parsley
- **2**   fresh jalapeños, seeded and finely chopped (see note, page 19)
- **½**   teaspoon salt
- **¼**   teaspoon ground cumin
- **4**   boneless pork top loin chops, cut 1 inch thick
- **1**   tablespoon olive oil
- **½**   teaspoon dried thyme, crushed
- **½**   teaspoon black pepper
- **½**   teaspoon lemon juice

1 For salsa, in a medium saucepan combine pineapple, black-eyed peas, red onion, sweet pepper, parsley, jalapeños, salt, and cumin. Cook on medium heat about 5 minutes or until heated through, stirring occasionally. Remove from heat; cover to keep warm.

2 Meanwhile, trim fat from chops. In a small bowl combine oil, thyme, pepper, and lemon juice. Brush evenly over both sides of each chop.

3 For a charcoal grill, grill chops on the rack of an uncovered grill directly over medium coals for 7 to 9 minutes or until chops are slightly pink in center and juices run clear (160°F), turning once halfway through grilling. (For a gas grill, preheat grill. Reduce heat to medium. Place chops on grill rack over heat. Cover and grill as above.)

4 Serve the chops with warm pineapple salsa.

PER SERVING 466 cal., 12 g total fat (3 g sat. fat), 93 mg chol., 661 mg sodium, 43 g carbo., 7 g fiber, 44 g pro.

Pork Chops with
Hot Pineapple Salsa

Mahogany-Glazed
Pork & Slaw

Mahogany-Glazed Pork & Slaw

A mixture of hoisin, vinegar, sesame oil, pepper, and garlic does double duty here—as a dressing for the slaw and as a glaze brushed on the meat the last few minutes of cooking.

PREP 15 minutes **GRILL** 12 minutes **MAKES** 4 servings

- ⅓ cup hoisin sauce
- 2 tablespoons cider vinegar
- ½ teaspoon toasted sesame oil
- ¼ teaspoon black pepper
- 2 cloves garlic, minced
- 3 cups packaged shredded broccoli (broccoli slaw mix)
- 2 pork shoulder blade steaks, cut ¾ inch thick

1 In a small bowl combine hoisin sauce, vinegar, sesame oil, pepper, and garlic. Toss half of the hoisin sauce mixture with the shredded broccoli. Cover and chill until ready to serve. Reserve remaining hoisin sauce mixture.

2 For a charcoal grill, grill steaks on the rack of an uncovered grill directly over medium coals for 12 to 14 minutes or until steaks are slightly pink in center and juices run clear (160°F), turning once and brushing occasionally with reserved hoisin sauce mixture during the last 2 to 3 minutes of grilling. (For a gas grill, preheat grill. Reduce heat to medium. Place steaks on grill rack over heat. Cover and grill as above.)

3 Serve pork steaks with slaw.

PER SERVING 414 cal., 18 g total fat (6 g sat. fat), 153 mg chol., 486 mg sodium, 14 g carbo., 3 g fiber, 47 g pro.

quick tip Pork shoulder blade steak is a nicely marbled piece of meat cut from the upper part of the pork shoulder. It has lots of flavor and takes particularly well to the intense flavors of Asian cuisine. If you can't find it, you can substitute pork chops.

Maple-&-Mustard-Glazed Ham Steak

A ham steak may be completely cooked before it hits the grill, but smoke and fire add a new dimension of flavor—especially when it's brushed with a buttery sweet glaze.

PREP 10 minutes **GRILL** 14 minutes **MAKES** 6 servings

- 1 1½- to 2-pound cooked center-cut ham slice, cut ½ to ¾ inch thick
- 2 tablespoons butter or margarine
- ¼ cup pure maple syrup or maple-flavor syrup
- 2 tablespoons brown mustard

1 For a charcoal grill, grill ham on the rack of an uncovered grill directly over medium coals for 14 to 18 minutes or until heated through (140°F). (For a gas grill, preheat grill. Reduce heat to medium. Place ham on grill rack over heat. Cover and grill as above.)

2 Meanwhile, for glaze, in a small saucepan melt butter. Remove saucepan from heat. Stir in syrup and mustard, whisking until smooth. Return saucepan to heat. Bring to boiling; reduce heat. Cook for 1 to 2 minutes more or until slightly thickened.

3 To serve, brush ham with glaze; pass remaining glaze.

PER SERVING 258 cal., 14 g total fat (6 g sat. fat), 75 mg chol., 1,575 mg sodium, 14 g carbo., 2 g fiber, 19 g pro.

Maple-&-Mustard-Glazed Ham Steak

Currant-Glazed Pork Burgers

Pork takes particularly well to sweet flavors. The currant jelly glaze for these burgers is infused with the sweet spices cinnamon and cloves.

PREP 15 minutes **GRILL** 14 minutes **MAKES** 4 sandwiches

¼	cup currant jelly
3	tablespoons ketchup
1	tablespoon cider vinegar
⅛	teaspoon ground cinnamon
	Dash ground cloves
1	egg, lightly beaten
3	tablespoons fine dry bread crumbs
2	tablespoons chopped onion
2	tablespoons milk
¼	teaspoon salt
¼	teaspoon dried thyme, crushed
⅛	teaspoon black pepper
1	pound lean ground pork
4	whole wheat hamburger buns, split
4	lettuce leaves (optional)

❶ For sauce, in a small saucepan combine currant jelly, ketchup, vinegar, cinnamon, and cloves. Cook and stir just until boiling. Remove from heat; cover to keep warm.

❷ In a medium bowl combine egg, bread crumbs, onion, milk, salt, thyme, and pepper. Add ground pork; mix well. Shape mixture into four ¾-inch-thick patties.

❸ For a charcoal grill, grill patties on the rack of an uncovered grill directly over medium coals for 14 to 18 minutes or until done (160°F), turning once halfway through grilling. Lightly toast buns on grill for 1 to 2 minutes. (For a gas grill, preheat grill. Reduce heat to medium. Place patties, then buns on grill rack over heat. Cover and grill as above.)

❹ If desired, arrange lettuce on bottom halves of buns. Top with burgers, sauce, and top halves of buns.

PER SANDWICH 347 cal., 11 g total fat (4 g sat. fat), 107 mg chol., 612 mg sodium, 43 g carbo., 3 g fiber, 21 g pro.

Brats with Mango Relish

Smoky bratwurst is perfectly paired with the sour flavor of sauerkraut—and, surprisingly, the sweetness of this grilled mango relish.

START TO FINISH 20 minutes **MAKES** 4 servings

1	large fresh mango, seeded, peeled, and halved
1	small red onion, cut in ½-inch slices
4	cooked smoked bratwurst (12 ounces)
4	hoagie buns, bratwurst buns, or other crusty rolls, split
2	hearts of romaine lettuce, halved
½	teaspoon Jamaican jerk seasoning
	Salt
	Black pepper

❶ Brush mango and onion with 1 tablespoon cooking oil.

❷ For a charcoal grill, grill mango halves, onion, and brats on the rack of uncovered grill directly over medium coals for 8 minutes or until mango and brats are brown and heated through and onion is crisp-tender, turning once halfway through grilling. Lightly toast buns for 1 to 2 minutes on grill. Set aside mango, onion, and brats.

❸ Lightly brush romaine with cooking oil. Grill 1 to 2 minutes directly over medium coals until light brown and wilted, turning once.

❹ For relish, chop grilled mango and onion. Combine in bowl with 1 tablespoon cooking oil, the jerk seasoning, salt, and pepper. Serve brats in buns with relish and romaine.

PER SERVING 478 cal., 31 g total fat (6 g sat. fat), 66 mg chol., 1,112 mg sodium, 35 g carbo., 2 g fiber, 15 g pro.

{ When in doubt about what to grill for guests, a two-fer of burgers and brats makes everyone happy. }

Halibut Veracruz

Halibut Veracruz

Serve this meaty Mexican fish dish with hot cooked rice and/or warmed tortillas.

PREP 20 minutes **GRILL** 4 minutes **MAKES** 4 servings

- 4 fresh or frozen halibut steaks (about 1½ pounds), mahi mahi, grouper, or tuna
- Salt
- Black pepper
- 1 14½-ounce can chopped tomatoes with green chiles, drained
- ¼ cup sliced green onions (2)
- 1 tablespoon olive oil
- 1 teaspoon minced garlic
- 1 teaspoon drained capers
- 1 teaspoon snipped fresh oregano or ½ teaspoon dried oregano, crushed
- ½ teaspoon snipped fresh thyme or ¼ teaspoon dried thyme, crushed
- Cooked rice (optional)
- Flour tortillas (optional)

1 Thaw fish, if frozen. Rinse fish; pat dry with paper towels. Sprinkle fish evenly with salt and pepper. In a small bowl combine drained tomatoes with green chiles, green onions, oil, garlic, capers, oregano, and thyme; set aside.

2 Tear a 36×18-inch piece of heavy-duty foil; fold in half to make an 18-inch square. Place fish steaks in center of foil. Top with tomato mixture. Bring up 2 opposite edges of foil; seal with a double fold. Fold remaining edges together to completely enclose fish, leaving space for steam to build.

3 For a charcoal grill, grill foil packet on the rack of an uncovered grill directly over medium coals for 4 to 6 minutes per ½-inch thickness of fish or until fish flakes easily when tested with a fork. (For a gas grill, preheat grill. Reduce heat to medium. Place foil packet on grill rack over heat. Cover and grill as above.) If desired, serve with rice and tortillas.

PER SERVING 254 cal., 7 g total fat (1 g sat. fat), 54 mg chol., 651 mg sodium, 8 g carbo., 2 g fiber, 36 g pro.

Orange & Dill Sea Bass

Instead of the more predictable combination of lemon, dill, and fish, this recipe takes a slightly sweeter turn, with a squeeze of fresh orange juice right before serving.

PREP 15 minutes **GRILL** 6 minutes **MAKES** 4 servings

- 4 5- to 6-ounce fresh or frozen sea bass or orange roughy fillets, cut ¾ inch thick
- 2 tablespoons snipped fresh dill
- 2 tablespoons olive oil
- ¼ teaspoon salt
- ¼ teaspoon white pepper
- 4 large oranges, cut into ¼-inch slices
- 1 orange, cut into wedges

1 Thaw fish, if frozen. Rinse fish; pat dry. In a small bowl stir together dill, oil, salt, and pepper. Brush both sides of fish fillets with dill mixture.

2 For a charcoal grill, arrange a bed of orange slices on a greased grill rack directly over medium coals. Arrange fish on orange slices. Cover and grill for 6 to 9 minutes or until fish begins to flake when tested with a fork (do not turn fish). (For a gas grill, preheat grill. Reduce heat to medium. Arrange orange slices and fish on greased grill rack over heat. Cover and grill as above.)

3 To serve, use a spatula to transfer fish and grilled orange slices to a serving platter. Squeeze the juice from orange wedges over the fish.

PER SERVING 268 cal., 10 g total fat (2 g sat. fat), 58 mg chol., 242 mg sodium, 18 g carbo., 3 g fiber, 28 g pro.

quick tip White pepper has a distinctive flavor that is especially nice with fish. Like black pepper, it is best when freshly ground. If you can, keep one pepper grinder in your kitchen filled with black peppercorns and another filled with white peppercorns.

Cilantro-Lime Trout

Lime and cilantro stand in for the more common lemon and parsley in this trout preparation.

PREP 15 minutes   **GRILL** 8 minutes   **MAKES** 4 servings

    4   8- to 10-ounce fresh or frozen dressed trout, heads removed
    3   tablespoons lime juice
    2   tablespoons olive oil
    2   tablespoons snipped fresh cilantro or parsley
    ½   teaspoon salt
    ¼   teaspoon cracked black pepper
        Lime wedges

1 Thaw trout, if frozen. Rinse trout; pat dry with paper towels. In a small bowl combine lime juice and oil. Brush the inside and outside of each trout with juice mixture. Sprinkle cilantro, salt, and pepper evenly inside the cavity of each fish.

2 For a charcoal grill, place trout in a well-greased grill basket. Place basket on the rack of an uncovered grill directly over medium coals. Grill for 8 to 12 minutes or until trout begins to flake when tested with a fork, turning basket once halfway through grilling. (For a gas grill, preheat grill. Reduce heat to medium. Place fish in well-greased grill basket. Place grill basket on grill rack over heat. Cover; grill as above.)

3 Serve trout with lime wedges.

PER SERVING 259 cal., 14 g total fat (3 g sat. fat), 83 mg chol., 342 mg sodium, 1 g carbo., 0 g fiber, 30 g pro.

---

quick tip   A grill basket is a handy tool to have if you grill a lot of fish. Trout, in particular, is a thin, delicate fish. A grill basket allows you to turn the fish while cooking without having it stick to the grill or break.

Salmon with Asian Glaze

The Pineapple Rice that accompanies the salmon would also be a delicious side dish with grilled pork or chicken.

PREP 20 minutes   **GRILL** 8 minutes   **MAKES** 4 servings

    1   recipe Pineapple Rice
    2   tablespoons hoisin sauce
    1   tablespoon soy sauce
  1½   teaspoons peanut oil
    1   teaspoon grated fresh ginger
    1   clove garlic, minced
    4   4-ounce fresh skinless salmon fillets, cut 1 inch thick

1 Prepare Pineapple Rice; cover and keep warm. Meanwhile, in a small bowl stir together hoisin sauce, soy sauce, peanut oil, ginger, and garlic; set aside.

2 Rinse salmon; pat dry with paper towels. For a charcoal grill, grill fish on the greased rack of an uncovered grill directly over medium coals for 8 to 12 minutes or until fish flakes easily with a fork, turning once halfway through grilling and brushing with sauce during the last 2 minutes of grilling. (For a gas grill, preheat grill. Reduce heat to medium. Place fish on greased grill rack over heat. Cover and grill as above.)

3 Serve salmon with Pineapple Rice.

PINEAPPLE RICE: In a medium saucepan combine 1 cup chicken broth, ¾ cup jasmine or long grain rice, and ½ cup pineapple juice. Bring to boiling; reduce heat. Simmer, covered, for 15 minutes. Stir in 1 cup frozen shelled green or sweet soybeans (edamame) and ½ cup sliced green onions. Cook 3 minutes more or until rice is tender. Stir in 1 cup bite-size pieces fresh pineapple. Makes about 4 cups.

PER SERVING 461 cal., 14 g total fat (3 g sat. fat), 61 mg chol., 670 mg sodium, 48 g carbo., 4 g fiber, 36 g pro.

{ Whether it comes from the sea or a mountain stream, fish makes a meal seem special. }

Honey, Lime &
Rum-Glazed Shrimp

Honey, Lime & Rum-Glazed Shrimp ♥

Extra-large shrimp take better to grilling than smaller shrimp because they are less likely to dry out—and more likely to stay nice and juicy—during cooking.

START TO FINISH 30 minutes   **MAKES** 4 servings

¼	cup honey
3	tablespoons lime juice
3	tablespoons dark rum
1	tablespoon orange juice
1½	teaspoons cornstarch
1	teaspoon grated fresh ginger
1	tablespoon snipped fresh cilantro
½	teaspoon finely shredded lime peel
½	teaspoon finely shredded orange peel
20	fresh extra-jumbo shrimp in shells (about 1¼ pounds), peeled and deveined
¼	teaspoon salt
¼	teaspoon black pepper

❶ For glaze, in a small saucepan combine honey, lime juice, rum, orange juice, cornstarch, and ginger. Cook and stir on medium heat until thickened and bubbly. Cook and stir for 2 minutes more. Cool to room temperature. Stir in cilantro, lime peel, and orange peel.

❷ Rinse shrimp; pat dry with paper towels. On four 10- to 12-inch skewers, thread shrimp, leaving ¼ inch between pieces. Season shrimp with salt and pepper. Remove and reserve half of the glaze. Brush shrimp with half of the glaze.

❸ For a charcoal grill, grill kabobs on the rack of an uncovered grill directly over medium coals for 2 to 3 minutes or until shrimp are opaque, turning once halfway through grilling. (For a gas grill, preheat grill. Reduce heat to medium. Place kabobs on grill rack over heat. Cover and grill as above.)

❹ Brush shrimp with the reserved glaze.

PER SERVING 248 cal., 2 g total fat (0 g sat. fat), 215 mg chol., 357 mg sodium, 21 g carbo., 0 g fiber, 29 g pro.

Grilled Scallop Kabobs ♥

Leaving some space between pieces of food on a kabob ensures that everything will cook properly.

PREP 15 minutes   **GRILL** 5 minutes   **MAKES** 4 servings

12	ounces fresh or frozen sea scallops
16	cherry tomatoes
1	medium yellow summer squash, halved lengthwise and sliced ½ inch thick
3	tablespoons bottled sesame-ginger stir-fry sauce

❶ Thaw scallops, if frozen. Rinse scallops; pat dry with paper towels. On eight 8-inch skewers, alternately thread scallops, cherry tomatoes, and squash, leaving ¼ inch between pieces.

❷ For a charcoal grill, grill kabobs on the greased rack of an uncovered grill directly over medium coals for 5 to 8 minutes or until scallops are opaque, turning once and brushing frequently with stir-fry sauce during the last half of grilling. (For a gas grill, preheat grill. Reduce heat to medium. Place kabobs on greased grill rack over heat. Cover and grill as above.)

PER SERVING 108 cal., 1 g total fat (0 g sat. fat), 28 mg chol., 421 mg sodium, 9 g carbo., 1 g fiber, 16 g pro.

quick tip   If using wooden skewers, soak them in water for at least 30 minutes before grilling.

Grilled Scallop Kabobs

Pita, Cheese & Veggie Grill

Blocks of feta cheese are warmed in a cast-iron skillet on the grill while the zucchini and onion grill over the grate.

START TO FINISH 20 minutes   **MAKES** 4 servings

1	8-ounce block feta cheese, quartered
1	medium zucchini, halved lengthwise
1	medium red onion, cut in ½-inch-thick slices
¼	cup Italian salad dressing
4	pita bread rounds
2	medium tomatoes, cut in wedges
1	tablespoon honey

1 Drizzle cheese, zucchini, and onion slices with half of the salad dressing. Sprinkle with salt and pepper.

2 On rack of charcoal grill place zucchini, onion slices, and a 6-inch cast-iron skillet (to heat for softening the cheese) directly over medium coals. Grill zucchini and onion for 8 minutes or until tender, turning once halfway through cooking time. Remove vegetables. Grill pita bread and tomatoes on grill rack for 2 minutes or until bread is toasted and tomatoes are lightly charred. Place cheese in hot skillet; heat for 1 to 2 minutes to soften. (For a gas grill, preheat grill. Reduce heat to medium. Place zucchini, onion slices, and a 6-inch cast-iron skillet over heat. Cover and grill as above.)

3 To serve, cut zucchini in chunks. Drizzle cheese, vegetables, pitas, and tomatoes with honey and remaining salad dressing.

PER SERVING 404 cal., 17 g total fat (9 g sat. fat), 50 mg chol., 1,352 mg sodium, 48 g carbo., 3 g fiber, 15 g pro.

Pita, Cheese & Veggie Grill

Zucchini Crab Cakes

Zucchini and green onion add a bit of color and some fresh crunch to these crab cakes that are topped with a yummy Tomato-Sour Cream Sauce.

PREP 20 minutes   **GRILL** 8 minutes   **MAKES** 4 servings

1	cup coarsely shredded zucchini
¼	cup thinly sliced green onions (2)
2	teaspoons cooking oil
1	egg, beaten
⅔	cup seasoned fine dry bread crumbs
1	tablespoon Dijon mustard
1	teaspoon snipped fresh thyme or ½ teaspoon dried thyme, crushed
⅛	to ¼ teaspoon cayenne pepper
8	ounces fresh lump crabmeat (1½ cups) or two 6-ounce cans crabmeat, drained, flaked, and cartilage removed
2	large red and/or yellow tomatoes, sliced ¼ inch thick
1	recipe Tomato-Sour Cream Sauce
	Lemon and/or lime wedges (optional)

1 In a medium skillet cook zucchini and green onions in hot oil over medium-high heat for 3 to 5 minutes or just until vegetables are tender and liquid is evaporated. Cool slightly.

2 In a large bowl combine egg, bread crumbs, mustard, thyme, and cayenne pepper. Add crabmeat and the zucchini mixture; mix well. Using about ¼ cup mixture per crab cake, shape into eight ½-inch-thick patties.

3 For a charcoal grill, grill crab cakes on the greased rack of an uncovered grill directly over medium coals for 8 to 10 minutes or until golden, turning once. (For a gas grill, preheat grill. Reduce heat to medium. Place crab cakes on greased grill rack over heat. Cover and grill as above.)

4 To serve, arrange tomato slices and crab cakes on plates. Serve with Tomato-Sour Cream Sauce and, if desired, lemon wedges.

TOMATO-SOUR CREAM SAUCE: In a small bowl stir together ½ cup sour cream, ¼ cup finely chopped yellow or red tomato, 1 tablespoon lemon or lime juice, and ⅛ teaspoon seasoned salt. Cover and chill until serving time. Makes ¾ cup.

PER SERVING 243 cal., 10 g total fat (4 g sat. fat), 120 mg chol., 835 mg sodium, 20 g carbo., 1 g fiber, 18 g pro.

For busy families, here's the way to cook: Stir together a few ingredients in the slow cooker before you leave the house for the day, then come home to a hot, healthful dinner that's ready to eat.

221

229

234

slow & simple

222

Easy Hungarian Paprikash

Serve this hearty beef dish with steamed green beans or broccoli. As an option to the noodles, serve it over hot cooked rice or mashed potatoes.

PREP 20 minutes   **COOK** 8 to 10 hours (low) or 4 to 5 hours (high)
COOKER SIZE 3½- or 4-quart   **MAKES** 8 servings

2	pounds lean beef stew meat
2	medium onions, sliced
1	cup chopped red or green sweet pepper (1 large)
1	4.5-ounce jar sliced mushrooms, drained
1	14.5-ounce can diced tomatoes, drained
1	10.75-ounce can condensed cream of mushroom soup
1	tablespoon paprika
1	teaspoon dried thyme, crushed
¼	teaspoon coarsely ground black pepper
8	cups hot cooked noodles
½	cup sour cream

❶ Cut meat into 1-inch pieces. Set aside. In the slow cooker combine onions, sweet pepper, meat, and mushrooms.

❷ In a medium bowl stir together tomatoes, mushroom soup, paprika, thyme, and black pepper. Pour over mixture in cooker.

❸ Cover and cook on low-heat setting for 8 to 10 hours or on high-heat setting for 4 to 5 hours. Serve meat mixture over hot cooked noodles. Top each serving with sour cream.

PER SERVING 452 cal., 12 g total fat (4 g sat. fat), 126 mg chol., 503 mg sodium, 50 g carbo., 4 g fiber, 34 g pro.

Cola Pot Roast

Browning the meat first gives it more flavor after it's cooked.

PREP 15 minutes   **COOK** 7 to 8 hours (low) or 3 ½ to 4 hours (high)
COOKER SIZE 4½- or 5-quart   **MAKES** 6 servings

1	2 ½- to 3-pound boneless beef chuck pot roast
	Nonstick cooking spray
2	16-ounce packages frozen stew vegetables
1	12-ounce can cola
1	envelope (1-ounce) onion soup mix
2	tablespoons quick-cooking tapioca

❶ Trim fat from meat. Lightly coat a large skillet with cooking spray; heat over medium heat. Brown roast on all sides in skillet.

❷ Place roast in slow cooker. Top with frozen vegetables. In a small bowl stir together cola, soup mix, and tapioca. Pour over meat and vegetables in cooker.

❸ Cover and cook on low-heat setting for 7 to 8 hours or on high-heat setting for 3 ½ to 4 hours.

PER SERVING 278 cal., 5 g total fat (2 g sat. fat), 75 mg chol., 582 mg sodium, 28 g carbo., 2 g fiber, 29 g pro.

Mushroom-Onion Pot Roast

This is the perfect dish for a cold fall or winter Sunday, when you can hang around the house reading and enjoying the delicious smell of pot roast bubbling away in the kitchen.

PREP 30 minutes   **COOK** 10 to 12 hours (low) or 5 to 6 hours (high)
COOKER SIZE 5- to 6-quart   **MAKES** 6 servings

1	3-pound boneless beef chuck pot roast
½	teaspoon salt
¼	teaspoon black pepper
2	tablespoons cooking oil
2	large onions, halved and sliced ¼ inch thick (about 4 cups)
3	cups small button mushrooms, sliced
1	10.5-ounce can condensed beef consommé
½	cup dry red wine
4	cloves garlic, minced
1	teaspoon dried thyme, crushed
2	tablespoons cornstarch
2	tablespoons cold water
2	cups refrigerated hot mashed potatoes
	Cooked buttered carrots (optional)

❶ Trim fat from meat. Sprinkle meat with salt and pepper. In an extra-large skillet brown roast on all sides in hot oil on medium heat; set aside. Place onions and mushrooms in the slow cooker. Top with meat. In a medium bowl stir together consommé, wine, garlic, and thyme. Pour over meat.

❷ Cover and cook on low-heat setting for 10 to 12 hours or high-heat setting for 5 to 6 hours.

❸ Place meat on a serving platter; keep warm. Transfer cooking liquid and vegetables to a medium saucepan. In a small bowl stir together cornstarch and the cold water; stir into saucepan. Cook and stir on medium heat until thickened and bubbly; cook and stir for 2 minutes more. Serve meat, vegetables, and sauce over hot mashed potatoes. If desired, serve with cooked buttered carrots.

PER SERVING 523 cal., 18 g total fat (5 g sat. fat), 135 mg chol., 958 mg sodium, 30 g carbo., 3 g fiber, 55 g pro.

Spanish Braised Short Ribs
with Orange Gremolata

Spanish Braised Short Ribs with Orange Gremolata

Gremolata—made from minced parsley, lemon peel, and garlic—is traditionally served as a fresh, bright flavor accompaniment to osso buco, or braised veal shanks. This version swaps orange for the lemon.

PREP 20 minutes **COOK** 7 to 8 hours (low) or 3½ to 4 hours (high)
COOKER SIZE 3½- or 4-quart **MAKES** 4 servings

2	pounds beef short ribs
	Salt
	Black pepper
1	large onion, cut into wedges
2	medium carrots, cut into 2-inch pieces
4	ounces cooked smoked chorizo sausage, casing removed and chopped
1	14.5-ounce can diced tomatoes, undrained
¼	cup white wine
¼	cup orange juice
2	teaspoons sherry vinegar
1	teaspoon paprika
2	bay leaves
3	tablespoons snipped fresh parsley
1	tablespoon minced garlic
1	tablespoon finely shredded orange peel

1 Sprinkle short ribs with salt and pepper.

2 In a slow cooker place onion, carrots, chorizo, and short ribs. Add undrained tomatoes, wine, orange juice, vinegar, paprika, and bay leaves.

3 Cover and cook on low-heat setting for 7 to 8 hours or on high-heat setting for 3½ to 4 hours. Discard bay leaves. Skim fat from sauce.

4 For gremolata, in a small bowl combine parsley, garlic, and orange peel. Serve short ribs, vegetables, and cooking liquid in shallow bowls; top with gremolata.

PER SERVING 360 cal., 20 g total fat (7 g sat. fat), 293 mg chol., 775 mg sodium, 15 g carbo., 4 g fiber, 27 g pro.

Asian Lettuce Wraps

These savory wraps make fun, interactive party food. Set out the meat and the lettuce and let guests make their own wraps. Have a bottle of Asian hot sauce on hand for those who like their food fiery.

PREP 20 minutes **COOK** 8 to 10 hours (low) or 4 to 5 hours (high) + 15 minutes (high) **COOKER SIZE** 3½- or 4-quart
MAKES 12 servings

1	3-pound boneless beef chuck pot roast
1½	cups diced jicama (1 small) or chopped celery (3 stalks)
½	cup chopped green onions (4)
¼	cup rice vinegar
¼	cup reduced-sodium soy sauce
2	tablespoons hoisin sauce
1	tablespoon finely chopped fresh ginger
½	teaspoon salt
½	teaspoon chili oil
¼	teaspoon black pepper
2	tablespoons cornstarch
2	tablespoons cold water
24	Bibb or Boston lettuce leaves

1 Trim fat from meat. If necessary, cut meat to fit into the slow cooker. Place meat in cooker. In a medium bowl combine jicama, green onions, vinegar, soy sauce, hoisin sauce, ginger, salt, chili oil, and pepper. Pour over meat.

2 Cover and cook on low-heat setting for 8 to 10 hours or on high-heat setting for 4 to 5 hours.

3 If using low-heat setting, turn to high-heat setting. In a small bowl combine cornstarch and water. Stir cornstarch mixture into liquid around the meat. Cover and cook about 15 minutes more or until thickened.

4 Remove meat from cooker. Using 2 forks, pull meat apart into shreds. Return meat to cooker. Spoon meat mixture onto lettuce leaves. Fold bottom edge of each lettuce leaf up and over filling. Fold in opposite sides; roll up from bottom.

PER SERVING 168 cal., 4 g total fat (1 g sat. fat), 67 mg chol., 401 mg sodium, 5 g carbo., 0 g fiber, 25 g pro.

quick tip If you don't have chili oil, you can substitute ½ teaspoon toasted sesame oil stirred together with ¼ teaspoon crushed red pepper flakes.

Tried-&-True Chili Mac

Kids seem to love pretty much anything with macaroni in it. Serve this chili mac with veggies and dip and you have a healthful, family-pleasing meal.

PREP 25 minutes **COOK** 4 to 6 hours (low) or 2 to 3 hours (high)
COOKER SIZE 3½- or 4-quart **MAKES** 8 servings

- 1½ pounds lean ground beef
- 1 cup onion, chopped (1 large)
- 3 cloves garlic, minced
- 1 15-ounce can chili beans in chili gravy, undrained
- 1 14.5-ounce can diced tomatoes and green chiles, undrained
- 1 cup low-sodium beef broth
- ¾ cup green sweet pepper, chopped (1 medium)
- 2 teaspoons chili powder
- 1 teaspoon ground cumin
- 8 ounces dried cavatappi or macaroni, cooked according to package directions
- ¼ cup shredded reduced-fat cheddar cheese

❶ In a large skillet cook ground beef, onion, and garlic on medium heat until meat is brown and onion is tender. Drain off fat.

❷ In a slow cooker combine meat mixture, undrained chili beans, undrained tomatoes and green chiles, broth, sweet pepper, chili powder, and cumin.

❸ Cover and cook on low-heat setting for 4 to 6 hours or on high-heat setting for 2 to 3 hours. Stir in cooked pasta.

❹ To serve, top each serving with some of the cheese.

PER SERVING 343 cal., 10 g total fat (4 g sat. fat), 58 mg chol., 510 mg sodium, 36 g carbo., 5 g fiber, 26 g pro.

Taco Chili

It doesn't get much simpler than this five-ingredient chili!

PREP 10 minutes **COOK** 4 to 6 hours (low) or 2 to 3 hours (high)
COOKER SIZE 3½- or 4-quart **MAKES** 4 to 6 servings

- 1 pound ground beef
- 1 1.2-ounce package taco seasoning mix
- 2 15-ounce cans chunky Mexican-style tomatoes
- 1 15-ounce can red kidney beans, undrained
- 1 15-ounce can whole kernel corn, undrained

❶ In a large skillet cook ground beef until brown; drain off fat.

❷ In a slow cooker combine the cooked ground beef, taco seasoning mix, undrained tomatoes, undrained beans, and undrained corn. Cover and cook on low-heat setting for 4 to 6 hours or on high-heat setting for 2 to 3 hours.

PER SERVING 464 cal., 17 g total fat (6 g sat. fat), 71 mg chol., 2,317 mg sodium, 50 g carbo., 9 g fiber, 33 g pro.

Beef & Red Bean Chili

In the age-old argument about whether there should be beans in chili, this savory bowl o' red suggests that it's actually a very tasty idea.

PREP 30 minutes **COOK** 10 to 12 hours (low) or 5 to 6 hours (high)
STAND 1 hour **COOKER SIZE** 3½- or 4-quart
MAKES 8 servings

- 1 cup dry red beans or dry red kidney beans
- 1 tablespoon olive oil
- 2 pounds boneless beef chuck pot roast, cut into 1-inch pieces
- 1 cup coarsely chopped onion
- 1 15-ounce can tomato sauce
- 1 14½-ounce can diced tomatoes with green chile peppers, undrained
- 1 14-ounce can reduced-sodium beef broth
- 2 to 3 canned chipotle chile peppers in adobo sauce, finely chopped, plus 2 teaspoons adobo sauce (see note, page 19)
- 2 teaspoons dried oregano, crushed
- 1 teaspoon ground cumin
- ¾ cup finely chopped red sweet pepper (1 medium) (optional)
- ¼ cup snipped fresh cilantro (optional)

❶ Rinse beans. Place beans in a large saucepan or Dutch oven. Add enough water to cover beans by 2 inches. Bring to boiling; reduce heat. Simmer, uncovered, for 10 minutes. Remove from heat. Cover; let stand for 1 hour.

❷ Meanwhile, in a large skillet heat oil on medium-high heat. Add half of the meat and the onion; cook and stir until meat is brown. Using a slotted spoon, transfer meat-onion mixture to the slow cooker. Repeat with remaining meat. Stir tomato sauce, undrained tomatoes, beef broth, chipotle peppers and adobo sauce, oregano, and cumin into mixture in slow cooker. Drain and rinse the beans; stir into mixture in cooker.

❸ Cover and cook on low-heat setting for 10 to 12 hours or on high-heat setting for 5 to 6 hours. If desired, top each serving with sweet pepper and cilantro.

PER SERVING 288 cal., 7 g total fat (2 g sat. fat), 67 mg chol., 702 mg sodium, 24 g carbo., 6 g fiber, 31 g pro.

Classic French Dips

Classic French Dips

Both the onions and the meat get meltingly tender with hours of slow, moist cooking. Serve these sandwiches with a green salad dressed with a French vinaigrette.

PREP 20 minutes **COOK** 9 to 10 hours (low) or 4½ to 5 hours (high)
COOKER SIZE 3½- to 5-quart **MAKES** 6 servings

- 1 large sweet onion (such as Vidalia, Maui, or Walla Walla), cut into ½-inch-thick slices and separated into rings (1 cup)
- 1 2- to 2½-pound fresh beef brisket or boneless beef bottom round roast
- 2 cloves garlic, minced
- 1 teaspoon dried thyme, marjoram, or oregano, crushed
- ½ teaspoon black pepper
- 1 14-ounce can low-sodium beef broth
- 2 tablespoons Worcestershire sauce
- 1 16-ounce loaf whole grain baguette-style bread, cut crosswise into 6 pieces and halved lengthwise, or 6 whole grain hoagie buns, split and, if desired, toasted

❶ Place onion slices in the slow cooker. Trim fat from beef. If necessary, cut beef to fit cooker. Place beef on top of onions. Sprinkle with garlic, thyme, and pepper. Pour beef broth and Worcestershire sauce over all.

❷ Cover and cook on low-heat setting for 9 to 10 hours for brisket or 8 to 9 hours for bottom round or on high-heat setting for 4½ to 5 hours for brisket or 4 to 4½ hours for bottom round.

❸ Transfer meat to a cutting board; thinly slice across the grain, removing any visible fat as you slice. Using a slotted spoon, remove onions from cooker.

❹ Divide sliced brisket and onion slices among bread bottoms. Add bread tops. Skim fat from cooking juices in cooker; pass juices for dipping sandwiches.

PER SERVING 339 cal., 7 g total fat (2 g sat. fat), 45 mg chol., 453 mg sodium, 39 g carbo., 9 g fiber, 33 g pro.

Green Chile Tamale Pie

This mélange of seasoned meats, beans, and vegetables is layered with slices of prepared polenta in this slow-cooked tamale pie.

PREP 30 minutes **COOK** 6 to 8 hours (low) or 3 to 4 hours (high)
COOKER SIZE 5- to 6-quart **MAKES** 8 to 10 servings

- 1 pound ground beef
- 1 pound bulk pork sausage
- 1 cup chopped onion (1 large)
- 3 cloves garlic, minced
- 1 15-ounce can pinto beans or black beans, rinsed and drained
- 1 cup frozen whole kernel corn
- 1 4-ounce can diced green chiles
- 1 teaspoon ground cumin
- 1 16-ounce tube refrigerated cooked polenta, cut into ¼-inch slices
- 1 8-ounce package shredded Monterey Jack cheese
- 1 8-ounce carton sour cream
- 1 tablespoon snipped fresh cilantro
- ½ teaspoon finely shredded lime peel

❶ In an extra-large skillet combine ground beef, sausage, onion, and garlic. Cook on medium heat until meat is brown and onion is tender. Drain off fat. In a large bowl combine meat mixture, beans, corn, chiles, and cumin.

❷ In the slow cooker layer half of the meat mixture, half of the polenta slices, and half of the cheese. Top with remaining meat mixture and remaining polenta slices.

❸ Cover and cook on low-heat setting for 6 to 8 hours or on high-heat setting for 3 to 4 hours. Uncover; top with remaining cheese. Let stand for 5 minutes or until cheese melts.

❹ In a small bowl stir together sour cream, cilantro, and lime peel. Serve with tamale pie.

PER SERVING 427 cal., 24 g total fat (13 g sat. fat), 79 mg chol., 660 mg sodium, 30 g carbo., 5 g fiber, 25 g pro.

{ An unwatched pot is a blessing on busy days. Fill it up and walk away—then come home to dinner. }

Lamb-Sausage Cassoulet

This classic French dish is traditionally cooked for hours in a Dutch oven in a low-temperature oven. The slow cooker accomplishes the same thing—and you don't have to hang around the house.

PREP 20 minutes   **COOK** 5 to 6 hours (low) or 2½ to 3 hours (high)
COOKER SIZE 4- to 5-quart   **MAKES** 6 servings

- 1 pound lean ground lamb, beef, pork, or turkey
- ¾ cup chopped onion (1 medium)
- 1 pound cooked smoked Polish sausage, cut into ½-inch-thick slices
- 3 15-ounce cans Great Northern beans, rinsed and drained
- 1 8-ounce can tomato sauce
- ¾ cup chicken broth
- ¼ cup dry white wine or chicken broth
- 2 tablespoons quick-cooking tapioca
- 2 bay leaves
- 1 clove garlic, minced
- ½ teaspoon dried thyme, crushed
- 1 tablespoon snipped fresh parsley

❶ In a large skillet cook lamb and onion until lamb is brown and onion is tender; drain well.

❷ In the slow cooker combine lamb mixture, sausage slices, beans, tomato sauce, broth, wine, tapioca, bay leaves, garlic, and thyme.

❸ Cover and cook on low-heat setting for 5 to 6 hours or on high-heat setting for 2½ to 3 hours.

❹ Discard bay leaves. Sprinkle lamb mixture with parsley.

PER SERVING 745 cal., 35 g total fat (13 g sat. fat), 102 mg chol., 1,480 mg sodium, 57 g carbo., 12 g fiber, 47 g pro.

quick tip   Ground lamb isn't always available. If not, ask your butcher to grind some for you from boneless leg of lamb or chops.

Mexican Tacos Carnitas

Pork shoulder roast is one of the best cuts for the slow cooker. It starts out tough but ends up juicy and butter-knife tender after long, moist cooking. Because it's inexpensive, it's a great choice for feeding a crowd.

PREP 25 minutes   **COOK** 10 to 12 hours (low) or 4½ to 5 hours (high)
OVEN 350°F   **COOKER SIZE** 3½- or 4-quart   **MAKES** 6 servings

- 1 tablespoon ground pasilla, New Mexico, or ancho chile pepper
- 1 teaspoon ground coriander
- 2 cloves garlic, minced
- 1 teaspoon snipped fresh oregano or ½ teaspoon dried oregano, crushed
- 1 teaspoon finely shredded orange peel
- ½ teaspoon black pepper
- ¼ teaspoon salt
- 1 2-pound boneless pork shoulder roast, cut into 2-inch pieces
- 2 large onions, cut into wedges
- 1 14-ounce can reduced-sodium chicken broth
- ¾ cup orange juice
- 12 4- to 6-inch corn tortillas
- ¼ cup coarsely chopped fresh cilantro
- ¼ cup sliced green onions (2)
- ⅓ cup bottled green salsa
  Lime wedges (optional)

❶ In a large bowl stir together ground pasilla pepper, coriander, garlic, oregano, orange peel, black pepper, and salt. Add pork to bowl; toss to coat with spices.

❷ In the slow cooker place pork mixture; top with onion wedges. Pour broth and orange juice over all.

❸ Cover and cook on low-heat setting for 10 to 12 hours or on high-heat setting for 4½ to 5 hours.

❹ Use a slotted spoon to remove meat from slow cooker. Using 2 forks, coarsely shred meat; discard any fat. Drizzle meat with some of the cooking liquid.

❺ Wrap tortillas in foil. Heat in a 350°F oven for 10 minutes or until warm. To serve, top each tortilla with ¼ cup of the meat, some cilantro, and finely chopped green onions. Serve with salsa and, if desired, lime wedges.

PER SERVING 331 cal., 10 g total fat (3 g sat. fat), 91 mg chol., 451 mg sodium, 27 g carbo., 2 g fiber, 33 g pro.

Cranberry-Orange Pork Chops

Cranberry-Orange Pork Chops

Pork is often paired with fruit. In this sweetly spiced dish, it's paired with both cranberries and fresh plums and/or apricots.

PREP 15 minutes   **COOK** 7 to 8 hours (low) or 3½ to 4 hours (high)
STAND 5 minutes   **COOKER SIZE** 3½- or 4-quart
MAKES 8 servings

- 2   cups coarsely chopped, peeled carrots
- 8   boneless pork loin chops, cut ¾ inch thick (about 1¾ pounds)
- 1   14-ounce can whole cranberry sauce
- 1   teaspoon finely shredded orange peel
- 2   tablespoons quick-cooking tapioca
- 1   teaspoon finely shredded lemon peel
- ¼   teaspoon ground cardamom
- 3   fresh plums and/or apricots, pitted and sliced (about 8 ounces)
- 4   cups hot cooked couscous or rice

1 Place carrots in the slow cooker. Place pork chops on top of carrots. Combine cranberry sauce, orange peel, tapioca, lemon peel, and cardamom; pour over meat.

2 Cover and cook on low-heat setting for 7 to 8 hours or on high-heat setting for 3½ to 4 hours.

3 Gently stir sliced fruit into pork mixture; turn off slow cooker. Cover; let stand for 5 minutes. Serve over cooked couscous or rice.

PER SERVING 323 cal., 4 g total fat (1 g sat. fat), 55 mg chol., 73 mg sodium, 47 g carbo., 3 g fiber, 22 g pro.

---

quick tip   Plums are in season May through October; apricots from May through August. Make this dish in that window of time for best results.

Apricot-Glazed Pork Roast

Serve this glazed pork roast with a mix of peas, snow peas, baby corn, and baby carrots.

PREP 15 minutes   **COOK** 10 to 12 hours (low) or 5 to 6 hours (high)
COOKER SIZE 3½- to 6-quart   **MAKES** 6 to 8 servings

- 1   3- to 3½-pound boneless pork shoulder roast
- 1   18-ounce jar apricot preserves
- 1   cup chopped onion (1 large)
- ¼   cup chicken broth
- 2   tablespoons Dijon mustard
     Hot cooked rice (optional
     Cooked mixed vegetables (optional))

1 Trim fat from roast. If necessary, cut roast to fit in a slow cooker. Place roast in slow cooker. In a small bowl combine apricot preserves, onion, broth, and mustard; pour over roast.

2 Cover and cook on low-heat setting for 10 to 12 hours or on high-heat setting for 5 to 6 hours.

3 Transfer roast to a serving plate. Skim fat from sauce. Spoon some of the sauce over roast. If desired, serve remaining sauce with hot cooked rice and mixed vegetables.

PER SERVING 456 cal., 10 g total fat (3 g sat. fat), 93 mg chol., 184 mg sodium, 61 g carbo., 2 g fiber, 29 g pro.

Apricot-Glazed Pork Roast

Spaghetti Sauce Italiano

When you get home after a long day away, all you have to do is cook up some pasta and toss a bagged salad with some dressing, and dinner's done.

PREP 25 minutes   **COOK** 8 to 10 hours (low) or 4 to 5 hours (high)
COOKER SIZE 3½- or 4-quart   **MAKES** 6 to 8 servings

1	pound bulk Italian sausage or ground beef
1	cup chopped onion (1 large)
2	cloves garlic, minced
2	14.5-ounce cans diced tomatoes, undrained
1	6-ounce can tomato paste
2	4-ounce cans mushroom stems and pieces, drained
1	bay leaf
2	teaspoons dried Italian seasoning, crushed
½	teaspoon salt
¼	teaspoon black pepper
1	cup chopped green sweet pepper (1 large)
12	to 16 ounces dried spaghetti, cooked and drained
	Finely shredded or grated Parmesan cheese (optional)

❶ In a large skillet cook the sausage, onion, and garlic on medium heat until meat is brown and onion is tender. Drain off fat; discard.

❷ Meanwhile, in the slow cooker stir together undrained tomatoes, tomato paste, mushrooms, bay leaf, Italian seasoning, salt, and black pepper. Stir in meat mixture.

❸ Cover and cook on low-heat setting for 8 to 10 hours or on high-heat setting for 4 to 5 hours. Stir in sweet pepper. Discard bay leaf. Serve meat mixture over hot cooked spaghetti. If desired, sprinkle with Parmesan cheese.

PER SERVING 553 cal., 23 g total fat (10 g sat. fat), 51 mg chol., 1,506 mg sodium, 62 g carbo., 6 g fiber, 27 g pro.

SPICY TOMATO-CREAM SAUCE: Prepare as above, except use hot Italian sausage and stir ½ cup whipping cream into sauce just before serving.

PER SERVING 622 cal., 30 g total fat (15 g sat. fat), 78 mg chol., 1,513 mg sodium, 62 g carb., 6 g fiber, 27 g pro.

Italian Braised Chicken with Fennel & Cannellini

Chicken drumsticks and thighs have more flavor than breast meat—but they also have more fat. Skinning them removes much of it, so you're left with lean, great-tasting chicken that stays juicy even after a long cooking time.

PREP 30 minutes   **COOK** 5 to 6 hours (low) or 2½ to 3 hours (high)
COOKER SIZE 3½- or 4-quart   **MAKES** 6 servings

2	to 2½ pounds chicken drumsticks and/or thighs, skin removed
¼	teaspoon salt
¼	teaspoon black pepper
1	15-ounce can cannellini beans, rinsed and drained
1	bulb fennel, cored and cut into thin wedges
1	medium yellow sweet pepper, seeded and cut into 1-inch pieces
1	medium onion, cut into thin wedges
3	cloves garlic, minced
1	teaspoon snipped fresh rosemary or ½ teaspoon dried rosemary, crushed
1	teaspoon snipped fresh oregano or ½ teaspoon dried oregano, crushed
¼	teaspoon crushed red pepper
1	14.5-ounce can diced tomatoes
½	cup dry white wine or reduced-sodium chicken broth
¼	cup tomato paste
¼	cup shaved Parmesan cheese
1	tablespoon snipped fresh parsley

❶ Sprinkle chicken pieces with salt and pepper. Place chicken in the slow cooker. Top with cannellini beans, fennel, sweet pepper, onion, garlic, rosemary, oregano, and crushed red pepper. In a medium bowl combine tomatoes, white wine, and tomato paste; pour over mixture in the slow cooker.

❷ Cover and cook on low-heat setting for 5 to 6 hours or on high-heat setting for 2½ to 3 hours.

❸ Sprinkle each serving with Parmesan cheese and parsley.

PER SERVING 225 cal., 4 g total fat (1 g sat. fat), 68 mg chol., 584 mg sodium, 23 g carbo., 7 g fiber, 25 g pro.

Chicken, Barley
& Leek Stew

Chicken à la King

This elegant dish is a great use of leftover chicken or turkey.

PREP 20 minutes   **COOK** 6 to 7 hours (low) or 3 to 3 ½ hours (high)
STAND 10 minutes   **COOKER SIZE** 4- to 5-quart
MAKES 8 to 10 servings

- 4 cups chopped cooked chicken or turkey
- 2 10.75-ounce cans condensed cream of chicken soup
- 2 4.5-ounce jars sliced mushrooms, drained
- ¾ cup chopped green sweet pepper (1 medium)
- ¾ cup chopped celery
- 1 5-ounce can (⅔ cup) evaporated milk
- ½ cup bottled roasted red sweet peppers, drained and coarsely chopped
- ½ cup chopped onion
- 3 tablespoons dry sherry or dry white wine
- 1 teaspoon dried basil, crushed
- ½ teaspoon black pepper
- 1 10-ounce package frozen peas
- 4 or 5 English muffins, split and toasted; 8 to 10 baked potatoes; or 4 to 5 cups hot cooked rice

1 In the slow cooker combine chicken, chicken soup, mushrooms, green sweet pepper, celery, evaporated milk, roasted sweet peppers, onion, sherry, basil, and black pepper.

2 Cover and cook on low-heat setting for 6 to 7 hours or on high-heat setting for 3 to 3 ½ hours. Turn off cooker. Stir in frozen peas. Cover and let stand for 10 minutes.

3 Serve chicken mixture over English muffin halves, baked potatoes, or hot cooked rice.

PER SERVING 357 cal., 12 g total fat (4 g sat. fat), 74 mg chol., 940 mg sodium, 31 g carbo., 5 g fiber, 28 g pro.

Chicken, Barley & Leek Stew

Get a generous dose of whole grains in this healthful stew.

PREP 25 minutes   **COOK** 4 to 5 hours (low) or 2 to 2 ½ hours (high)
COOKER SIZE 4- to 5-quart   **MAKES** 6 servings

- 1 pound skinless, boneless chicken thighs, trimmed and cut into 1-inch pieces
- 1 tablespoon olive oil
- 1 49-ounce can reduced-sodium chicken broth
- 1 cup regular barley (not quick-cooking)
- 3 medium leeks, halved lengthwise and sliced
- 2 medium carrots, thinly sliced
- 1½ teaspoons dried basil or Italian seasoning, crushed
- ¼ teaspoon cracked black pepper
  Slivered fresh basil or snipped fresh parsley (optional)

1 In a large skillet cook chicken in hot oil until brown on all sides. In the slow cooker combine chicken, chicken broth, barley, leeks, carrots, dried basil, and pepper.

2 Cover and cook on low-heat setting for 4 to 5 hours or on high-heat setting for 2 to 2 ½ hours or until barley is tender.

3 If desired, top with fresh basil or parsley before serving.

PER SERVING 248 cal., 6 g total fat (1 g sat. fat), 63 mg chol., 558 mg sodium, 63 g carbo., 6 g fiber, 22 g pro.

quick tip   Adding ingredients such as fresh herbs or spinach to the slow cooker right before serving preserves their vibrance and flavor and gives the slow-cooked dish the fresh touch it often needs.

{ Take a batch of chicken soup to an under-the-weather friend —even on the busiest of days. }

Chicken Merlot with Mushrooms

Make this recipe with Cabernet Sauvignon, Pinot Noir, or Zinfandel and it could simply be called "Chicken with Red Wine and Mushrooms."

PREP 25 minutes   **COOK** 5 to 6 hours (low) or 2 ½ to 3 hours (high) + 15 minutes (high)   **COOKER SIZE** 3 ½- to 5-quart
MAKES 6 servings

3	cups sliced fresh mushrooms (8 ounces)
1	cup chopped onion (1 large)
2	cloves garlic, minced
2 ½	to 3 pounds meaty chicken pieces (breast halves, thighs, and drumsticks), skinned
¾	cup reduced-sodium chicken broth
1	6-ounce can tomato paste
¼	cup Merlot or other dry red wine or chicken broth
1 ½	teaspoons dried basil, crushed
½	teaspoon salt
¼	teaspoon black pepper
2	tablespoons cornstarch
2	tablespoons cold water
3	tablespoons shredded Parmesan cheese

❶ In the slow cooker place mushrooms, onion, and garlic. Add chicken. In a medium bowl combine chicken broth, tomato paste, wine, basil, salt, and pepper. Pour over chicken in cooker.

❷ Cover and cook on low-heat setting for 5 to 6 hours or on high-heat setting for 2 ½ to 3 hours.

❸ Transfer chicken to a serving platter, reserving cooking liquid. Cover chicken with foil to keep warm.

❹ If using low-heat setting, turn to high-heat setting. In a small bowl combine cornstarch and water. Stir into liquid in cooker. Cover and cook about 15 minutes more or until thickened. Spoon sauce over chicken. Sprinkle with Parmesan cheese.

PER SERVING 249 cal., 8 g total fat (4 g sat. fat), 75 mg chol., 639 mg sodium, 13 g carbo., 2 g fiber, 30 g pro.

Chicken-Corn Chowder

When it takes 15 minutes or less to stir together a few ingredients in the slow cooker, it's definitely a task you can tackle before you leave the house for the day—and you're richly rewarded with dinner at the end of it.

PREP 15 minutes   **COOK** 4 to 6 hours (low) or 2 to 3 hours (high)
COOKER SIZE 3 ½- or 4-quart   **MAKES** 6 servings

1	pound skinless, boneless chicken thighs, cut into ½- to ¾-inch pieces
2	10.75-ounce cans condensed cream of potato or cream of chicken soup
1	11-ounce can whole kernel corn with sweet peppers, undrained
1 ½	cups sliced celery (3 stalks)
1	cup water
1	cup half-and-half or light cream

❶ In the slow cooker combine the chicken, soup, undrained corn, celery, and water.

❷ Cover and cook on low-heat setting for 4 to 6 hours or on high-heat setting for 2 to 3 hours.

❸ Stir half-and-half into slow cooker. Ladle chowder into 6 bowls.

PER SERVING 261 cal., 10 g total fat (5 g sat. fat), 86 mg chol., 1,029 mg sodium, 24 g carbo., 3 g fiber, 19 g pro.

Chicken Cassoulet-Style Soup

There are many versions of cassoulet—and dishes inspired by it, such as this soup—but all of them contain the same two ingredients: sausage and white beans.

PREP 25 minutes   **COOK** 5 to 7 hours (low) or 2 ½ to 3 ½ hours (high)
COOKER SIZE 3 ½- or 4-quart   **MAKES** 6 servings

1	pound boneless, skinless chicken thighs, cut into ½-inch pieces
8	ounces smoked turkey sausage, cut into ½-inch slices
1	26-ounce jar pasta sauce with red wine and herbs
1	15- to 19-ounce can white kidney (cannellini) beans, rinsed and drained
1 ⅓	cups water
1	teaspoon dried oregano, crushed

❶ In the slow cooker combine chicken, sausage, pasta sauce, beans, water, and oregano.

❷ Cover and cook on low-heat setting for 5 to 7 hours or on high-heat setting for 2 ½ to 3 ½ hours.

PER SERVING 286 cal., 7 g total fat (2 g sat. fat), 88 mg chol., 1,178 mg sodium, 33 g carbo., 9 g fiber, 30 g pro.

Smokin' Jambalaya

Smokin' Jambalaya

Fire-roasted tomatoes add a smoky touch to this New Orleans classic.

PREP 30 minutes **COOK** 6 to 8 hours (low) or 3 to 4 hours (high) + 30 minutes (high) **COOKER SIZE** 3½- or 4-quart **MAKES** 6 servings

1½	pounds skinless, boneless chicken thighs
4	ounces smoked turkey sausage
1	cup onion, chopped (1 large)
1	cup thinly sliced celery (2 stalks)
1	14.5-ounce can fire-roasted diced tomatoes, undrained
1	cup reduced-sodium chicken broth
2	tablespoons tomato paste
2	tablespoons quick-cooking tapioca, crushed
1	tablespoon Worcestershire sauce
1	tablespoon lemon juice
1	serrano pepper, seeded and finely chopped (see note, page 19)
3	cloves garlic, minced
½	teaspoon dried thyme, crushed
½	teaspoon dried oregano, crushed
¼	teaspoon cayenne pepper
⅛	teaspoon salt
8	ounces medium shrimp, peeled and deveined
½	cup yellow sweet pepper, chopped (1 small)
2	cups frozen cut okra
1	14.8-ounce pouch cooked long grain or brown rice

1 Cut chicken and sausage into bite-size pieces. In the slow cooker combine chicken, sausage, onion, and celery. Stir in undrained tomatoes, broth, tomato paste, tapioca, Worcestershire sauce, lemon juice, serrano pepper, garlic, thyme, oregano, cayenne pepper, and salt.

2 Cover and cook on low-heat setting for 6 to 8 hours or on high-heat setting for 3 to 4 hours.

3 If using low-heat setting, turn to high-heat setting. Stir in shrimp, sweet pepper, and okra. Cover and cook about 30 minutes more or until shrimp turn opaque.

4 Prepare rice according to package directions; serve with jambalaya.

PER SERVING 276 cal., 6 g total fat (1 g sat. fat), 112 mg chol., 490 mg sodium, 28 g carbo., 3 g fiber, 26 g pro.

Paella with Chicken & Shrimp

Because the shrimp is already cooked, add it at the very end of the cooking time—just to warm it up—so it doesn't overcook and get tough and rubbery.

PREP 25 minutes **COOK** 8 to 10 hours (low) or 4 to 5 hours (high) + 30 minutes(high) **STAND** 10 minutes **COOKER SIZE** 6-quart **MAKES** 10 servings

½	cup onion, chopped (1 medium)
¾	cup green sweet pepper, chopped (1 medium)
2	cloves garlic, minced
3	medium tomatoes, chopped
2	cups reduced-sodium chicken broth
1	cup water
2	teaspoons dried oregano, crushed
½	teaspoon salt
½	teaspoon ground turmeric
½	teaspoon black pepper
½	teaspoon bottled hot pepper sauce (optional)
3	pounds chicken thighs and drumsticks, skinned
8	ounces smoked turkey sausage link, halved lengthwise and sliced
2	cups uncooked long grain rice
8	ounces cooked, peeled and deveined shrimp (tails removed)
1	cup frozen peas

1 In the slow cooker place onion, sweet pepper, garlic, tomatoes, broth, water, oregano, salt, turmeric, black pepper, and hot pepper sauce, (if using); stir to combine. Top with chicken and sausage.

2 Cover and cook on low-heat setting for 8 to 10 hours or on high-heat setting for 4 to 5 hours. Stir in rice. If using low-heat setting, adjust to high-heat setting. Cover; cook 30 to 35 minutes more or until rice is tender. Stir in cooked shrimp and peas. Let stand, covered, for 10 minutes.

PER SERVING 312 cal., 5 g total fat (1 g sat. fat), 121 mg chol., 568 mg sodium, 36 g carbo., 2 g fiber, 28 g pro.

Moroccan Chicken Stew

Chicken breast meat will stay juicier in the slow cooker if it's cooked on the bone—as it is here.

PREP 30 minutes   **COOK** 6½ to 7 hours (low) or 3½ to 4 hours (high)
COOKER SIZE 6½- or 7-quart   **MAKES** 6 servings

4	carrots, peeled and sliced
2	large onions, halved and thinly sliced
6	small chicken breast halves, skinned (2½ to 3 pounds total)
½	teaspoon salt
⅓	cup raisins
⅓	cup dried apricots, coarsely chopped
1	14-ounce can reduced-sodium chicken broth
¼	cup tomato paste
2	tablespoons all-purpose flour
2	tablespoons lemon juice
2	cloves garlic, minced
1½	teaspoons ground cumin
1½	teaspoons ground ginger
1	teaspoon ground cinnamon
¾	teaspoon black pepper
2	cups hot cooked whole wheat couscous
3	tablespoons pine nuts, toasted
	Fresh cilantro sprigs (optional)

① Place carrots and onions in slow cooker. Sprinkle chicken with salt; add to cooker. Top chicken with raisins and apricots. In a medium bowl whisk together broth, tomato paste, flour, lemon juice, garlic, cumin, ginger, cinnamon, and pepper. Add to slow cooker.

② Cover and cook on low-heat setting for 6½ to 7 hours or on high-heat setting for 3½ to 4 hours. Serve in shallow bowls with couscous. Sprinkle with pine nuts and cilantro.

PER SERVING 338 cal., 5 g total fat (1 g sat. fat), 71 mg chol., 535 mg sodium, 41 g carbo., 6 g fiber, 35 g pro.

Clam Chowder

This low-fat and low-calorie chowder is deceptively creamy and rich-tasting. Fat-free half-and-half thickened with a little cornstarch provides the base.

PREP 25 minutes   **COOK** 4½ to 5 hours (low) or 2 to 2½ hours (high) + 30 minutes (high)   **COOKER SIZE** 3- to 4-quart   **MAKES** 8 servings

3	cups chopped celery (6 stalks)
1½	cups chopped onions (3 medium)
1	cup chopped carrots (2 medium)
2	8-ounce bottles clam juice
1	14-ounce can reduced-sodium chicken broth
1½	teaspoons dried thyme, crushed
½	teaspoon salt
½	teaspoon coarsely ground black pepper
1	cup fat-free half-and-half
2	tablespoons cornstarch
2	6.5-ounce cans chopped clams, drained
2	tablespoons dry sherry (optional)
4	slices turkey bacon, crisp-cooked, drained, and crumbled
	Chopped green onion (optional)

① In the slow cooker combine celery, onions, carrots, clam juice, broth, thyme, salt, and pepper.

② Cover and cook on low-heat setting for 4½ to 5 hours or on high-heat setting for 2 to 2½ hours.

③ If using low-heat setting, turn to high-heat setting. In a small bowl combine half-and-half and cornstarch. Stir half-and-half mixture, clams, and, if desired, sherry into cooker. Cover and cook for 30 minutes more. Sprinkle each serving with crumbled bacon and, if desired, green onion.

PER SERVING 144 cal., 2 g total fat (0 g sat. fat), 38 mg chol., 309 mg sodium, 14 g carbo., 2 g fiber, 15 g pro.

{ Slow cookers have a benefit in addition to convenience: Big-batch cooking usually means leftovers. }

Pasta with Eggplant Sauce

Pasta with Eggplant Sauce

Cubes of meaty eggplant stand in for meat in this vegetarian pasta sauce.

PREP 20 minutes   **COOK** 7 to 8 hours (low) or 3½ to 4 hours (high)
COOKER SIZE 3½- to 5-quart   **MAKES** 6 servings

- 1   medium eggplant
- ½   cup chopped onion (1 medium)
- 1   28-ounce can Italian-style tomatoes, undrained and cut up
- 1   6-ounce can Italian-style tomato paste
- 1   4-ounce can sliced mushrooms, drained
- 2   cloves garlic, minced
- ¼   cup dry red wine
- ¼   cup water
- 1½   teaspoons dried oregano, crushed
- ⅓   cup pitted kalamata olives or pitted ripe olives, sliced (optional)
- 2   tablespoons snipped fresh parsley
- Salt
- Black pepper
- 4   cups hot cooked penne pasta
- ¼   cup grated or shredded Parmesan cheese
- 2   tablespoons toasted pine nuts (see note, page 31) (optional)

❶ Peel eggplant, if desired; cut eggplant into 1-inch cubes. In the slow cooker combine eggplant, onion, undrained tomatoes, tomato paste, drained mushrooms, garlic, wine, water, and oregano.

❷ Cover and cook on low-heat setting for 7 to 8 hours or on high-heat setting for 3½ to 4 hours. Stir in olives (if using) and parsley. If desired, season to taste with salt and pepper. Serve over pasta; sprinkle with Parmesan cheese. If desired, garnish with pine nuts.

PER SERVING 249 cal., 3 g total fat (1 g sat. fat), 2 mg chol., 520 mg sodium, 46 g carbo., 6 g fiber, 9 g pro.

Curried Lentil Soup

Top each serving of this Indian-style soup with a spoonful of yogurt, if you like, to help cool the fire from the jalapeño and curry powder.

PREP 20 minutes   **COOK** 8 to 10 hours (low) or 4 to 5 hours (high)
COOKER SIZE 4- to 5-quart   **MAKES** 4 to 6 servings

- 1   pound sweet potatoes, peeled and coarsely chopped (2 medium)
- 1   cup dry brown or yellow lentils, rinsed and drained
- 1   cup onion, chopped (1 large)
- 1   medium jalapeño, seeded and finely chopped (see note, page 19)
- 3   cloves garlic, minced
- 1   14.5-ounce can diced tomatoes, undrained
- 3   14-ounce cans vegetable broth
- 1   tablespoon curry powder
- 1   teaspoon grated fresh ginger
- Plain yogurt or sour cream (optional)
- Small fresh chiles and/or crushed red pepper (optional)

❶ In the slow cooker combine sweet potatoes, lentils, onion, jalapeño, and garlic. Add undrained tomatoes, broth, curry powder, and ginger.

❷ Cover and cook on low-heat setting for 8 to 10 hours or on high-heat setting for 4 to 5 hours. If desired, top each serving with yogurt and garnish with chiles.

PER SERVING 316 cal., 2 g total fat (0 g sat. fat), 0 mg chol., 1,425 mg sodium, 60 g carbo., 18 g fiber, 18 g pro.

Split Pea Plus Soup

The "plus" in this super simple soup is the addition of smoked sausage, seasoned diced tomatoes, and shredded carrot to canned split pea with ham soup.

PREP 15 minutes   **COOK** 7 to 9 hours (low) or 3½ to 4½ (high)
COOKER SIZE 3½- or 4-quart   **MAKES** 6 servings

- 3   cups water
- 2   11.5-ounce cans condensed split pea with ham soup
- 1   14.5-ounce can diced tomatoes with garlic and onion, undrained
- 8   ounces cooked smoked sausage, sliced
- 1   cup purchased shredded carrot

❶ In the slow cooker combine water, soup, undrained tomatoes, sausage, and carrot.

❷ Cover and cook on low-heat setting for 7 to 9 hours or on high-heat setting for 3½ to 4½ hours.

PER SERVING 330 cal., 16 g total fat (6 g sat. fat), 32 mg chol., 1,724 mg sodium, 30 g carbo., 3 g fiber, 18 g pro.

A nearly endless selection of breads, spreads, fillings, and toppings makes sandwiches and pizza family-favorite foods—not to mention the fact that they offer up fork-free eating. Everyone likes that!

247

256

259

sandwiches & pizzas

244

Bean & Cheese Quesadillas

There's a surprise inside these savory quesadillas. Diced peaches add a little bit of sweetness to the filling. It's not so unlike having peaches or pineapple in salsa.

PREP 15 minutes **BAKE** 12 minutes **OVEN** 400°F
MAKES 4 servings

- ½   16-ounce can refried beans (¾ cup)
- 1   8-ounce can whole kernel corn, drained
- ¼   cup bottled salsa
- 1   canned chipotle chile pepper in adobo sauce, drained and chopped (optional) (see note, page 19)
- 8   8-inch flour tortillas
- 2   tablespoons cooking oil
- 1   cup packaged shredded broccoli (broccoli slaw mix)
- 1   4- to 4 ¼-ounce can diced peaches, drained
- 1   cup finely shredded Mexican cheese blend (4 ounces)
     Purchased guacamole dip, sour cream, and/or bottled salsa

❶ Preheat oven to 400°F. In a small bowl combine refried beans, corn, ¼ cup salsa, and, if desired, chipotle chile pepper. Brush 1 side of each tortilla with some of the oil. Spread bean mixture over the plain side of 4 tortillas; set aside.

❷ In another bowl combine broccoli slaw and peaches and spoon on top of bean mixture. Top with cheese. Top with remaining tortillas, oiled sides up; press down lightly. Place on a large baking sheet.

❸ Bake for 12 to 15 minutes or until golden brown and cheese is melted. Cut into quarters. Serve with guacamole dip, sour cream, and/or additional salsa.

PER SERVING 444 cal., 21 g total fat (7 g sat. fat), 25 mg chol., 825 mg sodium, 50 g carbo., 5 g fiber, 14 g pro.

Fruit & Cheese Pitas

Minus the lettuce, these fruit and cheese pockets make a filling, sustaining breakfast too.

START TO FINISH 20 minutes **MAKES** 2 servings

- ½   cup low-fat cottage cheese
- ½   cup shredded reduced-fat cheddar cheese (2 ounces)
- 2   kiwifruit, peeled and chopped, or ½ cup small strawberries, hulled and chopped
- ¼   cup drained pineapple tidbits
- 1   large whole wheat or regular pita bread round, halved crosswise
- 4   Bibb lettuce leaves
- 2   tablespoons sliced almonds, pecan pieces, or walnut pieces; toasted, if desired (optional) (see note, page 31)

❶ In a small bowl combine cottage cheese, cheddar cheese, kiwifruit, and pineapple. Stir gently to mix. Set aside.

❷ Line pita bread halves with Bibb leaves. Spoon some of the fruit and cheese mixture into each half. If desired, sprinkle with almonds. Serve immediately.

PER SERVING 271 cal., 8 g total fat (4 g sat. fat), 22 mg chol., 642 mg sodium, 36 g carbo., 5 g fiber, 18 g pro.

quick tip   These healthful pitas make a terrific lunch. To tote them somewhere, keep the bread, lettuce, filling, and almonds separate until it's time to eat or the pita will get soggy. The lettuce and filling should be refrigerated—the nuts and bread do not.

{ Cultures around the world love sandwiches—think of pitas, tortillas, crostini, and panini. }

Shrimp Quesadillas

Shrimp Quesadillas

Garlic or three-pepper hummus and marinated artichokes quickly add flavor to these seafood quesadillas.

START TO FINISH 20 minutes   **MAKES** 4 servings

  Nonstick cooking spray
4 8-inch vegetable tortillas
½ 7-ounce carton garlic or spicy three-pepper hummus (⅓ cup)
6 ounces peeled, deveined cooked medium shrimp
1 6-ounce jar marinated artichoke hearts or half a 16-ounce jar pickled mixed vegetables, drained and coarsely chopped
1 4-ounce package crumbled feta cheese

❶ Coat 1 side of each tortilla with cooking spray. Place tortillas, sprayed sides down, on work surface; spread with hummus. Top half of each tortilla with shrimp, artichokes, and cheese. Fold tortillas in half, pressing gently.

❷ Heat large nonstick skillet or griddle on medium heat for 1 minute. Cook quesadillas, two at a time, for 4 to 6 minutes or until golden brown and heated through, turning once.

PER SERVING 430 cal., 20 g total fat (7 g sat. fat), 108 mg chol., 1,098 mg sodium, 42 g carbo., 4 g fiber, 21 g pro.

---

quick tip Hummus is a handy ingredient to have around as a sandwich spread, party dip, or quick snack with veggies or crackers. Purchased hummus is convenient, but it's not inexpensive. The basic ingredients for hummus—canned chickpeas, lemon juice, olive oil, garlic, and tahini are relatively inexpensive. Make a big batch of hummus from your favorite recipe and freeze it in small containers. Thaw it in the refrigerator. The consistency will change slightly—it might get a little grainy—but after stirring, it will be nearly as smooth as when you first made it.

Tuna Bruschetta Sandwiches

Here's a new take on the classic tuna melt. Thick slices of Italian bread slathered with spinach artichoke dip, then topped with marinated tuna, sweet peppers, and cheese then broiled until bubbly.

START TO FINISH 20 minutes   **MAKES** 4 sandwiches

8 1-inch slices country Italian bread
1 8-ounce package frozen spinach-artichoke dip, thawed
2 5-ounce pouches lemon pepper marinated chunk light tuna
2 small red and/or yellow sweet peppers, cut into thin strips
1 cup shredded Italian cheese blend (4 ounces)

❶ Preheat broiler. Place bread on a baking sheet. Broil 4 inches from heat about 2 minutes or until toasted. Remove from oven.

❷ Turn bread slices over; spread with dip. Top with tuna, pepper strips, and cheese. Broil for 3 to 4 minutes or until cheese melts and mixture is heated through.

PER SANDWICH 488 cal., 15 g total fat (6 g sat. fat), 60 mg chol., 1,132 mg sodium, 47 g carbo., 3 g fiber, 40 g pro.

Turkey & Tomato Wraps

If you like cheese with your turkey and tomato, Swiss, Muenster, or provolone would be delicious in this wrap.

START TO FINISH 15 minutes   **MAKES** 4 wraps

4 butterhead lettuce leaves (Bibb or Boston)
4 ounces very thinly sliced cooked turkey breast
2 teaspoons honey mustard or low-fat mayonnaise dressing or salad dressing
1 small roma tomato, halved and very thinly sliced

❶ Place lettuce leaves on a flat surface. Cut leaves in half lengthwise and remove center vein.

❷ Place ½ ounce turkey on each leaf just below the center. Spread honey mustard over turkey. Top with tomato slices. Roll up, starting from a short side. Secure with wooden toothpicks.

PER WRAP 35 cal., 1 g total fat (0 g sat. fat), 11 mg chol., 338 mg sodium, 3 g carbo., 0 g fiber, 5 g pro.

Chicken & Hummus Pitas ♥

When the craving for a chicken gyro hits and there are no gyro stands in sight, these Greek-style sandwiches will fill the bill.

START TO FINISH 25 minutes **MAKES** 4 servings

- 1 tablespoon olive oil
- 1 teaspoon lemon juice
- ¼ teaspoon paprika
- Dash salt
- Dash ground black pepper
- 2 skinless, boneless chicken breast halves (about 12 ounces total)
- 2 large whole wheat pita bread rounds, halved
- ½ of a 7-ounce carton hummus
- ¾ cup coarsely chopped roma tomatoes
- ½ cup thinly sliced cucumber
- ⅓ cup plain lowfat yogurt

1 In a small bowl combine oil, lemon juice, paprika, salt, and pepper. Place chicken on the unheated rack of a broiler pan. Brush both sides of chicken with the oil mixture. Broil 4 to 5 inches from heat for 7 minutes. Turn chicken; broil 5 to 8 minutes more or until chicken is no longer pink. Cool slightly; cut into strips.

2 To serve, carefully open pita halves and spread hummus inside; stuff with chicken, tomatoes, cucumber, and yogurt.

PER SERVING 279 cal., 8 g total fat (1 g sat. fat), 51 mg chol., 328 mg sodium, 26 g carbo., 4 g fiber, 26 g pro.

Chicken Sandwiches

Though most sandwiches can be eaten with your fingers (that's kind of the point!), these towering beauties are a real knife-and-fork meal.

START TO FINISH 20 minutes **MAKES** 4 sandwiches

- 8 ounces asparagus spears, trimmed
- 2 tablespoons olive oil
- Salt
- Coarsely ground black pepper
- 4 4-inch portobello mushroom caps
- 4 skinless, boneless chicken breast halves (1 pound)
- 8 ½-inch slices country Italian bread*
- 1 8-ounce tub cream cheese spread with chive and onion

1 Tear off a 36×18-inch piece of heavy foil; fold in half to make an 18-inch square. Place asparagus in center of foil; drizzle with 1 teaspoon of the olive oil and sprinkle lightly with salt and pepper. Bring up opposite edges of foil and seal with a double fold. Fold remaining edges to completely enclose asparagus, leaving space for steam to escape. Set aside. Remove stems from mushrooms. Brush chicken and mushrooms with the remaining olive oil; sprinkle lightly with salt and pepper.

2 For a charcoal grill, place chicken, mushrooms, and foil packet with asparagus on the rack of an uncovered grill directly over medium coals. Grill for 12 to 15 minutes or until chicken is no longer pink (170°F) and mushrooms are tender, turning chicken and mushrooms once halfway through grilling. (For a gas grill, preheat grill. Reduce heat to medium. Place chicken, mushrooms, and foil packet on grill rack over heat. Cover; grill as above.) Remove chicken, mushrooms, and foil packet from grill; slice mushrooms.

3 Toast bread slices on grill rack for 1 to 2 minutes, turning once. Spread 1 side of each bread slice with cream cheese. On serving plates stack half of the bread slices, spread sides up, chicken, remaining bread slices, mushrooms, and asparagus.

PER SANDWICH 583 cal., 29 g total fat (15 g sat. fat), 121 mg chol., 751 mg sodium, 40 g carbo., 4 g fiber, 37 g pro.

*NOTE: If bread slices are too large, use halved slices of bread.

Chicken Sandwiches

Chicken Panini Sandwiches

Spicy Taco Tostadas

Chopped tomatoes and jalapeño add a fresh touch to a tub of refrigerated taco sauce with shredded chicken.

START TO FINISH 15 minutes **MAKES** 4 tostadas

- 1 18-ounce tub refrigerated taco sauce with shredded chicken
- 2 medium tomatoes, chopped
- 1 to 2 jalapeños, seeded and chopped (see note, page 19)
- 5 tostada shells
- 3 cups packaged shredded lettuce
   Shredded Mexican cheese blend (optional)

❶ In a large skillet heat the taco sauce with shredded chicken, tomato, and jalapeño on medium heat until heated through.

❷ Place 4 tostada shells on a serving platter. Top with shredded lettuce. Spoon chicken mixture on the lettuce. Coarsely crush the remaining tostada shell; sprinkle over taco mixture. If desired, sprinkle with cheese.

PER TOSTADA 236 cal., 8 g total fat (2 g sat. fat), 57 mg chol., 1,106 mg sodium, 25 g carbo., 5 g fiber, 15 g pro.

Spicy Taco Tostadas

Chicken Panini Sandwiches ♥

These Italian-style grilled sandwiches are one delicious way to serve leftover roast or grilled chicken.

START TO FINISH 20 minutes **MAKES** 4 sandwiches

- ⅓ cup fat-free mayonnaise dressing or salad dressing
- 2 cloves garlic, minced
- 1 teaspoon dried Italian seasoning, crushed
- 8 ½-inch-thick slices hearty multigrain bread
- 1½ cups sliced or shredded cooked chicken breast
- ½ cup bottled roasted red sweet peppers, drained and cut into strips
- 1 cup lightly packed fresh basil
- 4 teaspoons olive oil

❶ Preheat an electric sandwich press, a covered indoor grill, a grill pan, or a skillet. To assemble sandwiches, in a small bowl combine mayonnaise dressing, garlic, and Italian seasoning. Spread 1 side of each bread slice with the mayonnaise mixture. Layer chicken, roasted sweet peppers, and basil leaves on half of the bread slices. Top with the remaining bread slices, spread sides down. Brush top and bottom of each sandwich lightly with oil.

❷ Place sandwiches (half at a time, if necessary) in the sandwich press or indoor grill; cover and cook about 6 minutes or until bread is toasted. (If using a grill pan or skillet, place sandwiches on preheated grill pan or skillet. Weight sandwiches down and grill about 2 minutes or until bread is lightly toasted. Turn sandwiches over, weight down, and grill until the remaining side is lightly toasted.)

PER SANDWICH 312 cal., 9 g total fat (1 g sat. fat), 47 mg chol., 390 mg sodium, 35 g carbo., 9 g fiber, 25 g pro.

quick tip If you don't have leftover chicken breast, purchase a rotisserie chicken from the supermarket deli for the breast meat in these sandwiches. Use the thighs and drumsticks for another meal.

Horseradish Pork Wrap ♥

If you don't have cooked pork loin roast, you can certainly use leftover pork chops or pork tenderloin.

START TO FINISH 15 minutes   **MAKES** 4 servings

- ¼ cup light sour cream
- 1 tablespoon prepared horseradish
- 4 8-inch whole wheat flour tortillas
- 4 cups shredded romaine or fresh baby spinach
- 8 ounces cooked pork loin, thinly sliced
- 2 cups bite-size red sweet pepper strips

❶ In a small bowl combine sour cream and horseradish. Spread sour cream mixture on tortillas. Top with romaine, pork, and sweet pepper strips. Roll up tortillas.

PER SERVING 263 cal., 9 g total fat (3 g sat. fat), 35 mg chol., 373 mg sodium, 23 g carbo., 13 g fiber, 22 g pro.

quick tip   The sour cream-horseradish spread is also terrific on roast beef sandwiches or served as a sauce with grilled steak. If you like the fiery flavor of horseradish, add a little more to your taste.

Horseradish Pork Wrap

Ham & Cheese Pizza Tortillas

Using tomato-based pizza sauce will make these Italian-style tortilla stacks a little lighter than the Alfredo sauce.

PREP 15 minutes   **BAKE** 12 minutes   **MAKES** 8 servings

- ¼ cup purchased pesto
- 12 7- to 8-inch flour tortillas
- ½ pound finely chopped cooked ham (1½ cups)
- 2 cups shredded mozzarella cheese (8 ounces)
- 1 8-ounce can pizza sauce or ½ cup Alfredo pasta sauce

❶ Preheat oven to 425°F. Spread the pesto on 1 side of 4 tortillas. Top each with a second tortilla to make 4 stacks. Stir together the ham and half of the cheese. Sprinkle ham mixture over second layer of each tortilla stack. Top with the remaining tortillas. Spread top layer with pizza sauce or Alfredo sauce; sprinkle with remaining cheese.

❷ Place the tortilla stacks on an ungreased baking sheet. Bake for 12 to 15 minutes or until cheese is melted. To serve, cut each stack into wedges.

PER SERVING 315 cal., 16 g total fat (6 g sat. fat), 32 mg chol., 772 mg sodium, 26 g carbo., 1 g fiber, 16 g pro.

Curried Ham & Brie Sandwiches

A spread made of mango chutney, mayo, and curry powder livens up these ham and cheese sandwiches.

START TO FINISH 12 minutes   **MAKES** 4 sandwiches

- ¼ cup mango chutney
- 2 tablespoons mayonnaise or salad dressing
- ½ teaspoon curry powder
- 8 ½-inch slices country Italian bread
- ⅓ cup creamy-style Brie cheese or regular Brie cheese
- 12 ounces thinly sliced cooked ham
  Leaf lettuce, sliced tomato, and/or sliced sweet onion (optional)

❶ Place chutney in a small bowl; cut up any large fruit pieces. Stir in mayonnaise and curry powder. Set aside.

❷ Spread 4 of the bread slices with the Brie cheese. Top with ham. If desired, add lettuce, tomato, and/or onion. Spread chutney mixture on the remaining bread slices. Place bread slices, spread sides down, on top of sandwiches.

PER SANDWICH 363 cal., 18 g total fat (6 g sat. fat), 63 mg chol., 1,498 mg sodium, 30 g carbo., 3 g fiber, 20 g pro.

Ham & Pineapple Roll-Ups

Ham & Pineapple Roll-Ups

The combination of ham and pineapple isn't just for pizza. These crunchy, veggie-packed wraps feature the sweet and salty flavors of that classic combination too.

START TO FINISH 15 minutes **MAKES** 4 roll-ups

- 1 cup packaged shredded broccoli (broccoli slaw mix)
- ⅔ cup tub-style cream cheese spread with pineapple
- ½ cup chopped fresh pineapple
- ⅛ teaspoon black pepper
- 4 10-inch flour tortillas
- 1 9-ounce container thinly sliced deli-style cooked ham

❶ In a small bowl stir together shredded broccoli, ⅓ cup of the cream cheese spread, pineapple, and pepper; set aside.

❷ Spread flour tortillas with the remaining ⅓ cup cream cheese spread. Divide ham evenly among the tortillas. Spoon broccoli mixture on top of the ham. Roll up; cut in half crosswise to serve.

PER ROLL-UP 350 cal., 17 g total fat (9 g sat. fat), 61 mg chol., 1,013 mg sodium, 32 g carbo., 2 g fiber, 16 g pro.

Double Dill Ham & Slaw Sandwich

The "double dill" in these sandwiches is delivered in a slather of sour cream dill-flavored dip and in thin slices of crunchy dill pickles.

START TO FINISH 11 minutes **MAKES** 4 sandwiches

- 2 cups packaged shredded cabbage with carrot (coleslaw mix)
- ¼ cup sour cream dill-flavored dip
- 4 kaiser rolls, split
- 12 ounces thinly sliced cooked deli ham
- 8 thin lengthwise dill pickle slices

❶ In a medium bowl combine shredded cabbage and dill dip; spoon onto roll bottoms. Top with ham, pickle slices, and roll tops.

PER SANDWICH 300 cal., 7 g total fat (3 g sat. fat), 47 mg chol., 1,516 mg sodium, 35 g carbo., 2 g fiber, 21 g pro.

Salmon & Asparagus Wraps

These colorful wraps make elegant picnic food—and they can be made up to 6 hours before serving. If you're not eating them right way, be sure to keep them chilled.

START TO FINISH 25 minutes **MAKES** 4 servings

- 12 thin fresh asparagus spears (about 4 ounces)
- ½ cup tube-style cream cheese spread with chive and onion
- 2 teaspoons finely shredded lemon peel
- 2 tablespoons lemon juice
- ⅛ teaspoon cayenne pepper
- 6 ounces smoked salmon, flaked, with skin and bones removed
- 4 6- to 7-inch whole wheat flour tortillas
- 2 cups fresh spinach leaves
- ½ of a medium red sweet pepper, seeded and cut into thin bite-size strips

❶ Snap off and discard woody bases from asparagus. In a covered medium saucepan, cook asparagus spears in a small amount of boiling lightly salted water for 2 to 3 minutes or until crisp-tender. Drain and plunge into ice water to cool quickly. Drain again; pat dry with paper towels.

❷ In a medium bowl stir together cream cheese, lemon peel, lemon juice, and cayenne pepper. Fold in flaked salmon. Spread on tortillas. For wraps, arrange spinach, 3 of the asparagus spears, and one-fourth of the sweet pepper strips over salmon mixture on each tortilla. Roll up tortillas. If necessary, secure with toothpicks. Serve immediately or wrap in plastic wrap and chill up to 6 hours.

PER SERVING 298 cal., 14 g total fat (8 g sat. fat), 40 mg chol., 777 mg sodium, 27 g carbo., 3 g fiber, 13 g pro

Salmon & Asparagus Wraps

Beef & Cucumber Stacks

This hearty sandwich has a built-in salad: Thin slices of cucumber drizzled with a green onion-yogurt dressing adds crunch and freshness.

START TO FINISH 15 minutes **MAKES** 4 sandwiches

- 8 slices dark rye bread
- ¼ cup mayonnaise or salad dressing
- 8 ounces thinly sliced deli roast beef
- 1 small cucumber, very thinly sliced
- ½ cup plain yogurt
- ¼ cup sliced green onions (2)
- ½ teaspoon dried Italian seasoning
  Salt
  Black pepper

❶ If desired, toast bread. Place a slice of rye bread on each of 4 plates; spread with mayonnaise. Top with beef and cucumber.

❷ In a small bowl combine yogurt, green onions, and Italian seasoning; season to taste with salt and pepper. Spoon over cucumber. Top with remaining bread slices.

PER SANDWICH 377 cal., 15 g total fat (4 g sat. fat), 33 mg chol., 1,286 mg sodium, 37 g carbo., 4 g fiber, 19 g pro.

quick tip   Greek yogurt, which is thicker and more flavorful than regular plain yogurt, is increasingly available. If you can find it, try it in this recipe. It comes in both light and regular varieties.

Reuben Sandwiches

The story of the origin of the Reuben has two versions. Ones goes that it was invented by Arthur Reuben, owner of New York's now-defunct Reuben's delicatessen. The other claims that it was invented by Omaha wholesale grocer Reuben Kay to nosh on during a poker game with friends. Either way, it's a keeper.

PREP 10 minutes **COOK** 8 minutes **MAKES** 4 sandwiches

- 3 tablespoons butter or margarine, softened
- 8 slices dark rye or pumpernickel bread
- 3 tablespoons bottled Thousand Island or Russian salad dressing
- 6 ounces thinly sliced cooked corned beef
- 4 slices Swiss cheese (3 ounces)
- 1 cup sauerkraut, well drained

❶ Spread butter on 1 side of each bread slice and salad dressing on the other. With the buttered sides down, top 4 slices with meat, cheese, and sauerkraut. Top with remaining bread slices, dressing sides down.

❷ Preheat a large skillet on medium heat. Reduce heat to medium-low. Cook two of the sandwiches at a time on medium-low heat for 4 to 6 minutes or until the bread is toasted and the cheese melts, turning once. Repeat with remaining sandwiches.

PER SANDWICH 404 cal., 22 g total fat (10 g sat. fat), 64 mg chol., 2,508 mg sodium, 34 g carbo., 8 g fiber, 20 g pro.

Beef & Sweet Pepper Tortilla Wraps ♥

Pick your meat—beef, ham, or turkey—or combine them however you like.

START TO FINISH 15 minutes **MAKES** 6 wraps

- 3 7- or 8-inch flour tortilla wraps
- ½ 8-ounce tub light cream cheese with chives and onion or roasted garlic
- 18 to 24 fresh basil leaves
- ½ 7-ounce jar roasted red sweet peppers, well-drained and cut into ¼-inch strips
- 4 ounces thinly sliced cooked beef, ham, and/or turkey
- 1 tablespoon light mayonnaise or salad dressing

❶ Spread each tortilla with one-third of the cream cheese. Cover each with basil leaves, leaving a 1-inch border. Arrange pepper strips on basil leaves. Top with sliced meat. Spread mayonnaise onto meat.

❷ Tightly roll up each tortilla into a spiral; cut each wrap in half crosswise.

PER WRAP 135 cal., 6 g total fat (3 g sat. fat), 24 mg chol., 186 mg sodium, 10 g carbo., 1 g fiber, 8 g pro.

Sicilian-Style Pizza

Roasted Vegetable Pizza

The asparagus and squash are quick-"roasted" under the broiler, then the whole pizza takes another dash under the broiler—just 3 to 4 minutes—until it's heated through.

START TO FINISH 20 minutes **MAKES** 4 servings

- 12 ounces asparagus spears, trimmed and cut into 2-inch lengths
- 1 medium yellow summer squash, halved lengthwise and thinly sliced
- ⅓ cup bottled Italian salad dressing
- ½ of a 6.3-ounce container semisoft cheese with garlic and herb (about ½ cup)
- 1 12-inch Italian bread shell (such as Boboli)
- ½ cup finely shredded Parmesan cheese (2 ounces)

  Freshly ground black pepper

1 Preheat broiler. In a 15×10×1-inch baking pan combine asparagus, squash, and salad dressing. Broil 3 to 4 inches from heat for 6 minutes, stirring twice. Drain, reserving 2 tablespoons of the dressing. Place semisoft cheese in a small bowl; stir in hot reserved dressing until combined.

2 Place bread shell on a baking sheet. Spread with semisoft cheese mixture. Top with drained vegetables; sprinkle with Parmesan cheese and pepper.

3 Broil for 3 to 4 minutes or until heated through.

PER SERVING 458 cal., 22 g total fat (8 g sat. fat), 32 mg chol., 1,037 mg sodium, 49 g carbo., 3 g fiber, 18 g pro.

Sicilian-Style Pizza

Sicilians adore escarole—a dark leafy green that is equally delicious chopped and eaten fresh in a salad or cooked in garlic, olive oil, and a little bit of chicken broth.

PREP 15 minutes **COOK** 10 minutes **OVEN** 425°F
MAKES 4 servings

- 1 16-ounce Italian bread shell (such as Boboli)
- 3 medium red and/or yellow tomatoes, thinly sliced
- 1 cup fresh mozzarella, thinly sliced (4 ounces)
- ⅓ cup halved, pitted kalamata olives
- 1 tablespoon olive oil
- 1 cup coarsely chopped escarole or curly endive
- ¼ cup shredded Pecorino Romano or Parmesan cheese (1 ounce)

  Freshly ground black pepper

1 Preheat oven to 425°F. Place bread shell on an ungreased baking sheet or pizza pan. Top bread shell with tomatoes, mozzarella cheese, and olives. Drizzle oil over all.

2 Bake for 8 minutes. Carefully sprinkle with escarole; bake 2 minutes more. To serve, sprinkle with Pecorino Romano cheese and pepper.

PER SERVING 460 cal., 20 g total fat (5 g sat. fat), 31 mg chol., 936 mg sodium, 53 g carbo., 3 g fiber, 21 g pro.

{ When it's loaded with vegetables and has very little or no meat, pizza is fairly healthful. }

Garlic Veggie Pizza

Creamy garlic salad dressing steps into a new role on this all-vegetable pizza, serving as a flavorful white sauce alternative to red sauce.

PREP 20 minutes **BAKE** 12 minutes **OVEN** 450°F
MAKES 6 servings

- 1 12-inch Italian bread shell (such as Boboli)
- 1 tablespoon cooking oil
- ½ cup sweet onion, cut in thin wedges (1 medium)
- 1¼ cups zucchini, thinly sliced (1 medium)
- ½ cup red sweet pepper, cut into thin strips (1 small)
- ⅓ cup bottled creamy garlic or creamy roasted garlic salad dressing
- ¾ cup shredded mozzarella cheese (3 ounces)
- ½ cup crumbled basil and tomato feta cheese (2 ounces)

❶ Preheat oven to 450°F. Place bread shell on a baking sheet; set aside.

❷ In a large skillet heat oil on medium-high heat. Add onion. Cook and stir until onion is tender. Add zucchini and sweet pepper; cook 2 minutes more. Remove from heat.

❸ Spread salad dressing over bread shell; spoon on vegetable mixture. Combine mozzarella cheese and feta cheese. Sprinkle cheeses over vegetables.

❹ Bake for 12 minutes or until cheese melts and just begins to brown. To serve, cut into wedges.

PER SERVING 336 cal., 16 g total fat (4 g sat. fat), 20 mg chol., 735 mg sodium, 37 g carbo., 2 g fiber, 14 g pro.

quick tip   If you want to use fresh mozzarella instead of preshredded brick mozzarella on this pizza, you can actually shred fresh mozzarella. For easier shredding, make sure the cheese is refrigerator-cold.

Italian Vegetable Pesto Pizza

You can really use any kind of richly flavored black olives on this pizza, including Niçoise—or even regular ripe olives.

START TO FINISH 20 minutes **OVEN** 450°F **MAKES** 4 servings

- 1 12-inch Italian bread shell (such as Boboli)
- ⅓ cup refrigerated basil pesto
- 2 medium roma tomatoes, thinly sliced
- ½ cup chopped yellow sweet pepper (1 small)
- ¼ cup pitted kalamata olives, halved
- 1 cup shredded Italian cheese blend (4 ounces)

❶ Preheat oven to 450°F. Place bread shell on a baking sheet. Spread bread shell with pesto. Top with tomatoes, sweet pepper, olives, and cheese. Bake for 10 to 12 minutes or until cheese melts.

PER SERVING 566 cal., 28 g total fat (4 g sat. fat), 32 mg chol., 1,072 mg sodium, 59 g carbo., 1 g fiber, 25 g pro.

Stuffed Spinach Pizza

This is like a giant pizza pillow. A filling of vegetables, sauce, and cheese is sandwiched between two layers of crust. After it's baked, it's cut in squares and served with hot pizza sauce for dipping.

START TO FINISH 30 minutes **OVEN** 450°F
MAKES 6 to 8 servings

- 1 6-ounce package fresh spinach leaves, coarsely chopped (6 cups)
- 2 cups shredded mozzarella cheese (8 ounces)
- 1 16-ounce jar pizza sauce
- 1 teaspoon bottled hot pepper sauce (optional)
- 2 13.8-ounce cans refrigerated pizza dough
- 6 ounces sliced provolone cheese
- ¼ cup shredded Parmesan cheese

❶ Preheat oven to 450°F. In a very large bowl combine spinach, mozzarella, 1 cup pizza sauce, and, if desired, hot pepper sauce. Set aside.

❷ Grease a 13×9×2-inch baking pan. On a lightly floured surface roll 1 pizza crust into a 17×13-inch rectangle. Place in pan, pressing crust over the bottom and up the sides. Line bottom of crust with provolone cheese slices. Spread spinach mixture over provolone. On the lightly floured surface roll second crust into a 13×9-inch rectangle. Place over spinach mixture. Pinch edges of crusts together to seal. Prick top of crust all over with a fork.

❸ Bake for 20 minutes or until crust is deep golden brown. Remove pizza from oven. Sprinkle with Parmesan cheese. Let stand a few minutes to melt cheese. Heat remaining pizza sauce and pass with pizza.

PER SERVING 539 cal., 23 g total fat (11 g sat. fat), 44 mg chol., 1,139 mg sodium, 58 g carbo., 4 g fiber, 27 g pro.

Grilled Mexican Pizza

Grilled Mexican Pizza

Save a little prep time by buying precooked and crumbled bacon—or even the real bacon bits that are on the market now. Look for them in the aisle with the salad dressings.

PREP 20 minutes   **GRILL** 6 minutes   **MAKES** 8 servings

4	6- to 7-inch whole wheat pita bread rounds
2	large red and/or yellow tomatoes, sliced
6	ounces Monterey Jack cheese with jalapeño peppers, shredded
⅓	cup sliced green onions (3)
¼	cup bottled sliced pickled jalapeños
1	tablespoon cooking oil
1	tablespoon fresh lime juice
1	teaspoon ground cumin
¼	teaspoon salt
¼	teaspoon cracked black pepper
1	medium avocado, halved, seeded, peeled, and sliced
6	slices bacon, crisp-cooked, drained, and crumbled

❶ For a charcoal grill, place pita rounds on the rack of a covered grill directly over low coals. Cover; grill for 2 minutes. Turn pita rounds over and arrange tomato slices over the toasted sides of rounds. Sprinkle with cheese. Cover; grill for 4 minutes more or until rounds are lightly toasted and cheese is melted. (For a gas grill, preheat grill. Reduce heat to low. Cover and grill as above.)

❷ Meanwhile, in a medium bowl combine green onions, jalapeños, oil, lime juice, cumin, salt, and black pepper.

❸ Remove rounds from grill. Top with avocado slices and sprinkle with bacon.

PER SERVING 252 cal., 14 g total fat (6 g sat. fat), 24 mg chol., 499 mg sodium, 22 g carbo., 5 g fiber, 11 g pro.

Caesar Salmon Pizzas

Thin wedges of this elegant pizza make a nice addition to an appetizer buffet.

PREP 15 minutes   **BAKE** 8 minutes   **OVEN** 400°F
MAKES 2 pizzas

2	6-inch Italian bread shells (such as Boboli)
¼	cup bottled creamy Caesar salad dressing
2	cups torn fresh spinach
2	ounces smoked salmon, flaked and skin and bones removed
¼	cup walnut pieces, toasted (see note, page 31)
¼	cup finely shredded Parmesan cheese (1 ounce)
2	tablespoons thinly bias-sliced green onion (1)
1	teaspoon drained capers (optional)

❶ Preheat oven to 400°F. Lightly spread bread shells with some of the Caesar dressing. Place bread shells on a baking sheet.

❷ Top bread shells with spinach, salmon, walnuts, half of the Parmesan cheese, the green onion, and, if desired, capers.

❸ Bake for 8 to 10 minutes or just until heated through. Drizzle with remaining Caesar dressing; sprinkle with remaining Parmesan cheese.

PER PIZZA 652 cal., 39 g total fat (6 g sat. fat), 19 mg chol., 1,480 mg sodium, 54 g carbo., 4 g fiber, 26 g pro.

---

quick tip   Fresh spinach is lovely on this pizza, but if you want a little more flavor, you could substitute watercress or arugula. Both have a nice peppery bite that goes nicely with the salmon.

{ The fun of pizza is its versatility. Any flatbread works—and the topping choices are nearly infinite. }

Tuna Alfredo Pizza

Capers are delicious with tuna. Sprinkle a few of the piquant little buds onto the pizza after you add the zucchini and before you add the cheese, if you like.

START TO FINISH 20 minutes   **OVEN** 425°F   **MAKES** 4 servings

- 1   12-inch Italian bread shell (such as Boboli)
- ⅔   cup refrigerated light Alfredo pasta sauce
- 1   5-ounce pouch lemon pepper marinated chunk light tuna, flaked
- 1   small zucchini or yellow summer squash, thinly sliced
- ⅓   cup finely shredded Parmesan cheese
       Freshly ground black pepper

❶ Preheat oven to 425°F. Place bread shell on a pizza pan or a large baking sheet. Spread with Alfredo sauce. Top with tuna and zucchini; sprinkle with Parmesan cheese and pepper.

❷ Bake for 10 to 12 minutes or until heated through.

PER SERVING 438 cal., 12 g total fat (4 g sat. fat), 42 mg chol., 1,100 mg sodium, 54 g carbo., 0 g fiber, 30 g pro.

Tuna Alfredo Pizza

Chicken Salad Pita Pizzas

Watch these pizzas carefully after you put them under the broiler. If they cook for much more than a minute or so, the greens will be beyond wilted.

START TO FINISH 20 minutes   **MAKES** 4 pizza

- 4   pita bread rounds
- 4   cups packaged torn mixed salad greens
- 3   tablespoons bottled reduced-calorie creamy Caesar salad dressing
- 1   6-ounce package refrigerated Southwest-flavor cooked chicken breast strips
- 1   cup shredded Italian cheese blend (4 ounces)

❶ Preheat broiler. Arrange pita bread rounds on a large baking sheet. In a large bowl toss together mixed greens and salad dressing; pile on the pita rounds. Top with chicken and cheese.

❷ Broil 4 inches from heat for 1 to 1½ minutes or until cheese begins to brown and greens begin to wilt. Serve with knives and forks.

PER PIZZA 340 cal., 11 g total fat (5 g sat. fat), 49 mg chol., 1,124 mg sodium, 37 g carbo., 2 g fiber, 23 g pro.

Alfredo Chicken Pita Pizzas

Alfredo-sauced chicken pizza is a popular choice at restaurants. Here's an easy way to make it at home.

START TO FINISH 20 minutes   **OVEN** 450°F   **MAKES** 4 servings

- 4   large pita bread rounds
- ½   cup refrigerated Alfredo pasta sauce
- 1   6-ounce package refrigerated cooked chicken breast strips
- ½   cup roasted red sweet peppers, cut into thin strips
- ¼   cup sliced green onions (2)
- 1   cup finely shredded Italian cheese blend

❶ Preheat oven to 450°F. Place pita bread rounds on a large baking sheet. Bake for 6 to 8 minutes or until light brown. Spread tops of pitas with Alfredo pasta sauce. Top with chicken breast strips, roasted sweet peppers, green onions, and cheese.

❷ Bake for 6 to 8 minutes more or until heated through and cheese melts.

PER SERVING 387 cal., 15 g total fat (8 g sat. fat), 65 mg chol., 1,123 mg sodium, 39 g carbo., 2 g fiber, 24 g pro.

Greek Pita Pizzas

Chicken Satay Pizza

If you love cilantro, sprinkle some of the chopped fresh herb over the top of this pizza after it comes out of the oven.

START TO FINISH 20 minutes   **OVEN** 425°F   **MAKES** 4 servings

- 1   **12-inch Italian bread shell (such as Boboli)**
- ¼   **cup bottled peanut sauce**
- 1   **6-ounce package refrigerated cooked chicken breast strips**
- ½   **cup packaged coarsely shredded fresh carrot**
- 1   **cup shredded Monterey Jack cheese (4 ounces)**
- ¼   **cup sliced green onion and/or chopped peanuts (optional)**

❶ Preheat oven to 425°F. Place bread shell on a 12-inch pizza pan or large baking sheet. Spread peanut sauce over bread shell. Top with chicken and carrot. Sprinkle with cheese and, if desired, green onion and/or peanuts.

❷ Bake, uncovered, for 10 to 12 minutes or until heated through and cheese melts.

PER SERVING 500 cal., 18 g total fat (6 g sat. fat), 56 mg chol., 1,509 mg sodium, 56 g carbo., 0 g fiber, 30 g pro.

---

quick tip   Much of Thai food is known for its blend of sweet and spicy flavors. Here the peanut sauce is sweet, and—depending on the type you buy—a little bit hot. Taste it first. If you like more kick, stir in a little bit of cayenne or crushed red pepper before you spread it on the bread shell.

Greek Pita Pizzas

The toppings on these Mediterranean-style pita pizzas include ground meat cooked in a rosemary-infused tomato sauce, kalamata olives, and (of course!) feta cheese.

PREP 25 minutes   **BAKE** 5 minutes   **OVEN** 400°F
MAKES 4 servings

- 6   **ounces lean ground beef or lamb**
- ¼   **cup finely chopped onion**
- 2   **cloves garlic, minced**
- 1   **8-ounce can tomato sauce**
- 1   **teaspoon snipped fresh rosemary or ¼ teaspoon dried rosemary, crushed**
- 2   **6-inch whole wheat or white pita bread rounds**
- ½   **cup shredded part-skim mozzarella cheese (2 ounces)**
- ½   **cup shredded fresh spinach**
- 1   **small tomato, seeded and chopped**
- ¼   **cup crumbled feta cheese (1 ounce)**
- 12   **pitted kalamata or ripe olives, quartered**

❶ Preheat oven to 400°F. In a medium nonstick skillet cook ground beef, onion, and garlic until meat is brown; drain off fat. Stir tomato sauce and rosemary into meat mixture in skillet. Bring to boiling; reduce heat. Simmer, uncovered, for 2 minutes.

❷ Carefully split pita bread rounds in half horizontally; place pita halves, rough sides up, in a single layer on a large baking sheet. Bake for 3 to 4 minutes or until lightly toasted.

❸ Top toasted pita bread with meat mixture; sprinkle with mozzarella cheese. Bake for 2 to 3 minutes more or until cheese melts. Remove from oven. Top with spinach, tomato, feta cheese, and olives; serve immediately.

PER SERVING 251 cal., 10 g total fat (4 g sat. fat), 42 mg chol., 739 mg sodium, 25 g carbo., 4 g fiber, 16 g pro.

> Italian, Greek, or Indian?
> A little creativity allows your pizza
> to speak any language you want.

Greek-Style Pizza

Here's a new approach to a meat-and-potatoes meal. Roast beef, potatoes, spinach, and feta cheese are layered on a chewy flatbread then baked until hot.

START TO FINISH 25 minutes **MAKES** 4 servings

2	cups packaged refrigerated diced potatoes with onion
1	tablespoon olive oil
4	flatbread or pita rounds
	Olive oil
4	ounces crumbled feta cheese with garlic and herb
2	cups fresh spinach
12	ounces thinly sliced deli low-sodium roast beef
	Sliced baby sweet peppers (optional)
	Crushed red pepper (optional)

1 In a large skillet cook potatoes in 1 tablespoon oil on medium heat for 5 minutes or until tender; set aside.

2 Meanwhile, heat broiler. Place flatbread on extra-large baking sheet; lightly brush bread with oil. Top with half of the cheese. Broil 3 to 4 inches from heat for 2 to 3 minutes or until cheese begins to melt. Top barely melted cheese with spinach, roast beef, potatoes, and remaining cheese.

3 Broil 3 to 5 minutes or until heated through. Drizzle with additional olive oil. If desired, top with pepper slices and crushed red pepper.

PER SERVING 555 cal., 24 g total fat (11 g sat. fat), 96 mg chol., 1,243 mg sodium, 57 g carbo., 1 g fiber, 30 g pro.

Chili Mac Pizza

Taco pizza is a mainstay of pizza parlors all over the country—why not a chili mac pie?

PREP 15 minutes **BAKE** 15 minutes **OVEN** 400°F
MAKES 6 servings

12	ounces ground beef
1	tablespoon chili seasoning mix
1	15-ounce can chili beans, undrained
1	14.5-ounce can diced tomatoes with green chiles
1	11-ounce can whole kernel corn with red and green sweet peppers
1	cup cooked macaroni (optional)
1	12-inch purchased pizza crust
1½	cups shredded Monterey Jack cheese with jalapeños or regular Monterey Jack cheese
	Crumbled tortilla chips
	Shredded lettuce (optional)
	Sour cream (optional)
	Salsa (optional)

1 Preheat oven to 400°F. In a large skillet cook ground beef until brown; drain off fat. Stir in chili seasoning. Add undrained chili beans, tomatoes, corn, and macaroni (if using). Heat to boiling; reduce heat and simmer, uncovered, for 5 minutes.

2 Place pizza crust on a large baking sheet. Spoon meat mixture over crust. Sprinkle with cheese. Bake for 15 minutes. Add tortilla chips and, if desired, lettuce, sour cream, and salsa before serving.

PER SERVING 581 cal., 26 g total fat (10 g sat. fat), 71 mg chol., 1,377 mg sodium, 59 g carbo., 6 g fiber, 32 g pro.

{ *Pizza started out as street food. Neapolitans still enjoy a single slice as they stroll through the city.* }

Barbecue Skillet Pizza

Cheeseburger Pizza

How can kids resist a dish that combines their two favorite foods? Serve it with baby carrots and dip.

PREP 20 minutes **BAKE** 8 minutes **OVEN** 425°F
MAKES 4 servings

8	ounces ground beef
½	cup onion, chopped (1 medium)
1½	cups shredded cheddar cheese (6 ounces)
2	tablespoons ketchup
1	tablespoon sweet pickle relish
1	tablespoon yellow mustard
1	12-inch thin crust Italian bread shell (such as Boboli)

❶ Heat oven to 425°F. In a large skillet cook ground beef and onion until meat is brown and onion is tender; drain off fat. Stir in ½ cup of cheese, ketchup, pickle relish, and mustard. Cook and stir until the cheese melts. Remove from heat.

❷ Place bread shell on a baking sheet. Spread meat mixture on bread shell. Sprinkle with remaining 1 cup cheese.

❸ Bake for 8 to 10 minutes or until heated through and cheese melts. Cut into 8 wedges.

PER SERVING 528 cal., 27 g total fat (14 g sat. fat), 83 mg chol., 870 mg sodium, 41 g carbo., 2 g fiber, 29 g pro.

Easy Barbecued Pork Pizza

For a fresh crunch, top each serving with a spoon or two of prepared coleslaw right before serving.

PREP 15 minutes **BAKE** 12 minutes **OVEN** 425°F
MAKES 8 servings

1	17- to 18-ounce package refrigerated BBQ sauce with cooked shredded pork
1	tablespoon cooking oil
2	medium red and/or yellow sweet peppers, cut into thin strips
1	medium onion, cut into thin wedges
1	12-inch Italian bread shell (such as Boboli)
1	cup shredded Monterey Jack cheese

❶ Preheat oven to 425°F. Heat shredded pork according to package directions.

❷ In a large skillet heat oil on medium heat. Add sweet pepper and onion; cook about 5 minutes or until crisp-tender.

❸ Place the Italian bread shell on a large baking sheet. Spoon shredded pork over the bread shell, spreading evenly to the edges. Top with sweet pepper and onion. Sprinkle with cheese.

❹ Bake for 12 minutes or until cheese melts and the edge of the crust is light brown.

PER SERVING 318 cal., 11 g total fat (3 g sat. fat), 33 mg chol., 862 mg sodium, 39 g carbo., 1 g fiber, 17 g pro.

Barbecue Skillet Pizza

This deep-dish barbecued-beef pizza uses refrigerated biscuits as a crust.

START TO FINISH 30 minutes **MAKES** 6 servings

1	18-ounce tub refrigerated barbecue sauce with shredded beef
1	cup chopped green sweet pepper (1 large)
1	cup onion, chopped (1 large)
1	7.5-ounce package refrigerated biscuits (10)
1	cup shredded cheddar cheese (4 ounces)
1½	cups shredded lettuce
2	roma tomatoes, chopped

❶ In a large microwave-safe bowl combine shredded beef, green pepper, and onion. Microwave, covered, on high for 3 minutes, stirring once. Meanwhile, lightly grease a heavy large skillet with flared sides. Press biscuits into the bottom and halfway up the sides of the skillet, moistening edges of biscuits and pressing to seal.

❷ Cook crust, covered, on medium heat for 3 minutes. Check crust and press with fork to seal any holes. Spoon beef mixture into partially cooked crust. Sprinkle with cheese. Cook, covered, for 9 to 14 minutes more or until edges of crust are light brown.

❸ Loosen edges and carefully slide pizza onto serving platter. Sprinkle with lettuce and tomatoes. Cut into wedges.

PER SERVING 313 cal., 11 g total fat (5 g sat. fat), 41 mg chol., 1,358 mg sodium, 38 g carbo., 3 g fiber, 18 g pro.

quick tip It's important to use a skillet with flared rather than straight sides to make this skillet pizza. It's far easier to slide the pizza out of a pan with flared edges than it is to remove it from one with straight sides. If a straight-sided skillet is all you have, serve the pizza right from the pan.

Savory Focaccia Pie

You can use either sweet or hot Italian sausage for this focaccia pie. If you want to lighten it up just a bit, look for Italian sausage made with ground turkey.

START TO FINISH 25 minutes   **OVEN** 250°F   **MAKES** 4 servings

- ¾   cup oil-packed dried tomato halves with Italian herbs (3 ounces)
- 1   12-inch round rosemary or garlic focaccia
- 8   ounces bulk Italian sausage
- 1   4-ounce package baby spinach (4 cups)
- 2   ounces goat cheese (chèvre) or feta cheese

❶ Preheat oven to 250°F. Drain tomatoes, reserving oil. Place focaccia on a large baking sheet; brush with 2 teaspoons of the oil from the tomatoes. Cut into 8 wedges. Arrange wedges in a circle. Place in oven to warm.

❷ Meanwhile, in an extra-large skillet cook sausage on medium-high heat until no longer pink, breaking up with a wooden spoon. Drain off fat, reserving 2 teaspoons of the drippings in the skillet. Cook spinach in drippings just until wilted.

❸ Turn oven to broil. Top warmed focaccia with cheese, dried tomatoes, sausage, and spinach. Broil 4 to 5 inches from heat for 3 to 5 minutes or until cheese is softened and toppings are heated through. If desired, drizzle wedges with additional oil from tomatoes.

PER SERVING 548 cal., 29 g total fat (10 g sat. fat), 64 mg chol., 1,006 mg sodium, 55 g carbo., 2 g fiber, 22 g pro.

---

quick tip   Choose a focaccia bread with a flat top, not rounded, which will help the toppings stay on better; or trim off the rounded top using a serrated knife.

Canadian Bacon Pizza

The winning combination of Canadian bacon and artichokes is featured on this simple pizza.

PREP 15 minutes   **BAKE** 15 minutes   **OVEN** 350°F
MAKES 4 to 6 servings

- 1   16-ounce package Italian bread shell (such as Boboli)
- 1   6-ounce jar marinated artichoke hearts
- 1   5.2-ounce container semisoft cheese with garlic and herb
- 1   3.5-ounce package pizza-style Canadian-style bacon (1½-inch diameter)
- 1   medium green, red, or yellow sweet pepper, cut into bite-size strips

❶ Preheat oven to 350°F. Place the bread shell on a large baking sheet. Drain artichoke hearts, reserving 2 teaspoons of the marinade. Coarsely chop artichokes; set aside. In a small bowl combine cheese and reserved marinade.

❷ Spread half the cheese mixture over bread shell; top with Canadian bacon, sweet pepper, and artichoke hearts. Spoon remaining cheese mixture by teaspoons over toppings. Bake for 15 minutes or until heated through.

PER SERVING 529 cal., 24 g total fat (9 g sat. fat), 54 mg chol., 1,136 mg sodium, 58 g carbo., 2 g fiber, 23 g pro.

{ Whether it's fat and chewy or thin and crispy, pizza is the one food that pleases everyone. }

Even the best main dishes need something on the side. Round out dinner with a salad, vegetable, rice, pasta, or bread that features fresh, creative flavor combinations and good nutrition.

276 **280** **292**

tasty side dishes

299

Broccoli Slaw

A combination of shredded cabbage and shredded broccoli gives this colorful slaw extra crunch and nutrition.

START TO FINISH 10 minutes   **MAKES** 6 to 8 servings

- ⅓ cup mayonnaise or salad dressing
- 2 tablespoons cider vinegar
- 1 teaspoon sugar
- 1 teaspoon caraway seeds
- ½ teaspoon salt
- ½ 16-ounce package (4 cups) broccoli slaw mix
- ½ 16-ounce package (4 cups) shredded cabbage with carrot (coleslaw mix)
- 2 tablespoons thinly sliced green onion

❶ In a very large bowl stir together mayonnaise, vinegar, sugar, caraway seeds, and salt. Add broccoli slaw mix, coleslaw mix, and green onion; toss to coat. Serve immediately or cover and chill up to 12 hours.

PER SERVINGS 115 cal., 10 g total fat (1 g sat. fat), 9 mg chol., 291 mg sodium, 6 g carbo., 2 g fiber, 1 g pro.

---

quick tip   The dressing in this recipe features the traditional balance of vinegar to sugar. If you like your slaw a little sweeter, increase the sugar by ½ teaspoon or so.

Broccoli Slaw

Roasted Asparagus ♥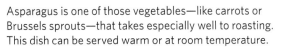

Asparagus is one of those vegetables—like carrots or Brussels sprouts—that takes especially well to roasting. This dish can be served warm or at room temperature.

PREP 10 minutes   **ROAST** 15 minutes   **OVEN** 450°F
MAKES 4 servings

- 1 pound fresh asparagus, trimmed
- ⅛ teaspoon black pepper
- 1 tablespoon olive oil
- 3 tablespoons grated Parmesan cheese

❶ Preheat oven to 450°F. Place asparagus in a 2-quart baking dish. Sprinkle with black pepper. Drizzle with olive oil. Roast, uncovered, for 15 minutes or until crisp-tender, using tongs to lightly toss twice during roasting. Transfer asparagus to a warm serving platter. Sprinkle with cheese.

PER SERVING 58 cal., 5 g total fat (1 g sat. fat), 3 mg chol., 59 mg sodium, 3 g carbo., 1 g fiber, 3 g pro.

Asparagus with Almond Sauce ♥

Elegant, perfectly cooked spears of asparagus are drizzled with a nutty lemon-butter sauce right before serving. Try this side with grilled or roasted salmon or chicken.

START TO FINISH 15 minutes   **MAKES** 4 servings

- 1 pound fresh asparagus, trimmed
- 2 tablespoons sliced almonds
- 1 tablespoon butter
- ½ cup chicken broth
- 1 teaspoon cornstarch
- 2 teaspoons lemon juice
  Dash black pepper

❶ In a large saucepan cook asparagus, covered, in boiling lightly salted water for 3 to 5 minutes or until crisp-tender. Drain well; transfer to a serving platter. Keep warm.

❷ Meanwhile, for sauce, in a large skillet cook and stir almonds in hot butter on medium heat for 2 to 3 minutes or until golden. In a small bowl stir together broth, cornstarch, lemon juice, and pepper; add to skillet. Cook and stir until thick and bubbly. Cook and stir 1 minute more. Spoon sauce over asparagus.

PER SERVING 76 cal., 5 g total fat (2 g sat. fat), 8 mg chol., 143 mg sodium, 6 g carbo., 3 g fiber, 3 g pro.

Garlicky Broccoli Rabe

Garlicky Broccoli Rabe ♥ 🎬

This is delicious as a side dish, but you can also toss it with hot cooked rigatoni or orecchiette pasta to make it a meatless main dish. If it seems a little dry, toss the mixture with a little chicken broth. Sprinkle with a little freshly grated Parmesan cheese on each serving.

START TO FINISH 20 minutes   **MAKES** 6 servings

- 2   **pounds broccoli rabe**
- 1   **large red sweet pepper, cut into bite-size strips**
- 1   **teaspoon dried basil, crushed**
- ¼   **teaspoon salt**
- 3   **cloves garlic, minced**
- 2   **tablespoons olive oil**
- **Crushed red pepper**
- **Lemon wedges**

1 Wash broccoli rabe; remove and discard woody stems. Coarsely chop the leafy greens; set aside florets and chopped leaves.

2 In a large skillet cook and stir sweet pepper, basil, salt, and garlic in hot oil on medium-high heat for 2 minutes. Add broccoli rabe. Using tongs, toss and cook vegetables for 4 to 6 minutes or until broccoli rabe is crisp-tender. Transfer to serving dish. Sprinkle with crushed red pepper. Serve with lemon wedges.

PER SERVING 103 cal., 5 g total fat (1 g sat. fat), 0 mg chol., 178 mg sodium, 7 g carbo., 4 g fiber, 6 g pro.

---

quick tip   Broccoli rabe, also known as rapini, is a pleasantly bitter green that is in peak season in the spring. When choosing broccoli rabe, look for slender, firm stalks; crisp, green leaves; and florets that are tightly closed.

Saucepan Baked Beans 🎬

Most baked-bean dishes have to be simmered for hours in the oven. This one takes less than 30 minutes from start to finish and tastes just as good with a pulled pork sandwich.

PREP 10 minutes   **COOK** 10 minutes   **MAKES** 6 servings

- 1   **16-ounce can pork and beans in tomato sauce**
- 1   **15-ounce can navy or Great Northern beans, rinsed and drained**
- ¼   **cup ketchup**
- 2   **tablespoons maple syrup or packed brown sugar**
- 2   **teaspoons dry mustard**
- ¼   **cup chopped purchased cooked bacon, warmed**

1 In a medium saucepan combine pork and beans, navy beans, ketchup, maple syrup, and dry mustard. Bring mixture to boiling; reduce heat. Simmer, uncovered, about 10 minutes or until desired consistency, stirring frequently. Top with bacon.

PER SERVING 211 cal., 3 g total fat (1 g sat. fat), 5 mg chol., 870 mg sodium, 39 g carbo., 8 g fiber, 11 g pro.

---

quick tip   If you like a little heat (of the tongue-tingling variety) in your baked beans, stir one finely chopped chipotle pepper in adobo sauce into the bean mixture before simmering.

Saucepan Baked Beans

Sweet-and-Sour Cabbage ♥

Serve this tangy-sweet dish with baked pork chops, roasted pork loin, or grilled, boiled, or baked German sausages such as bratwurst.

START TO FINISH 15 minutes   **MAKES** 4 servings

3	tablespoons packed brown sugar
3	tablespoons vinegar
3	tablespoons water
4	teaspoons vegetable oil
¼	teaspoon caraway seeds
¼	teaspoon salt
	Dash black pepper
3	cups shredded red or green cabbage
¾	cup chopped apple

❶ In a large skillet combine brown sugar, vinegar, water, oil, caraway seeds, salt, and pepper. Cook for 2 to 3 minutes or until hot and brown sugar is dissolved, stirring occasionally.

❷ Stir in the cabbage and apple. Cook, covered, on medium-low heat about 5 minutes or until cabbage is crisp-tender, stirring occasionally. Serve with a slotted spoon.

PER SERVING 109 cal., 5 g total fat (1 g sat. fat), 0 mg chol., 163 mg sodium, 17 g carbo., 2 g fiber, 1 g pro.

---

quick tip   Shred the cabbage for this dish on a box grater, with a good sharp chef's knife, or—perhaps easiest—in a food processor.

Butter-Glazed Carrots

If you can't get the kids to eat their vegetables, try this dish—or the maple-glazed version. They'll be singing the praises of bunny food in no time.

START TO FINISH 18 minutes   **MAKES** 4 servings

1	pound carrots, peeled and cut into ½-inch-thick diagonal slices
2	tablespoons butter, softened
1	to 2 teaspoons dried tarragon or basil, crushed
	Salt and black pepper

❶ In a medium saucepan cook carrots, covered, in ½ cup boiling water for 8 to 10 minutes or just until carrots are tender; drain off water.

❷ Add butter and tarragon to the saucepan. Stir until combined; if necessary heat on low heat to melt butter completely. Season to taste with salt and pepper.

PER SERVING 98 cal., 6 g total fat (4 g sat. fat), 15 mg chol., 261 mg sodium, 11 g carbo., 3 g fiber, 1 g pro.

MAPLE-GLAZED CARROTS: Prepare as above, except use 1 tablespoon butter, omit the herb, and add 2 tablespoons pure maple syrup and 1 tablespoon sesame seeds, toasted.

MICROWAVE DIRECTIONS: In a microwave-safe baking dish or casserole combine carrots and ¼ cup water. Microwave, covered, on high for 7 to 9 minutes or until carrots are tender, stirring once. Drain off water. Add butter and tarragon to the baking dish. Stir until combined; if necessary, microwave for 10 to 20 seconds more to melt butter completely. Season to taste with salt and pepper.

{ Though the main dish is usually given the most thought, a stellar side makes a meal special. }

Fresh Fruit with
Citrus Mint Dressing

Fresh Fruit with Citrus Mint Dressing ♥ 🎬

This light, cool dish is refreshingly delicious with grilled chicken or salmon for dinner. It would also make a nice addition to a brunch buffet featuring an egg dish such as a strata or frittata.

START TO FINISH 20 minutes   **MAKES** 6 servings

- ¼ cup orange juice
- 1 tablespoon snipped fresh mint
- 1 teaspoon honey
- 4 cups assorted fresh fruit (such as cut-up pineapple, halved or quartered strawberries, quartered kiwifruit slices, cut-up papaya, and/or cut-up mango)

1 For dressing, in a medium bowl whisk together orange juice, mint, and honey. Add fruit to dressing; toss lightly to coat.

PER SERVING 58 cal., 0 g total fat, 0 mg chol., 3 mg sodium, 13 g carbo., 2 g fiber, 1 g pro.

MAKE-AHEAD DIRECTIONS: Prepare as directed. Cover and chill up to 4 hours, stirring occasionally.

---

quick tip   If you are in an especially big hurry, save prep time on most fruit or vegetable salads by picking up the ingredients at the salad bar at your supermarket deli. You'll find abundant cut-up fresh fruit such as pineapple, melon, mango, papaya, and washed and hulled strawberries.

Skillet Scalloped Corn

Serve this shortcut scalloped corn with smoked turkey breast, meaty slices of ham, or pork chops.

START TO FINISH 15 minutes   **MAKES** 4 servings

- 2 teaspoons butter
- ½ cup crushed rich round, wheat, or rye crackers
- 1 11-ounce can whole kernel corn with sweet peppers, drained
- 1 7- to 8.75-ounce can whole kernel corn with sweet peppers, whole kernel corn, or white (shoepeg) corn, drained
- 2 1-ounce slices process Swiss cheese, torn
- ⅓ cup milk
- ⅛ teaspoon onion powder
  Dash black pepper

1 For topping, in a large skillet melt butter on medium heat. Add 2 tablespoons of the crushed crackers to the skillet. Cook and stir until lightly brown; remove and set aside.

2 In the same skillet combine remaining crushed crackers, corn, cheese, milk, onion powder, and pepper. Cook, stirring frequently, until cheese melts. Transfer to a serving dish; sprinkle with crumb topping.

PER SERVING 183 cal., 9 g total fat (4 g sat. fat), 18 mg chol., 704 mg sodium, 19 g carbo., 2 g fiber, 6 g pro.

Skillet Scalloped Corn

Farm-Style Green Beans

These homey, bacon-topped green beans are absolutely delicious with roasted chicken.

START TO FINISH 25 minutes **MAKES** 4 servings

8	ounces fresh green beans
2	slices bacon, cut up
1	medium onion, thinly sliced (about 1 cup)
½	cup fresh sliced mushrooms
1½	cups chopped tomato or one 14 ½-ounce can diced tomatoes, drained
¼	teaspoon salt*

❶ Trim green beans and leave whole or cut into 1-inch pieces. In a saucepan cook the beans, covered, in a small amount of boiling salted water for 10 minutes or until crisp-tender; drain.

❷ Meanwhile, in a large skillet cook bacon on medium heat until crisp. Remove bacon, reserving drippings. Drain bacon on paper towels; set aside. Cook onion and mushrooms in reserved drippings on medium heat until tender. Add tomato and salt. Cook, uncovered, 2 to 3 minutes or until most of the liquid is absorbed.

❸ Transfer beans to a serving platter or bowl. Top with onion mixture. Sprinkle bacon over the vegetables.

PER SERVING 132 cal., 9 g total fat (3 g sat. fat), 13 mg chol., 312 mg sodium, 10 g carbo., 3 g fiber, 4 g pro.

*NOTE: Omit salt if using canned tomatoes.

Farm-Style Green Beans

Grilled-Onion Salad with Grape Tomatoes & Cabrales Cheese

Cabrales is an intensely flavored Spanish blue cheese. If you are a fan of pungent blue cheese, you will love it. If you prefer a milder blue, consider Danish blue or Gorgonzola.

PREP 20 minutes **GRILL** 10 minutes **MAKES** 8 servings

3	tablespoons olive oil
1	tablespoon sherry vinegar
¼	teaspoon salt
¼	teaspoon ground cumin
⅛	teaspoon paprika
⅛	teaspoon freshly ground black pepper
2	large red onions, sliced ¼ inch thick, or 6 red boiling onions, quartered lengthwise
1	tablespoon olive oil
6	cups torn watercress, arugula, or spinach
1½	cups grape or cherry tomatoes, halved (if desired)
½	cup crumbled Cabrales or other blue cheese (2 ounces)

❶ For dressing, in a screw-top jar combine the 3 tablespoons oil, the vinegar, salt, cumin, paprika, and pepper. Cover and shake well.

❷ Brush red onion pieces with the 1 tablespoon oil. For a charcoal grill, place onions on the rack of an uncovered grill directly over medium coals. Grill about 10 minutes or until onions are softened and slightly charred, turning once halfway through grilling. (For a gas grill, preheat grill. Reduce heat to medium. Add onions to grill rack over heat. Cover and grill as above.) Separate onion slices into rings.

❸ In a large bowl combine grilled onions, watercress, and tomatoes. Pour dressing over watercress mixture; toss gently to coat. Arrange on a large serving platter. Sprinkle with cheese.

PER SERVING 115 cal., 9 g total fat (3 g sat. fat), 6 mg chol., 204 mg sodium, 6 g carbo., 1 g fiber, 4 g pro.

Grilled-Onion Salad
with Grape Tomatoes
& Cabrales Cheese

Mixed Greens Salad
with Pears

Mixed Greens Salad with Pears 🍲

If you don't want to make your own vinaigrette, a bottled balsamic or champagne vinaigrette would work beautifully on this salad.

START TO FINISH 15 minutes   **MAKES** 6 servings

- 1   5-ounce bag spring mix salad greens
- 2   medium fresh pears, cored and sliced
- 2   ounces Gruyère cheese, cubed
- 1   recipe White Wine Vinaigrette
     Fresh pear, thinly sliced (optional)

1 In a large bowl combine salad greens, sliced pears, and cheese. Drizzle with vinaigrette and toss to coat. If desired, garnish each salad with additional pear slices.

WHITE WINE VINAIGRETTE: In a screw-top jar combine 3 tablespoons salad oil; 2 tablespoons white wine vinegar; 1 tablespoon honey; ¼ teaspoon dried basil or oregano, crushed; ⅛ teaspoon salt; ⅛ teaspoon dry mustard; and ⅛ teaspoon black pepper. Cover and shake to combine.

PER SERVING 148 cal., 10 g total fat (3 g sat. fat), 10 mg chol., 85 mg sodium, 12 g carbo., 2 g fiber, 3 g pro.

---

quick tip   This is a lovely salad to serve in the fall, when pears are in season. When buying pears, look for firm, unblemished skin. Pears are not usually ripe right from the store. Let them sit on the counter for a couple of days until they are fragrant and yield to gentle pressure—then refrigerate until you are ready to use them.

Creamed Peas & New Potatoes

Old-fashioned and comforting, this two-vegetable side dish is just the thing to serve with roast beef for a Sunday supper.

START TO FINISH 30 minutes   **MAKES** 4 servings

- 1   pound tiny new potatoes (10 to 12)
- 1½   cups shelled peas or frozen loose-pack peas
- ¼   cup chopped onion
- 1   tablespoon butter or margarine
- 1   tablespoon all-purpose flour
- ½   teaspoon salt
     Dash black pepper
- 1   cup milk
     Snipped fresh chives or dill (optional)

1 Scrub potatoes; cut any large potatoes in half. Peel a narrow strip from around the center of each whole potato. In a medium saucepan cook potatoes, covered, in a small amount of boiling salted water for 8 minutes. Add fresh peas and cook for 10 to 12 minutes more or until tender. (If using frozen peas, cook potatoes 14 minutes; add peas and cook 4 to 5 minutes more.) Drain; return vegetables to saucepan.

2 Meanwhile, in a small saucepan cook onion in hot butter until tender. Stir in flour, salt, and pepper. Add milk all at once. Cook and stir until thickened and bubbly. Cook and stir 1 minute more. Stir into potatoes and peas; heat through. Season to taste. If desired, sprinkle with chives.

PER SERVING 194 cal., 5 g total fat (3 g sat. fat), 13 mg chol., 358 mg sodium, 31 g carbo., 5 g fiber, 8 g pro.

{ When planning a meal, be sure to include a variety of tastes, textures, and temperatures. }

Chunky Mustard Potato Salad

This picnic-perfect potato salad can be made and chilled for up to 24 hours before serving. It's a popular choice to take to a potluck barbecue on a busy weekend.

PREP 15 minutes   **MAKES** 10 servings

1	20-ounce package refrigerated new potato wedges
¼	teaspoon salt
½	cup green onions, sliced (4)
¼	cup coarsely chopped dill pickles
¼	cup chopped roasted sweet red pepper
¼	cup chopped celery
¼	cup cooked bacon crumbles
2	tablespoons Dijon mustard
½	teaspoon salt
¼	teaspoon black pepper
½	cup mayonnaise or salad dressing

❶ Place potatoes in a large saucepan. Add enough water to cover potatoes; add ¼ teaspoon salt. Bring to boiling; reduce heat. Simmer, covered for 5 minutes. Drain well; rinse with cold water and drain again.

❷ Meanwhile, in a very large serving bowl combine green onions, pickles, red pepper, celery, bacon crumbles, mustard, ½ teaspoon salt, and black pepper. Stir in potatoes. Add mayonnaise and mix gently. If desired, chill up to 24 hours.

PER SERVING 131 cal., 9 g total fat (1 g sat. fat), 6 mg chol., 457 mg sodium, 8 g carbo., 2 g fiber, 3 g pro.

---

quick tip   Different varieties of potatoes are best used for specific dishes. New potatoes or waxy white potatoes hold their shape best when boiled, they are the right choice for potato salads. Idaho or russet potatoes get mushy and fall apart in potato salad—but they make beautiful french fries and mashed potatoes.

Garlic & Pepper Stir-Fry

Serve this Asian-style side with grilled fish or chicken.

START TO FINISH 25 minutes   **MAKES** 4 servings

2	tablespoons soy sauce
1	teaspoon toasted sesame oil
¼	teaspoon cracked black pepper
1	tablespoon cooking oil
3	cloves garlic, minced
2	cups red, yellow, and/or green sweet peppers, cut into bite-size strips; broccoli pieces, carrot slices; and/or sugar snap peas (stems and ends removed)
1	medium onion, sliced and separated into rings
2	cups sliced fresh mushrooms
	Sesame seeds, toasted (see note, page 31)

❶ In a small bowl stir together soy sauce, sesame oil, and black pepper; set aside. In an extra-large skillet heat cooking oil on high heat for 1 minute. Add garlic; cook and stir for 1 minute. Add peppers and onion; cook and stir for 3 minutes. Add mushrooms; cook and stir for 2 to 3 minutes more or until vegetables are crisp-tender.

❷ Add soy sauce mixture to skillet or wok. Cook and stir to coat vegetables. Transfer mixture to a serving dish. Sprinkle with sesame seeds.

PER SERVING 95 cal., 6 g total fat (1 g sat. fat), 0 mg chol., 464 mg sodium, 8 g carbo., 2 g fiber, 4 g pro.

Garlic & Pepper Stir-Fry

Chunky Mustard
Potato Salad

Sugar Snap Peas with
Orange-Ginger Butter

Shredded Hash Browns

This is the real deal—crispy and delicious homemade hash browns. This version is spiked with a little hot chile.

START TO FINISH 25 minutes   **MAKES** 2 or 3 servings

- 3   or 4 small russet or white potatoes (about 12 ounces total)
- ¼   cup finely chopped onion
- 1   small fresh jalapeño, banana pepper, or Anaheim chile pepper, seeded and chopped (see note, page 19) (optional)
- ¼   teaspoon salt
- ⅛   teaspoon coarsely ground black pepper
- 2   tablespoons butter, cooking oil, or margarine
    Fresh sage leaves (optional)

1 Peel potatoes and coarsely shred using the coarsest side of the shredder (you should have about 2 cups shredded potatoes). Rinse shredded potatoes in a colander; drain well and pat dry with paper towels. In a medium bowl combine shredded potatoes, onion, jalapeño, salt, and black pepper.

2 In a large nonstick skillet melt butter on medium heat. Carefully add potato mixture, pressing into an even pancake-like round (7 to 8 inches in diameter). Using a spatula, press potato mixture firmly. Cover and cook on medium heat about 8 minutes or until golden brown. Check occasionally and reduce heat, if necessary, to prevent overbrowning.

3 Using 2 spatulas or a spatula and fork, turn the hash browns. (If you're not sure you can turn in a single flip, cut into quarters and turn by sections.) Cook, uncovered, for 5 to 7 minutes more or until golden brown and crisp. Remove from skillet; cut into wedges. If desired, garnish with fresh sage.

PER SERVING 168 cal., 9 g total fat (1 g sat. fat), 0 mg chol., 197 mg sodium, 19 g carbo., 2 g fiber, 3 g pro.

---

quick tip   Shredded potato dishes such as hash browns or potato pancakes turn out best when there is very little water left in the potatoes before cooking. To maximize the crispiness of hash browns, roll the shredded and rinsed potatoes in a clean cotton kitchen towel, then wring them out over the sink to extract as much water as possible before proceeding with the recipe.

Herbed Potatoes ▣

No time to peel and shred potatoes? These nicely seasoned potatoes start with frozen hash browns that get dolled up with herbs and cheese.

START TO FINISH 27 minutes   **MAKES** 4 servings

- 3   green onions, sliced
- ½   teaspoon dried Italian seasoning, crushed
- 1   tablespoon butter
- 4½   cups frozen loose-pack hash brown potatoes
- ¼   teaspoon salt
- ⅓   cup grated Parmesan cheese
- 1   tablespoon snipped fresh parsley

1 In a large nonstick skillet cook green onions and Italian seasoning in butter on medium heat about 2 minutes or until onions are tender. Stir in frozen potatoes and salt. Cook about 15 minutes or until potatoes are tender and lightly browned, stirring twice. Stir in Parmesan cheese and parsley.

PER SERVING 257 cal., 7 g total fat (4 g sat. fat), 13 mg chol., 354 mg sodium, 44 g carbo., 4 g fiber, 8 g pro.

Sugar Snap Peas with Orange-Ginger Butter ♥

A quick gingery glaze of butter and marmalade enhances the naturally sweet flavor of sugar snap peas.

START TO FINISH 25 minutes   **MAKES** 4 servings

- 3   cups fresh sugar snap peas or frozen sugar snap peas
- 1   teaspoon grated fresh ginger
- 1   tablespoon butter or margarine
- 1   tablespoon orange marmalade or peach preserves
- 1   teaspoon cider vinegar
- ⅛   teaspoon black pepper

1 Remove strings and tips from peas. Cook fresh peas, covered, in a small amount of boiling salted water for 3 to 5 minutes or until crisp-tender. (Cook frozen peas according to the package directions.) Drain well.

2 Meanwhile, in a small saucepan cook ginger in hot butter for 1 minute. Stir in marmalade, vinegar, and pepper; cook and stir until marmalade melts. Pour marmalade mixture over hot cooked peas; toss to coat.

PER SERVING 58 cal., 3 g total fat (2 g sat. fat), 8 mg chol., 25 mg sodium, 7 g carbo., 1 g fiber, 1 g pro.

Summer Squash Toss ♥ 🎬

Serve this side with a grilled steak and some Texas toast.

START TO FINISH 25 minutes   **MAKES** 8 servings

- 1   medium red onion, cut into thin wedges
- 1   tablespoon olive oil or vegetable oil
- 3   medium zucchini and/or yellow summer squash, halved lengthwise and cut into ¼-inch slices (about 5 cups)
- ½   teaspoon salt
- ¼   teaspoon black pepper
- 2   tablespoons snipped fresh basil, thyme, and/or parsley
- 2   ounces goat cheese (chévre), crumbled

❶ In an extra-large skillet cook onion in hot oil on medium-high heat for 7 minutes, stirring occasionally. Add zucchini, salt, and pepper to skillet; reduce heat to medium. Cook, uncovered, about 8 minutes or until vegetables are crisp-tender, stirring occasionally. Sprinkle with herbs and cheese.

PER SERVING 52 cal., 3 g total fat (1 g sat. fat), 3 mg chol., 179 mg sodium, 4 g carbo., 1 g fiber, 2 g pro.

quick tip   When you're cooking in a skillet, it's important to use the correct size pan—and not just because the food will spill out if the pan is too small. If the pan is too large, the food may stick and burn or the food will steam instead of cooking properly. In this recipe, that means instead of having a nice crisp brown edge, the squash could get soggy and too soft—and you don't want that.

Broiled Summer Squash & Onions

Equally good served warm or at room temperature, this dish can be made outdoors on the grill too.

PREP 10 minutes   **BROIL** 8 minutes   **MAKES** 4 servings

- ¼   cup bottled olive oil vinaigrette or balsamic vinaigrette salad dressing
- ½   teaspoon dried basil or oregano, crushed
- ⅛   teaspoon black pepper
- 2   medium yellow summer squash or zucchini, quartered lengthwise
- 1   small onion, cut into thin wedges
     Shredded Parmesan or crumbled blue cheese (optional)
     Toasted pine nuts (see note, page 31) (optional)

❶ In a small bowl whisk together salad dressing, basil, and pepper. Brush summer squash and onion with some of the salad dressing mixture.

❷ Place summer squash and onion on the unheated rack of a broiler pan. Broil about 4 inches from the heat for 8 to 10 minutes or until crisp-tender, turning and brushing occasionally with salad dressing mixture.

❸ Cut broiled vegetables into bite-size pieces; transfer to a serving bowl. Toss with any remaining salad dressing mixture. If desired, top with cheese and/or nuts.

PER SERVING 91 cal., 8 g total fat (1 g sat. fat), 0 mg chol., 77 mg sodium, 4 g carbo., 1 g fiber, 1 g pro.

{ Even adamant vegetable avoiders warm up to the mild flavor of zucchini and summer squash. }

Summer Tomato Salad

Summer Tomato Salad

Make this salad when you arrive home from the farmer's market with a bushel basket full of ripe summer tomatoes and have to so something with them, fast.

START TO FINISH 30 minutes   **MAKES** 6 servings

- 1   recipe Tarragon Vinaigrette
- 3   cups mesclun salad greens
- 2   medium red tomatoes, cut into wedges or sliced
- 2   medium yellow or heirloom green tomatoes, cut into 8 wedges each
- 1   cup red or yellow cherry tomatoes, halved if desired
- 1   small red onion, cut into paper-thin slices
- ¼   teaspoon coarse salt
- ¼   teaspoon freshly ground black pepper

❶ Prepare Tarragon Vinaigrette; set aside. Divide the greens among 6 salad plates. Arrange the tomatoes on and around the greens. Top each serving with onion slices. Sprinkle with salt and pepper. Drizzle with some of the dressing. Store any remaining dressing, covered, in the refrigerator up to 1 week.

TARRAGON VINAIGRETTE: In a screw-top jar combine ½ cup olive oil, ¼ cup red or white wine vinegar, 1 tablespoon finely chopped fresh tarragon, 1 tablespoon finely chopped fresh chives, and ½ teaspoon Dijon mustard. Cover and shake well.

PER SERVING 192 cal., 19 g total fat (3 g sat. fat), 0 mg chol., 109 mg sodium, 7 g carbo., 2 g fiber, 2 g pro.

Basil Quinoa Salad

Basil Quinoa Salad

Quinoa is an ancient South American grain. It is lower in carbohydrates than most grains and is considered to contain a complete protein. It has a nutty flavor and a texture similar to couscous.

START TO FINISH 30 minutes   **MAKES** 6 servings

- 1   cup fresh basil leaves
- 2   tablespoons grated Parmesan cheese
- 2   tablespoons lemon juice
- 2   tablespoons olive oil
- 4   cloves garlic, minced
- ½   teaspoon salt
- ¼   teaspoon black pepper
- 2   cups cooked quinoa*
- 1   15-ounce can red kidney beans, rinsed and drained
- 1   cup chopped yellow sweet pepper (1 large)
- ½   cup chopped, seeded tomato (1 medium)
- ½   cup sliced green onions (4)
- 4   cups torn Bibb lettuce

❶ Place basil in a food processor. Add Parmesan cheese, lemon juice, olive oil, garlic, salt, and black pepper. Cover and process until nearly smooth, stopping to scrape down sides as needed; set aside.

❷ In a large bowl stir together cooked quinoa, beans, sweet pepper, tomato, and green onions. Add basil mixture; stir to coat.

❸ Serve quinoa mixture over torn lettuce.

PER SERVING 177 cal., 6 g total fat (1 g sat. fat), 1 mg chol., 332 mg sodium, 24 g carbo., 8 g fiber, 8 g pro.

*NOTE: To make 2 cups cooked quinoa, in a fine strainer rinse ½ cup quinoa under cold running water; drain. In a small saucepan combine 1¼ cups water, quinoa, and ¼ teaspoon salt. Bring to boiling; reduce heat. Cover and simmer for 15 minutes. Let stand to cool slightly. Drain off remaining liquid.

Spanish-Style Rice 🍲

Next time you make tacos at home, instead of opening up a can of Spanish rice or refried beans, make this fresher alternative. It cooks undisturbed for 20 minutes, giving you time to get everything else ready.

START TO FINISH 30 minutes **MAKES** 4 servings

- 1   14.5-ounce can Mexican-style stewed tomatoes, cut up (undrained)
- ½   cup water
- 1   teaspoon chili powder
- ½   cup uncooked long grain rice
- ¼   teaspoon salt
- ⅛   teaspoon black pepper
       Several dashes bottled hot pepper sauce (optional)
- ¼   cup chopped pimiento-stuffed olives or chopped pitted ripe olives
- ½   cup shredded cheddar cheese

❶ In a medium saucepan combine tomatoes, water, chili powder, rice, salt, pepper, and, if desired, hot pepper sauce. Bring to boiling; reduce heat. Simmer, covered, about 20 minutes or until rice is tender and most of the liquid is absorbed. Stir in olives. Sprinkle with cheese.

PER SERVING 185 cal., 6 g total fat (3 g sat. fat), 15 mg chol., 590 mg sodium, 25 g carbo., 2 g fiber, 6 g pro.

Spanish-Style Rice

Heavenly Couscous

Bits of dried apricot give this fragrant couscous sweetness and a delightfully chewy texture. It's delicious with chicken.

START TO FINISH 15 minutes **MAKES** 4 servings

- 1   cup couscous
- ¼   teaspoon salt
- 1   cup boiling water
- 1   teaspoon butter
- ¼   cup slivered almonds
- ¼   cup snipped dried apricots
- ½   teaspoon finely shredded orange peel
       Fine orange peel curls (optional)

❶ In a medium bowl mix couscous and salt. Gradually add boiling water. Let stand until liquid is absorbed, about 5 minutes.

❷ Meanwhile, in a small skillet cook and stir almonds in hot butter on medium heat until almonds are light golden brown. Remove almonds from skillet to cool. Fluff couscous with a fork. Add apricots, orange peel, and toasted almonds to couscous. Fluff again. If desired, sprinkle with orange peel curls. Serve immediately.

PER SERVING 250 cal., 5 g total fat (1 g sat. fat), 2 mg chol., 163 mg sodium, 42 g carbo., 4 g fiber, 8 g pro.

quick tip   Most of the dried apricots you find in the supermarket are treated with sulfites to help them retain their bright color and plumpness. If you or someone you cook for has an adverse reaction to sulfites—and many people do—look for untreated dried apricots at a health food store. They will be darker in color and won't be as moist as the treated apricots, but they taste just as good.

Five-Minute Pilaf

Pasta with Pepper-Cheese Sauce

A hollandaise sauce mix and bottled roasted red peppers make whipping up this creamy pasta dish a snap.

START TO FINISH 25 minutes   **MAKES** 4 to 6 servings

8   ounces dried medium shell macaroni, mostaccioli, or cut ziti pasta

1   0.9- to 1.25-ounce package hollandaise sauce mix

1   cup bottled roasted red sweet peppers, drained and chopped

½   cup shredded Monterey Jack cheese with jalapeño chile peppers (2 ounces)

1 Cook pasta according to package directions. Drain well and return pasta to pan.

2 Meanwhile, for sauce, prepare hollandaise sauce according to package directions, except use only 2 tablespoons butter. Stir in roasted red peppers. Remove pan from heat. Add cheese to sauce, stirring until cheese melts. Add sauce to pasta in pan; toss to coat.

PER SERVING 384 cal., 13 g total fat (8 g sat. fat), 36 mg chol., 407 mg sodium, 53 g carbo., 2 g fiber, 13 g pro.

Five-Minute Pilaf ♥ 🎬

Have everything else you're serving on the table—and everyone you're serving sitting at it—before you stir together this pilaf. It's that fast.

START TO FINISH 5 minutes   **MAKES** 6 servings

1   8.8-ounce pouch cooked brown rice (about 2 cups)

2   cups frozen Italian-blend vegetables or frozen zucchini and yellow summer squash

¼   cup refrigerated reduced-fat basil pesto

2   tablespoons pine nuts or chopped walnuts, toasted (see note, page 31)

1 In a large microwave-safe bowl combine brown rice and frozen vegetables. Cover bowl. Microwave on high for 4 to 5 minutes or until vegetables are crisp-tender and mixture is heated through, stirring once or twice during cooking. Stir in pesto. To serve, sprinkle with pine nuts.

PER SERVING 136 cal., 6 g total fat (1 g sat. fat), 3 mg chol., 110 mg sodium, 17 g carbo., 2 g fiber, 4 g pro.

Pesto Macaroni Salad

Getting kids involved with cooking is a fun way to get them interested in eating good food. Ask your little chef to tear up the basil leaves for this salad.

START TO FINISH 30 minutes   **MAKES** 14 servings

3   cups dried bow tie and/or wagon wheel pasta

5   ounces fresh green beans, trimmed and cut into 1-inch pieces (about 1 cup)

1   pound small fresh mozzarella balls, drained and sliced

1   7-ounce container purchased refrigerated basil pesto

½   cup fresh basil leaves, torn

½   teaspoon fine sea salt

1 Cook macaroni according to package directions; drain. Rinse with cold water; drain again. In a saucepan cook beans, covered, in a small amount of boiling salted water for 10 to 15 minutes or until crisp tender; drain. Rinse with cold water; drain again.

2 In a large bowl combine macaroni, green beans, mozzarella, and pesto. Stir in basil and salt. Serve immediately or chill up to 2 hours before serving.

PER SERVING 249 cal., 14 g total fat (4 g sat. fat), 26 mg chol., 255 mg sodium, 20 g carbo., 1 g fiber, 11 g pro.

Pesto Macaroni Salad

Curried Seed Rolls ♥

Purchased whole grain rolls get a South Asian twist from curry butter and a mango-chutney accompaniment.

START TO FINISH 17 minutes   **OVEN** 375°F   **MAKES** 8 rolls

  2   tablespoons butter
  ¼   teaspoon curry powder
      Dash garlic powder
  1   to 2 tablespoons mixed seeds (such as cumin seeds, sesame seeds, poppy seeds, and/or dill seeds)
  8   purchased whole grain or whole wheat dinner rolls
      Butter (optional)
      Mango chutney or other fruit chutney (optional)

❶ Preheat oven to 375°F. Place melted butter, curry powder, and garlic powder in a small shallow dish. Place seeds in another small shallow dish or on waxed paper. Dip tops of rolls into melted butter, then dip into seeds. Place rolls on an ungreased baking sheet.

❷ Bake for 7 to 9 minutes or until hot. Serve warm. If desired, serve with additional butter and chutney.

PER ROLL 104 cal., 4 g total fat (2 g sat. fat), 8 mg chol., 158 mg sodium, 15 g carbo., 2 g fiber, 3 g pro.

---

quick tip   Mango chutney may be the most familiar type of chutney, but it's not the only type. There are many kinds of fruit chutneys on the market. Some of them are made from one kind of fruit, while others are made from a blend of fruits. Fruits that are commonly cooked into chutneys include peaches, passion fruit, dates, apples, pears, and cranberries.

Corn Bread

Sometimes you want it plain and simple—and sometimes you want it gussied up. Among the classic recipe and the five flavorful variations that follow, there is a corn bread to suit any dish or occasion.

PREP 10 minutes   **BAKE** 15 minutes   **OVEN** 400°F
MAKES 8 to 10 wedges

  1   cup all-purpose flour
  ¾   cup cornmeal
  2   to 3 tablespoons sugar
  2 ½ teaspoons baking powder
  ¾   teaspoon salt
  1   tablespoon butter
  2   eggs
  1   cup milk
  ¼   cup cooking oil or melted butter

❶ Preheat oven to 400°F. In a medium bowl stir together the flour, cornmeal, sugar, baking powder, and salt; set aside.

❷ Add the 1 tablespoon butter to an 8×8×2-inch baking pan, a 9×1½-inch round baking pan, or a large cast-iron skillet. Place pan in the preheated oven about 3 minutes or until butter melts. Remove pan from oven; swirl butter to coat bottom and sides of pan.

❸ Meanwhile, in a small bowl beat eggs with a fork; stir in milk and oil. Add egg mixture to flour mixture all at once; stir just until moistened (batter should be lumpy). Pour batter into the hot pan. Bake for 15 to 20 minutes or until a wooden toothpick inserted near the center comes out clean. Serve warm.

PER WEDGE 219 cal., 10 g total fat (3 g sat. fat), 60 mg chol., 390 mg sodium, 26 g carbo., 1 g fiber, 5 g pro.

DOUBLE CORN BREAD: Prepare as above, except fold ½ cup frozen whole kernel corn, thawed, into the batter.

GREEN CHILE CORN BREAD: Prepare as above, except fold 1 cup shredded cheddar cheese or Monterey Jack cheese (4 ounces) and one 4-ounce can diced green chile peppers, drained, into the batter.

SWEET PEPPER CORN BREAD: Prepare as above, except fold ½ cup chopped red sweet pepper into the batter.

GREEN ONION-BACON CORN BREAD: Prepare as above, except fold ⅓ cup crumbled cooked bacon and ¼ cup sliced green onion into the batter.

CORN MUFFINS: Prepare as above, except omit the 1 tablespoon butter. Spoon batter into 12 greased 2½-inch muffin cups, filling each two-thirds full. Bake in the preheated oven about 15 minutes or until light brown and a wooden toothpick inserted in the centers comes out clean. Makes 12 muffins.

Focaccia Breadsticks

Cheese-Garlic Crescents

The cheese and garlic at the center of these flaky crescents comes from semisoft cheese flavored with garlic and herbs.

PREP 15 minutes **BAKE** 11 minutes **OVEN** 375°F
MAKES 8 rolls

- 1   8-ounce package (8) refrigerated crescent rolls
- ¼   cup semisoft cheese with garlic and herb
- 2   tablespoons finely chopped walnuts, toasted (see note, page 31)
      Nonstick cooking spray
      Milk
- 1   tablespoon seasoned fine dry bread crumbs

❶ Preheat oven to 375°F. Unroll crescent rolls; divide into 8 triangles. In a small bowl stir together cheese and walnuts. Place a rounded measuring teaspoon of the cheese mixture near the center of the wide end of each crescent roll. Roll up, starting at the wide end.

❷ Lightly coat a baking sheet with cooking spray. Place the rolls, point sides down, on the prepared baking sheet. Brush tops lightly with milk; sprinkle with bread crumbs.

❸ Bake about 11 minutes or until bottoms are browned. Serve warm.

PER ROLL 141 cal., 10 g total fat (3 g sat. fat), 6 mg chol., 254 mg sodium, 12 g carbo., 0 g fiber, 3 g pro.

Cheddar Garlic Biscuits

Brushing garlic butter on the warm, just-baked biscuits makes them especially fragrant.

START TO FINISH 15 minutes **OVEN** 425°F **MAKES** 10 biscuits

- 2   cups packaged biscuit mix
- ½   cup shredded cheddar cheese (2 ounces)
- ⅔   cup milk
- 2   tablespoons butter, melted
- ¼   teaspoon garlic powder

❶ Preheat oven to 425°F. Grease a baking sheet; set aside.

❷ In a large bowl combine biscuit mix and cheese; add milk. Stir to combine. Drop dough from rounded tablespoons onto prepared baking sheet. Bake for 8 to 9 minutes or until biscuits are golden.

❸ Meanwhile, in a small bowl combine melted butter and garlic powder; brush over hot biscuits. Serve warm.

PER BISCUIT 155 cal., 8 g total fat (4 g sat. fat), 14 mg chol., 367 mg sodium, 16 g carbo., 1 g fiber, 4 g pro.

Focaccia Breadsticks

With some savory flavorings and a twist or two, refrigerated pizza dough is transformed into these yummy breadsticks. Serve them as a side or as a nibble at a party.

PREP 15 minutes **BAKE** 12 minutes **OVEN** 350°F
MAKES 10 breadsticks

- ¼   cup oil-packed dried tomatoes
- ¼   cup grated Romano or Parmesan cheese
- 2   teaspoons water
- 1½   teaspoons snipped fresh rosemary or ½ teaspoon dried rosemary, crushed
- ⅛   teaspoon cracked black pepper
- 1   13.8-ounce package refrigerated pizza dough

❶ Preheat oven to 350°F. Lightly grease a baking sheet; set aside.

❷ Drain dried tomatoes, reserving oil; finely snip tomatoes. In a small bowl combine tomatoes, 2 teaspoons of the reserved oil, the Romano cheese, water, rosemary, and pepper. Set aside.

❸ On a lightly floured surface unroll the pizza dough. Roll the dough into a 10×8-inch rectangle. Spread the tomato mixture crosswise over half of the dough. Fold plain half of dough over filling; press lightly to seal edges. Cut the folded dough lengthwise into ten ½-inch strips. Fold each strip in half and twist two or three times. Place 1 inch apart on a prepared baking sheet.

❹ Bake for 12 to 15 minutes or until golden brown. Serve warm or cool on a wire rack.

PER BREADSTICK 95 cal., 3 g total fat (1 g sat. fat), 2 mg chol., 157 mg sodium, 15 g carbo., 1 g fiber, 3 g pro.

---

quick tip   Refrigerated pizza dough is a wonderful thing to keep on hand—a culinary blank slate. You can make it savory, as was done in this recipe, or you can make it sweet. Instead of the cheese and tomato mixture, spread the strips with a combination of a little melted butter, brown sugar, and cinnamon (maybe some chopped walnuts or pecans) and you have got a pretty good approximation of a cinnamon roll.

Keep dessert sweet and simple with this collection of special treats that relies on no-fuss ingredients such as packaged mixes, purchased doughs, and flavor-packed ingredients.

306

310

322

sweet tooth desserts

318

Crispy Chocolate Chewies

These chocolate-coconut-pecan-flavored cookies look and taste a bit like miniature German chocolate cakes.

PREP 20 minutes **BAKE** 10 minutes per batch
OVEN 350°F **MAKES** about 40 cookies

1	package 2-layer-size German chocolate cake mix
½	cup butter, melted
1	egg
¼	cup milk
¾	cup crisp rice cereal
¼	cup flaked coconut
1	cup canned coconut-pecan frosting
	Flaked coconut, toasted (see note, page 31)

❶ Preheat oven to 350°F. In a large mixing bowl combine cake mix, melted butter, egg, and milk. Beat on low until smooth. Stir in cereal and the ¼ cup coconut. Drop dough by rounded teaspoons 2 inches apart onto an ungreased cookie sheet.

❷ Bake for 10 to 12 minutes or until bottoms are light brown. Let stand for 1 minute on cookie sheet. Transfer to a wire rack and let cool. Spread cookies with coconut-pecan frosting. Sprinkle with toasted coconut.

PER COOKIE 108 cal., 5 g total fat (5 g sat. fat), 11 mg chol.,132 mg sodium, 15 g carbo., 0 g fiber, 1 g pro.

Gooey Brownie Cups

Brownie chunks, marshmallows, peanut butter-flavored pieces, and peanuts are warmed in the oven until everything is melty—then topped with ice cream and chocolate syrup.

PREP 10 minutes **BAKE** 7 minutes **OVEN** 350°F
MAKES 4 servings

4	purchased unfrosted chocolate brownies, cut into irregular-size chunks
1	cup tiny marshmallows
¼	cup peanut butter-flavored pieces and/or milk chocolate pieces
2	tablespoons chopped cocktail peanuts
	Chocolate or vanilla ice cream
	Chocolate-flavored syrup

❶ Preheat oven to 350°F. In a large bowl toss together brownie chunks, marshmallows, peanut-flavored pieces, and peanuts. Divide among 4 individual baking dishes.

❷ Bake for 7 to 8 minutes or until heated through and marshmallows are golden brown. Serve with ice cream and drizzle with chocolate syrup.

PER SERVING 581 cal., 28 g total fat (9 g sat. fat), 63 mg chol., 280 mg sodium, 78 g carbo., 3 g fiber, 9 g pro.

Easy 'Mallow Cookies ♥

These pretty and whimsical cookies are perfect for a little girl's tea party.

START TO FINISH 30 minutes **MAKES** 16 cookies

16	maraschino cherries with stems
⅓	cup marshmallow creme
1	tablespoon finely chopped maraschino cherries
32	vanilla wafers
4	ounces vanilla-flavor candy coating, coarsely chopped

❶ Place cherries with stems on paper towels; drain well. Line a cookie sheet with waxed paper; set aside. In a small bowl stir together marshmallow creme and chopped cherries. Spread 1 level teaspoon of the marshmallow mixture on bottoms of half of the vanilla wafers. Top with the remaining wafers, bottom sides down. Place on the prepared cookie sheet.

❷ In a small saucepan cook and stir candy coating on low heat until melted. Cool slightly.

❸ Dip half of each cookie into melted coating; let excess drip back into pan. Return dipped cookie to the cookie sheet. Holding each cherry by the stem, dip bottom of cherry into melted coating. Place on the dipped portion of a cookie; hold for several seconds or just until set. Let stand until coating is completely set.

PER COOKIE 126 cal., 5 g total fat (3 g sat. fat), 0 mg chol., 37 mg sodium, 20 g carbo., 0 g fiber, 1 g pro.

Easy 'Mallow Cookies

Crispy Chocolate Chewies

Soda Fountain Ice Cream Pie

Soda Fountain Ice Cream Pie

Crushed sugar ice cream cones are the secret to the crunchy crust for this luscious ice cream pie.

PREP 20 minutes **FREEZE** 9½ hours **STAND** 15 minutes
MAKES 10 servings

- 1½ cups crushed rolled sugar ice cream cones (12 cones)
- ¼ cup sugar
- ½ cup butter, melted
- 3 cups fresh strawberries
- 1 quart vanilla ice cream
- ⅓ cup malted milk powder
- ½ cup finely chopped fresh strawberries
- 1 recipe Sweetened Whipped Cream (optional)
  Malted milk balls, coarsely chopped (optional)
  Fresh strawberries (optional)
  Hot fudge ice cream topping (optional)

❶ For crust, in a medium bowl combine crushed cones and sugar. Drizzle with melted butter; toss gently to coat. Press mixture evenly onto bottom of an 8- or 9-inch springform pan. Cover and freeze about 30 minutes or until firm.

❷ Meanwhile, place the 3 cups strawberries in a blender. Cover and blend until smooth.

❸ In a chilled large bowl stir ice cream with a wooden spoon until softened. Stir in ½ cup of the pureed strawberries and the malted milk powder. Spoon half of the mixture over crust, spreading evenly. Cover and freeze for 30 minutes. (Cover and freeze remaining ice cream mixture.)

❹ Spoon remaining pureed strawberries over ice cream layer. Cover and freeze for 30 minutes more. Stir remaining ice cream mixture to soften. Spoon over strawberry layer, spreading evenly. Top with the ½ cup chopped strawberries. Cover and freeze about 8 hours or until firm.

❺ Let pie stand at room temperature for 15 minutes before serving. Cut into wedges. If desired, top with Sweetened Whipped Cream, chopped malted milk balls, and additional strawberries. If desired, serve with hot fudge topping.

PER SERVING 307 cal., 17 g total fat (10 g sat. fat), 52 mg chol., 178 mg sodium, 37 g carbo., 2 g fiber, 4 g pro.

SWEETENED WHIPPED CREAM: In a chilled mixing bowl add 1 cup whipping cream, 2 tablespoons sugar, and ½ teaspoon vanilla. Beat on medium until soft peaks form.

Blackberry Cream Pie

A slice of this gorgeous frozen cheesecakelike pie is welcome sight on a warm summer night.

PREP 10 minutes **BAKE** 5 minutes **FREEZE** 4 to 24 hours
OVEN 375°F **MAKES** 8 servings

- 1 9-inch purchased graham cracker crumb pie shell
- 1 egg white, beaten
- 1 cup whipping cream
- 1 8-ounce package cream cheese, softened
- 1 10-ounce jar blackberry or black raspberry spread
  Fresh blackberries or black raspberries, lemon peel twist, and/or mint leaves (optional)
  Whipped cream (optional)

❶ Preheat oven to 375°F. Brush pie shell with beaten egg white. Bake for 5 minutes. Cool on a wire rack.

❷ In a medium mixing bowl beat whipping cream on medium-high until stiff peaks form; set aside.

❸ In a large mixing bowl beat cream cheese on medium-high until smooth. Add blackberry spread. Beat on low just until combined. Fold in whipped cream. Spoon mixture into pie shell. Cover and freeze for 4 to 24 hours or until firm. If desired, garnish with fresh black berries, lemon peel twist, and/or mint, and whipped cream.

PER SERVING 294 cal., 21 g total fat (13 g sat. fat), 83 mg chol., 114 mg sodium, 23 g carbo., 0 g fiber, 7 g pro.

Blackberry Cream Pie

Quick Ice Cream Sandwiches

Chopped malted milk balls add a surprising crunch to the strawberry ice cream filling for these yummy sandwiches.

START TO FINISH 15 minutes   **MAKES** 6 servings

- 1   pint strawberry ice cream, softened
- ½   cup chopped malted milk balls
- 12   soft chocolate, oatmeal, or chocolate chip cookies
- ⅓   cup fudge ice cream topping

❶ In a chilled medium bowl stir ice cream just enough to soften, pressing it against the side of the bowl with a wooden spoon. Stir in malted milk balls.

❷ To assemble sandwiches spoon ice cream mixture onto the flat sides of 6 cookies. Spread fudge topping onto flat sides of the remaining 6 cookies. Place cookies, fudge sides down, on top of ice cream.

❸ Wrap each ice cream sandwich in plastic wrap. Freeze at least 6 hours or until firm.

PER SERVING 677 cal., 33 g total fat (21 g sat. fat), 76 mg chol., 559 mg sodium, 88 g carbo.,1 g fiber, 8 g pro.

Quick Ice Cream Sandwiches

Brie Apple Quesadillas

Of course, quesadillas make a lovely dessert—when they're filled with Brie, apples, and walnuts and drizzled with caramel sauce.

START TO FINISH 20 minutes   **OVEN** 400°F
MAKES 4 quesadillas

- 4   7- to 8-inch flour tortillas
- 1   tablespoon butter or margarine, melted
- 4   ounces Brie cheese, cut into ¼-inch slices (remove rind, if desired) or 1 cup shredded cheddar cheese
- 2   large cooking apples (such as Granny Smith), peeled, cored, and very thinly sliced
- ½   cup chopped walnuts
- 2   tablespoons packed brown sugar
- 2   to 3 tablespoons caramel-flavor ice cream topping

❶ Preheat oven to 400°F. Brush 1 side of each tortilla with melted butter. Place tortillas, buttered sides down, on a large baking sheet. Place cheese on one half of each tortilla. Arrange apples and walnuts on top of cheese. Sprinkle with brown sugar. Fold other half of each tortilla over apple-nut mixture.

❷ Bake for 8 to 10 minutes or until golden brown and cheese melts. Transfer quesadillas to a serving platter or dessert plates. Drizzle caramel topping over quesadillas.

PER QUESADILLA 462 cal., 23 g total fat (8 g sat. fat), 36 mg chol., 487 mg sodium, 54 g carbo., 3 g fiber, 13 g pro.

Cannoli

You can decorate the filled ends of these pastries with miniature chocolate chips or chopped pistachio nuts—the Italians do it both ways.

START TO FINISH 15 minutes   **MAKES** 6 servings

- ¾   cup ricotta cheese
- ⅓   cup miniature semisweet chocolate pieces
- 3   tablespoons sugar
- ¾   teaspoon vanilla
- ¼   teaspoon ground cinnamon
- ¾   cup frozen whipped dessert topping, thawed
- 6   purchased cannoli shells

❶ In a small bowl combine ricotta, chocolate pieces, sugar, vanilla, and cinnamon. Fold in whipped topping. Spoon mixture into a heavy plastic bag.

❷ Snip off corner of bag; pipe filling into shells. If desired, sprinkle additional chocolate pieces on filling.

PER SERVING 263 cal., 16 g total fat (6 g sat. fat), 16 mg chol., 36 mg sodium, 26 g carbo., 2 g fiber, 6 g pro.

Crepes with Maple-Pear Sauce

Crepes with Maple-Pear Sauce

If you can splurge for it, use pure maple syrup in this dessert. The maple flavor will be so much more pronounced and intense.

START TO FINISH 10 minutes   **MAKES** 5 servings

- 1   **15.25-ounce can pear slices, drained**
- 1   **cup pure maple syrup or maple-flavor syrup**
- 1   **4- to 4.5-ounce package (10 crepes) ready-to-use crepes**
- ½   **cup chopped pecans, toasted (see note, page 31)**
        Powdered sugar (optional)

1 In a small saucepan combine pear slices and maple syrup; heat through on medium-low heat.

2 Meanwhile, fold crepes into quarters; arrange on a serving platter. Pour hot pear mixture over crepes. Sprinkle with pecans. If desired, sprinkle with powdered sugar.

PER SERVING 344 cal., 10 g total fat (1 g sat. fat), 36 mg chol., 77 mg sodium, 63 g carbo., 2 g fiber, 3 g pro.

Nutty Maple Pudding

Pecans and pears make this pudding a fitting dessert for a fall dinner.

START TO FINISH 20 minutes   **OVEN** 350°F   **MAKES** 4 servings

- ½   **cup pecan pieces**
- ½   **cup whipping cream**
- 1   **4-serving-size package vanilla or white chocolate instant pudding and pie filling mix**
- 2   **cups milk**
- 3   **tablespoons pure maple syrup (optional)**
- 1   **medium pear, cored and thinly sliced**
- ⅓   **cup pure maple syrup**

1 Preheat oven to 350°F. Spread pecan pieces in a shallow baking pan. Bake for 5 to 10 minutes or until toasted. Cool on wire rack.

2 Meanwhile, in a chilled medium mixing bowl beat whipping cream on medium until soft peaks form (tips curl); set aside. Prepare pudding mix according to package directions, using the 2 cups milk. If desired, stir in the 3 tablespoons maple syrup. Fold whipped cream into pudding mixture.

3 Divide pudding mixture among 4 dessert dishes. Top with pear slices. In a small bowl combine the toasted pecans and the ⅓ cup maple syrup. Spoon pecan mixture over pudding and pear slices.

PER SERVING 447 cal., 24 g total fat (9 g sat. fat), 51 mg chol., 424 mg sodium, 56 g carbo., 3 g fiber, 6 g pro.

Chocolate-Ricotta Phyllo Shells ♥

You can use either regular or Dutch-process cocoa powder in these tiny tarts. Dutch-process has a more mellow flavor and lighter color than regular cocoa powder.

START TO FINISH 20 minutes   **MAKES** 15 miniature tarts

- ¾   **cup ricotta cheese**
- 1   **tablespoon sugar**
- 1   **teaspoon unsweetened cocoa powder**
- ¼   **teaspoon vanilla**
- 3   **tablespoons miniature semisweet chocolate pieces**
- 1   **2.1-ounce package baked miniature phyllo shells (15)**

1 For filling, in a medium bowl combine ricotta cheese, sugar, cocoa powder, and vanilla. Stir until smooth. Fold in 2 tablespoons of the chocolate pieces.

2 Using 2 spoons, scoop the filling into phyllo shells. Top with remaining chocolate pieces. Serve immediately or cover and chill up to 2 hours.

PER TART 62 cal., 3 g total fat (1 g sat. fat), 6 mg chol., 20 mg sodium, 6 g carbo., 0 g fiber, 2 g pro.

---

quick tip   If you want to be sure the phyllo shells stay as crisp as possible but you want to make these (mostly) ahead, simply make the filling and cover and refrigerate it until serving time. It only takes 5 minutes to fill and top the tarts.

Chocolate-Ricotta Phyllo Shells

Individual Brownie Trifles

Some fruits naturally pair with chocolate. Most notably, orange, cherry, strawberry, and—as in these individual trifles—raspberries.

START TO FINISH 20 minutes   **MAKES** 4 servings

- ⅔   **cup whipping cream**
- 1   **tablespoon sugar**
- ¼   **teaspoon vanilla**
- 8   **2×2-inch purchased baked brownies, crumbled into pieces (about 2 cups)**
- 2   **cups fresh raspberries or dark sweet cherries, pitted**
- 1   **cup chocolate ice cream topping**
  Unsweetened cocoa powder (optional)

1 In a chilled large mixing bowl combine whipping cream, sugar, and vanilla. Beat on medium until soft peaks form; set aside.

2 Divide of the crumbled brownies between 4 large parfait glasses or water goblets. Layer half the raspberries, ice cream topping, and whipped cream among the glasses, creating layers. Repeat layers with remaining brownies, raspberries, ice cream topping, and whipped cream. If desired, sprinkle with cocoa powder. Serve immediately or cover and chill up to 4 hours.

PER SERVING 627 cal., 29 g total fat (13 g sat. fat), 90 mg chol., 240 mg sodium, 88 g carbo., 7 g fiber, 9 g pro.

---

quick tip   When a recipe calls for beating whipping cream until "soft peaks form," it means a peak will hold its shape but not appear stiff. Be careful you don't beat beyond that or you'll wind up with butter.

Creamy Parfaits

Mascarpone is an Italian double- or triple-cream cheese that is most familiar as a key ingredient in tiramisu. If it is not in the regular dairy section, look for it in the specialty cheese case of your supermarket. If you can't find it there, regular cream cheese works fine too.

START TO FINISH 20 minutes   **MAKES** 4 servings

- 1   **4-serving-size package French vanilla instant pudding and pie filling mix**
- 1   **cup milk**
- ½   **cup mascarpone or cream cheese, softened**
- ¼   **cup whipping cream**
- 1   **cup crushed biscotti or shortbread cookies (5 biscotti or 16 shortbread cookies)**
- 1   **cup fresh berries (such as blueberries, raspberries, and/or hulled, sliced strawberries)**

1 Prepare pudding mix according to package directions using the 1 cup milk. Stir mascarpone cheese until smooth. Gradually stir ½ cup of the pudding into mascarpone cheese. Fold pudding-cheese mixture into the remaining pudding.

2 In a chilled small mixing bowl beat whipping cream on medium until soft peaks form. Fold whipped cream into pudding mixture; set aside.

3 To assemble parfaits, arrange half the crushed biscotti in 4 parfait glasses or water goblets. Add half the berries to each glass. Spoon half the pudding mixture on top. Repeat with remaining crushed biscotti, berries, and pudding. Serve immediately or cover and chill up to 4 hours.

PER SERVING 492 cal., 25 g total fat (14 g sat. fat), 74 mg chol., 510 mg sodium, 61 g carbo., 2 g fiber, 12 g pro.

{ *Dessert leaves a lasting impression—it's the last course of the meal. Make it a good one.* }

Cinnamon Toasted Pound Cake
& Strawberries

Cinnamon Toasted Pound Cake & Strawberries

This is truly a last-minute dessert, but it doesn't look or taste that way. Toasting brings out the best qualities of purchased pound cake—and so does topping it with beautiful, cinnamon-spiced fresh strawberries.

START TO FINISH 15 minutes   **MAKES** 6 servings

½	teaspoon ground cinnamon
1	tablespoon sugar
3	cups strawberries, washed and quartered
¼	cup strawberry jam
1	tablespoon lemon juice
1	10.75-ounce frozen pound cake, thawed and cut into 12 slices
2	tablespoons butter, softened
	Frozen whipped dessert topping, thawed

❶ In a small bowl stir together cinnamon and sugar. In a large bowl toss together strawberries, jam, lemon juice, and 1 teaspoon of the cinnamon-sugar mixture until berries are well coated.

❷ Toast pound cake slices. Spread 1 side of each slice with butter. Sprinkle with remaining cinnamon-sugar mixture. To serve, place 2 pound cake slices on each of 6 plates. Top with strawberries and whipped topping.

PER SERVING 875 cal., 56 g total fat (31 g sat. fat), 378 mg chol., 540 mg sodium, 135 g carbo., 5 g fiber, 13 g pro.

---

quick tip When strawberries are at peak season in May and early June, look for a pick-your-own patch nearby. If you don't want to pick your own, you can often buy pints of berries that were already picked. There is nothing equal to the taste and aroma of perfectly ripe strawberries. You know they're good when they're red all the way through.

Bananas Suzette

A bit of a cross between Bananas Foster and Crepes Suzette, this dessert is a delicious, contrasting combination of warm glazed bananas with cold vanilla ice cream.

START TO FINISH 15 minutes   **MAKES** 4 servings

2	ripe, yet firm, medium bananas
¼	cup orange juice
3	tablespoons sugar
1	tablespoon butter or margarine
¼	cup dried tart cherries
⅛	teaspoon ground nutmeg
2	cups vanilla ice cream

❶ Bias-slice each banana into 8 pieces. In a large skillet combine orange juice, sugar, and butter. Cook about 1 minute on medium-low heat or until butter melts and sugar dissolves. Add the bananas and cherries; cook for 2 to 4 minutes more or just until bananas are tender, stirring once. Stir in nutmeg.

❷ To serve, divide vanilla ice cream among 4 dessert bowls. Spoon bananas and sauce over ice cream.

PER SERVING 302 cal., 11 g total fat (7 g sat. fat), 39 mg chol., 83 mg sodium, 51 g carbo., 3 g fiber, 3 g pro.

Bananas Suzette

Blueberry-Lemon Tarts ♥

When you want "just a bite of dessert," look no further than these lovely little tarts.

START TO FINISH 10 minutes   **MAKES** 15 tarts

- ⅓ cup sour cream
- ⅓ cup purchased lemon curd or orange curd
- 1 2.1-ounce package miniature phyllo dough shells (15)
- ¼ cup fresh blueberries
  Sifted powdered sugar (optional)

❶ In a small bowl stir together sour cream and lemon or orange curd. Divide sour cream mixture among phyllo dough shells. Top with blueberries. If desired, sprinkle with powdered sugar.

PER TART 56 cal., 2 g total fat (1 g sat. fat), 7 mg chol., 18 mg sodium, 8 g carbo., 1 g fiber, 1 g pro.

Chocolate-Peanut Butter Ice Cream Sandwiches

Kids will go crazy for these ice cream sandwiches that feature a flavor combination of a certain famous candy cup.

START TO FINISH 15 minutes   **MAKES** 4 servings

- 1 pint tin roof sundae or other chocolate swirl premium ice cream
- 8 3½-inch purchased peanut butter cookies
- ¼ cup miniature semisweet chocolate pieces or crushed chocolate-covered crisp peanut butter candy

❶ Place a scoop of ice cream on the bottom of 4 cookies. Top with remaining 4 cookies, flat sides down. Press gently to force ice cream to the edges of the cookies. Place chocolate pieces in a shallow dish. Roll edges of ice cream sandwiches in the chocolate pieces to coat. Freeze for 5 minutes or until firm.

PER SERVING 625 cal., 36 g total fat (17 g sat. fat), 123 mg chol., 312 mg sodium, 65 g carbo., 2 g fiber, 11 g pro.

Mocha Pound Cake

Chocolate-and-coffee cream cheese filling and a slice of fresh orange are sandwiched between two delicate slices of toasted pound cake in this 20-minute dessert.

START TO FINISH 20 minutes   **MAKES** 4 servings

- ½ of a 10.75-ounce frozen pound cake, thawed
- 3 tablespoons sugar
- 2 tablespoons unsweetened cocoa powder
- 1 teaspoon instant coffee crystals
- ⅓ cup milk
- 1 3-ounce package cream cheese, softened
- 1 medium orange
  Orange slices, cut into eighths, or orange peel curls (optional)

❶ Preheat broiler. Cut pound cake into 8 thin slices; place on a baking sheet. Broil 3 to 4 inches from heat for 1 to 2 minutes per side or until toasted. In a small bowl whisk together sugar, cocoa powder, and coffee crystals. Gradually whisk in milk until smooth.

❷ In a medium mixing bowl beat cream cheese on medium until smooth. Gradually beat in the milk mixture until smooth, scraping sides of bowl as needed.

❸ Peel orange and cut crosswise into 4 slices. Place a pound cake slice on each of 4 dessert plates. Top each with an orange slice and the cream cheese mixture. Add remaining pound cake slices. If desired, garnish with additional orange slice pieces.

PER SERVING 291 cal., 16 g total fat (10 g sat. fat), 109 mg chol., 224 mg sodium, 35 g carbo., 2 g fiber, 5 g pro.

quick tip   To make an orange peel curl garnish, use a zester with a large hole or a vegetable peeler to make long, thin strips of orange peel. Wrap the peel tightly around a pencil or chopstick and let stand at room temperature for 30 minutes or until curl holds its shape. Remove curl from the pencil or chopstick.

{ Whether it's light or decadent, a bite of something sweet signals the end of the meal. }

Easy Topped Cupcakes
with German Chocolate
Ice Cream Frosting

Easy Topped Cupcakes

Cake and ice cream take are worthy of a celebration in these ice cream sundae-topped cupcakes.

PREP 30 minutes **FREEZE** 4 hours **OVEN** 350°F
MAKES 12 cupcakes

- 1 recipe ice cream frosting
- 1 package 2-layer-size desired flavor cake mix

1 Prepare and freeze ice cream frosting as directed. Meanwhile, line twenty-four 2½-inch muffin cups with paper bake cups or lightly grease muffin cups; set aside.

2 Prepare and bake cake mix according to package directions for cupcakes. Cool cupcakes in pans on wire racks for 5 minutes. Remove cupcakes from pans; cool completely on wire racks.

3 Remove paper bake cups, if using, from 12 of the cupcakes. Save remaining cupcakes for another use. Place the 12 cupcakes on individual plates or in shallow bowls. Top each cupcake as directed in the frosting recipes below. Serve immediately.

GERMAN CHOCOLATE ICE CREAM FROSTING: In your freezer, prepare a flat space large enough for a large baking sheet. Line a large baking sheet with waxed paper; set aside. Use an ice cream scoop to form twelve 2- to 3-inch-diameter scoops of chocolate ice cream. Drop scoops onto prepared baking sheet. Cover and freeze 4 hours or up to 3 days. To serve, place a scoop of ice cream on each cupcake. Drizzle with ¾ cup caramel ice cream topping, sprinkle with ¾ cup toasted pecan pieces and toasted flaked coconut (see note, page 31), and ½ cup miniature chocolate chips.

PER CUPCAKE 411 cal., 51 g total fat (12 g sat. fat), 80 mg chol., 261 mg sodium, 43 g carbo., 2 g fiber, 6 g pro.

BANANA SPLIT FROSTING: Prepare German Chocolate Ice Cream Frosting as directed, except substitute strawberry or banana split ice cream for the chocolate ice cream. Serve as directed, except drizzle with ¾ cup chocolate fudge ice cream topping and sprinkle with 1 cup chopped banana and ¾ cup chopped dry-roasted peanuts instead of the caramel topping, pecans, chocolate chips, and coconut.

ICE CREAM SUNDAE FROSTING: Prepare German Chocolate Ice Cream Frosting as directed, except substitute vanilla bean, vanilla fudge, or cherry vanilla ice cream for the chocolate ice cream. Serve as directed, using ¾ cup ice cream topping (such as chocolate fudge, caramel, chocolate mocha, butterscotch, or strawberry). Top with Sweetened Whipped Cream, ¾ cup chopped honey-roasted peanuts, and, if desired, drained maraschino cherries.

SWEETENED WHIPPED CREAM: In a chilled mixing bowl add 1 cup whipping cream, 2 tablespoons sugar, and ½ teaspoon vanilla. Beat on medium speed until soft peaks form.

quick tip   Assemble only as many desserts as you are going to serve at one time. Store unfrosted cupcakes in an airtight container at room temperature up to 3 days or freeze up to 3 months. Thaw frozen cupcakes before serving.

Quick Cherry Crisp

The filling for this stovetop fruit crisp is made only with real fruit, a little sugar, and cornstarch for thickener. The "crisp" comes in the form of crumbled cookies and toasted nuts.

START TO FINISH 20 minutes **MAKES** 4 servings

- ⅓ to ½ cup sugar
- 1 tablespoon cornstarch
- 4 cups frozen unsweetened pitted tart red cherries
- 1 cup crumbled shortbread cookies
- 2 tablespoons butter or margarine, melted
- ¼ cup pecans or almonds, toasted and chopped (see note, page 31)

  Ice cream (optional)

1 In a small bowl combine sugar and cornstarch. In a large saucepan sprinkle cornstarch mixture over cherries; stir to combine. Cook and stir on medium heat about 10 minutes or until thickened and bubbly. Cook and stir for 2 minutes more.

2 Meanwhile, in a medium bowl thoroughly combine crumbled cookies, butter, and nuts.

3 Spoon mixture into 4 dishes. Top each serving with cookie mixture. If desired, serve with ice cream.

PER SERVING 362 cal., 17 g total fat (6 g sat. fat), 20 mg chol., 152 mg sodium, 52 g carbo., 4 g fiber, 4 g pro.

Quick Cherry Crisp

Quick Apple Crisp

Prepared apple pie filling is warmed and given a flavor boost from ground ginger and vanilla—then simply topped with crunchy granola and a scoop of vanilla ice cream.

START TO FINISH 15 minutes **MAKES** 4 servings

1	**21-ounce can apple pie filling**
¼	**cup dried cranberries**
¼	**teaspoon ground ginger or cinnamon**
¼	**teaspoon vanilla**
1	**cup granola**
1	**pint vanilla ice cream**

❶ In a medium saucepan combine pie filling, dried cranberries, and ginger; heat through on medium-low heat, stirring occasionally. Remove from heat; stir in vanilla. Spoon into 4 bowls. Top each serving with granola. Serve with ice cream.

PER SERVING 507 cal., 15 g total fat (8 g sat. fat), 68 mg chol., 113 mg sodium, 88 g carbo., 6 g fiber, 9 g pro.

quick tip If it's in your budget, buy real vanilla extract. It's more expensive than the imitation stuff, but one sniff of the real thing and you'll understand why it makes your baked goods taste so much better than imitation.

Quick Apple Crisp

Stovetop Peach-Raspberry Cobbler ♥

Puff pastry thaws in about 45 minutes at room temperature, so even when you need a last-minute dessert, this fresh and pretty cobbler is a tasty possibility.

START TO FINISH 20 minutes **OVEN** 375°F **MAKES** 4 servings

1	**teaspoon sugar**
	Dash ground cinnamon
½	**of a sheet frozen puff pastry, thawed according to package directions**
1	**egg, lightly beaten**
3	**tablespoons sugar**
1	**tablespoon cornstarch**
¼	**teaspoon ground cinnamon**
1	**16-ounce package frozen unsweetened peach slices**
1	**cup fresh raspberries**
½	**cup water**
	Vanilla ice cream (optional)

❶ Preheat oven to 375°F. For puff pastry twists, in a small bowl combine the 1 teaspoon sugar and the dash cinnamon. Place puff pastry on a clean work surface. Brush pastry with beaten egg. Sprinkle with cinnamon-sugar mixture. Cut the pastry lengthwise into 4 strips; cut each strip in half crosswise. Twist strips; place on a greased baking sheet. Bake for 15 minutes or until brown and puffed.

❷ Meanwhile, in a large saucepan combine the 3 tablespoons sugar, the cornstarch, and the ¼ teaspoon cinnamon. Add frozen peaches, half of the raspberries, and the water. Cook on medium heat until mixture is thickened and bubbly. Cook and stir for 2 minutes more. Remove from heat. Stir in the remaining raspberries.

❸ Divide fruit mixture among 4 dessert dishes. Top with puff pastry. If desired, serve with ice cream.

PER SERVING 159 cal., 4 g total fat (1 g sat. fat), 53 mg chol., 34 mg sodium, 30 g carbo., 4 g fiber, 3 g pro.

Double Berry Soup

Quick Strawberry Cheesecake

This no-bake cheesecake is made parfait-style. A sweetened Brie and cream cheese mixture is layered in parfait glasses alternately with fresh strawberries and butter toffee-glazed and sliced almonds.

START TO FINISH 20 minutes   **MAKES** 4 servings

- 2   ounces Brie cheese, softened
- 1   3-ounce package cream cheese, softened
- 2   to 3 tablespoons sugar
- 1   teaspoon lemon juice
- 2   cups fresh strawberries, hulled and sliced
- ½   cup butter toffee-glazed sliced almonds
      Honey (optional)

❶ Remove and discard the rind from the Brie cheese. In a medium mixing bowl beat Brie, cream cheese, sugar, and lemon juice on medium until almost smooth. Set aside.

❷ Divide strawberries, cheese mixture, and almonds among 4 parfait glasses, alternating layers of berries, cheese, and almonds. If desired, drizzle each serving with honey.

PER SERVING 249 cal., 18 g total fat (7 g sat. fat), 38 mg chol., 213 mg sodium, 17 g carbo., 3 g fiber, 7 g pro.

Double Berry Soup

This two-berry soup is served warm, with a scoop of citrus sorbet for contrast.

START TO FINISH 20 minutes   **MAKES** 4 servings

- 2   cup sliced strawberries
- 2   cups blueberries
- ¾   cup orange juice
- ¼   cup sugar
- 2   cups lemon or other citrus sorbet
      Fresh mint leaves (optional)

❶ In a medium saucepan combine strawberries, blueberries, orange juice, and sugar. Cook on medium heat for 4 to 5 minutes or just until bubbly, stirring occasionally. Remove from heat. Let stand about 5 minutes to slightly cool.

❷ Ladle the soup into 4 shallow dessert bowls. Top each with a scoop of sorbet. If desired, garnish with fresh mint.

PER SERVING 244 cal., 1 g total fat (0 g sat. fat), 0 mg chol., 27 mg sodium, 61 g carbo., 4 g fiber, 1 g pro.

Caramelized Apples with Ice Cream

These skillet-cooked apples are much quicker to make than baked apples.

START TO FINISH 20 minutes   **MAKES** 6 servings

- ⅓   cup sugar
- 1   teaspoon ground cinnamon
- 1   tablespoon butter
- 3   firm cooking apples (such as Braeburn or Jonagold), halved lengthwise and cored
- ½   cup water
- 3   cups vanilla ice cream
      Purchased cookies (optional)

❶ In a shallow bowl combine sugar and cinnamon; reserve 1 tablespoon. In an extra-large skillet melt butter on medium heat. Press the cut side of each apple half into the remaining cinnamon-sugar mixture. Place apples, cut sides down, in the hot skillet. Sprinkle with remaining cinnamon-sugar mixture.

❷ Cook apples for 7 to 8 minutes or until apples begin to brown. Add ½ cup water. Cover; reduce heat to low. Simmer for 5 to 7 minutes, adding more water if sugar begins to burn.

❸ Arrange 2 apple halves on each of 4 plates; drizzle with sauce from skillet. Serve with ice cream. Sprinkle with reserved cinnamon-sugar mixture. If desired, serve with cookies.

PER SERVING 304 cal., 11 g total fat (7 g sat. fat), 33 mg chol., 58 mg sodium, 51 g carbo., 4 g fiber, 2 g pro.

Caramelized Apples with Ice Cream

Piecrust Cookies ♥

If your mother baked when you were a child, these simple spiced cookies made from piecrust may remind you of what she did with the pie dough scraps—much to your great joy.

PREP 15 minutes   **BAKE** 8 minutes   **OVEN** 400°F
MAKES about 25 cookies

- ½   of a 15-ounce package rolled refrigerated unbaked piecrust (1 crust)
- 1   tablespoon butter or margarine, melted
- 2   tablespoons packed brown sugar
- ½   to 1 teaspoon pumpkin pie spice or apple pie spice

1 Preheat oven to 400°F. Unroll piecrust according to package directions using the microwave method. Place on a lightly floured surface. Brush piecrust with melted butter. Sprinkle with brown sugar and pie spice.

2 Use a pastry wheel or pizza cutter to cut dough into 1½- to 2-inch squares (some of the edges may be smaller). Place on a ungreased large cookie sheet, leaving a small space between pastries.

3 Bake about 8 minutes or until golden brown. Serve warm or cool.

PER COOKIE 47 cal., 3 g total fat (1 g sat. fat), 3 mg chol., 35 mg sodium, 5 g carbo., 0 g fiber, 0 g pro.

---

quick tip   For any cookie that is baked on an ungreased baking sheet—and that's most cookies—it's a good idea to line the baking sheet with parchment paper before putting the cookies on it. Parchment keeps the cookies from sticking and makes cleanup a snap. Most of the time, you can simply toss the parchment paper and give the baking sheet a quick washing with hot water.

Warm Spiced Peaches ♥

Make this simple (and healthful!) microwave dessert when peaches are at their very best—in late July through early September. The quality of the fruit is so good then, they need very little embellishment.

START TO FINISH 15 minutes   **MAKES** 4 servings

- 3   ripe medium peaches, peeled and sliced
- 1   tablespoon sugar
- ½   teaspoon ground cinnamon
- ½   teaspoon finely shredded orange peel
- ½   teaspoon vanilla
- ¼   teaspoon ground nutmeg
- 1   6-ounce carton vanilla yogurt

1 In a medium bowl combine peaches, sugar, cinnamon, orange peel, vanilla, and nutmeg; toss gently to combine. Divide among four 5-inch individual quiche dishes or 10-ounce custard cups.

2 Place dishes, two at a time, in a microwave. Microwave on high for 1 to 1½ minutes or until warm. Serve with yogurt.

PER SERVING 95 cal., 1 g total fat (0 g sat. fat), 2 mg chol., 28 mg sodium, 20 g carbo., 2 g fiber, 3 g pro.

Fruit Bowl Sundaes

There may not be ice cream in these sundaes, but you won't miss it. Sliced strawberries and bananas are topped off with chocolate whipped cream studded with pieces of crushed chocolate sandwich cookies.

START TO FINISH 15 minutes   **MAKES** 4 sundaes

- ⅓   cup whipping cream
- 2   tablespoons chocolate-flavor syrup
- 2   chocolate-with-white-filling sandwich cookies, crushed
- 2   medium bananas, sliced
- 1   cup strawberries, sliced
- 2   tablespoons shredded coconut, toasted (see note, page 31)

1 In a chilled medium mixing bowl beat whipping cream with chilled beaters on medium until soft peaks form (tips curl). By hand, gradually fold chocolate syrup into whipped cream until smooth. Fold in cookie pieces.

2 Divide bananas and strawberries among 4 dessert dishes. Spoon whipped cream mixture on each serving. Sprinkle with coconut.

PER SUNDAE 188 cal., 10 g total fat (6 g sat. fat), 27 mg chol., 45 mg sodium, 27 g carbo., 2 g fiber, 2 g pro.

INDEX

Note: Boldfaced page numbers indicate photographs.